English
Revision for Junior Certificate
Higher Level

English Revision for Junior Certificate Higher Level

John G. Fahy

Gill & Macmillan

Gill & Macmillan Ltd
Hume Avenue
Park West
Dublin 12

with associated companies throughout the world
www.gillmacmillan.ie

© John Fahy 1994, 2000
0 7171 3018 5
Design and print origination in Ireland by
O'K Graphic Design, Dublin

The paper used in this book is made from the wood pulp of managed forests.
For every tree felled, at least one tree is planted, thereby renewing natural resources.

All rights reserved. No part of this publication may be copied, reproduced or transmitted
in any form or by any means, without permission of the publishers
or else under the terms of any licence permitting limited copying
issued by the Irish Copyright Licensing Agency,
The Writers' Centre, Parnell Square, Dublin 1.

Contents

PAPER I

Section 1. Reading
Examination hints	1
Examination questions	2
Sample answers	3

Section 2. Personal writing
Overview of grammar, style, and spelling
Words—recognition	7
The sentence—syntax	8
Construction of elegant sentences	11
Paragraphs	14
Style	16
Spelling: some rules	18

Categories of prose writing
Descriptive prose—characterisation	24
Autobiography	55
The short story	67
Diary writing	82
Speech writing	88
The essay	94
The personal experience essay	104
Satirical writing	110
Personal writing—examination hints	112

Section 3. Functional writing
Report writing	116
Writing instructions	121
Accurate description of a scene	122
Agenda and minutes of a meeting	125
Letters	126
Filling application forms	137
Curriculum vitae	139

Section 4. The media
Newspaper writing
Writing the news	140
Editorials	146
Feature articles	149
Letters to a newspaper	151
Reviews	158

Reading an advertisement   162
Persuasive writing	169

PAPER II

Examination hints: Paper II	173

Section 5. Drama
Drama check-list	174
Examination questions	176
Sample answers	182

Section 6. Poetry
Poetry check-list	184
Examination questions (unseen poetry)	186
Sample answers	187
Examination questions (studied poems)	189
Sample answer	189

Section 7. Fiction: novels and short stories
Fiction check-list	194
Examination questions	196
Sample answers	198

Examination papers   200

ACKNOWLEDGMENTS

For permission to reproduce copyright material grateful acknowledgment is made to the following:

Hamish Hamilton for extracts from *A Year in Provence* by Peter Mayle; Wolfhound for extracts from *The Green Guide for Ireland* by John Gormley; André Deutsch for an extract from *Home Before Night* by Hugh Leonard; The Hogarth Press for an extract from *Cider with Rosie* by Laurie Lee; John Murray for an extract from *A Place Apart* by Dervla Murphy; J.M. Dent for extracts from *A Prospect of the Sea* and *Memories of Christmas* by Dylan Thomas; Granta books for 'Subterranean Gothic' by Paul Theroux from *The Best of Granta Travel*; Methuen for an extract from *A Portrait of the Artist as a Young Girl* by Edna O'Brien; Michael Longley for *Crossing the Lisburn Road*; Hodder and Stoughton for 'Mrs Pulaska' by Christopher Burns from *Telly Stories: the best of BBC Radio's Recent Short Fiction* edited by Duncan Minshell; Blackstaff Press for *Secrets* by Bernard MacLaverty; Pan Books for extracts from the *Diary of Anne Frank*; Picador for *A Cool and Logical Analysis of the Bicycle Menace* by P.J. O'Rourke; The Irish Times for 'On Your Way' by Orla Bourke, 'The Telephone' by Kevin Myers and 'Migraine' by Kathryn Holmquist; Educational Company of Ireland for 'On Donkeys' from *Half in Earnest* by John D. Sheridan; Hamish Hamilton for 'The Dog that Bit People' from *The Thurber Carnival* by James Thurber; Macmillan for an extract from 'A Straight Choice' by Tony Runham; Brian Lennon for extracts from *The Career Handbook*; Weidenfeld and Nicolson for extracts from *The Letters of Evelyn Waugh* edited by Mark Amory.

For assistance with advertisements thanks are due to DDFH and B, Peter Owens, Burrell Marketing and Publicity and Hibernian Life.

For permission to reproduce photographs acknowledgment is made to The Irish Times, Camera Press, Bill Doyle and Lensmen.

The publishers have made every effort to trace copyright holders, but if they have inadvertently overlooked any, they will be pleased to make the necessary arrangements at the first opportunity.

Section 1 Reading

The skill of good reading, i.e. accurate, fast and sensitive comprehension of a piece of writing, is vital to the subject. It is important in all areas of the course—drama, poetry, media, and fiction—and has a central part in the examination. Reading skills are tested formally in Section 1 of Paper I but also play a vital role in the answering of unseen drama, poetry and fiction extracts in Paper II.

This book provides you with a method or framework for approaching the reading question in an examination, with sample answers to the 1992 reading question, and with *many opportunities to develop this skill through the reading questions on the extracts in the personal writing section*.

Examination Hints

1. Read the piece at least THREE TIMES: (*a*) for the overall outline and general idea of it; (*b*) for more detail. Then read the questions, and (*c*) have a final read with an eye on answering the questions.

2. What EXACTLY are you being asked to answer? Write out or underline the key words or phrases in the question. For example, in question (i), page 3, '*attitude* of the London lawyer to the French' is the key phrase. Keep to that point.

3. How many PARTS to the question? They may not be marked (a) and (b). For example, question (iii), page 3, has two parts: '*a keen eye for observation* and *a talent for humorous description.*' Answer all parts, as if the question was marked (a) and (b).

4. ANSWER FULLY. Use *all* points and examples in the text that can be mustered to support an answer.

5. Keep it RELEVANT. To keep you on the right track, it may help to use the terms of the question in your answer. For example, 'attitude' or a synonym for it (word of the same meaning) should crop up a good deal in answers to (i) and (ii) below.

2 READING

> **EXAM HINTS**
>
> **6.** Justify your answer in each case by REFERENCE TO THE TEXT or with a short quotation, except where the question asks for 'your own words'!
>
> **7.** Paragraph your answer—one paragraph for each major point you make.

Examination Questions [40 marks]

Read carefully the following passage and then answer the questions that follow it. [Junior Certificate examination, 1992]

A YEAR IN PROVENCE

The passage (slightly adapted) is taken from *A Year in Provence* by Peter Mayle. The writer is an Englishman who went with his wife to live in Provence in the south of France. In this book he describes some of their experiences there over a period of a year.

Our friend, the London lawyer, a man steeped in English reserve, was watching what he called 'the antics of the French' from the Fin de Siècle café in Cavaillon. It was a market day, and the pavement was a human traffic jam, slow-moving, jostling and chaotic.

'Look over there,' he said, as a car stopped in the middle of the street while the driver got out to embrace an acquaintance, 'they're always mauling each other. See that? Men kissing. Damned unhealthy, if you ask me.' He snorted into his beer, his sense of propriety outraged by such deviant behaviour, so alien to the respectable Anglo-Saxon.

It had taken some months to get used to the Provençal delight in physical contact. Like everyone brought up in England, I had absorbed certain social mannerisms. I had learned to keep my distance, to offer a nod instead of a handshake, to ration kissing to female relatives and to confine any public demonstrations of affection to dogs. To be engulfed by a Provençal welcome, as thorough and searching as being frisked by airport security guards, was, at first, a startling experience. Now I enjoyed it, and I was fascinated by the niceties of the social ritual, and the sign language which is an essential part of any Provençal encounter.

When two unencumbered men meet, the least there will be is the conventional handshake. If the hands are full, you will be offered a little finger to shake. If the hands are wet and dirty, you will be offered a forearm or an elbow. Riding a bicycle or driving a car does not excuse you from the obligation to touch hands, and so you will see perilous contortions being performed on busy streets as hands grope through car windows and across handlebars to find each other. And this is only the first and most restrained level of acquaintance. A closer relationship requires more demonstrative acknowledgement.

As our lawyer friend had noticed, men kiss other men. They squeeze shoulders, slap backs, pummel kidneys, pinch cheeks. When a Provençal man is truly pleased to see you, there is a real possibility of coming away from his clutches with superficial bruising.

The risk of bodily damage is less where women are concerned, but an amateur can easily make a social blunder if he miscalculates the required number of kisses. In my early days of discovery, I would plant a single kiss, only to find that the other cheek was being proffered as I was drawing back. Only snobs kiss once, I was told. I then saw what I assumed to be the correct procedure—the triple kiss, left-right-left, so I tried it on a Parisian friend. Wrong again. She told me that triple-kissing was a low Provençal habit, and that two kisses were enough among civilized people. The next time I saw my neighbour's wife, I kissed her twice. 'No,' she said, 'three times.'

I now pay close attention to the movement of the female head. If it stops swivelling after two kisses, I am almost sure I've filled my quota, but I stay poised for a third in case the head should keep moving.

Answer ALL the questions which follow.
(i) What is the attitude of the London lawyer to the French, as revealed in paragraphs 1 and 2 of the above passage? (13)
(ii) What similarities and/or differences do you find between the writer's attitude to the French and that of his friend the lawyer? (13)
(iii) 'The writer has a keen eye for observation and a talent for humorous description.' Do you think this statement is true? Give reasons for your answer. (14)

Sample answers

(i) The London lawyer is a very shy, reserved man who disapproves of the behaviour of the French. We know this because he uses the word 'antics', which suggests absurd carry-on, to describe their manners.

He shows an even stronger negative attitude in the second paragraph. He describes the French open embracing as 'mauling', a word that has suggestions of a rugby scrum. He demonstrates this very contemptuous attitude by snorting into his beer. The writer even goes so far as to say that the London lawyer considered the French behaviour 'deviant' or abnormal.

(ii) The very reserved London lawyer finds this open embracing by the French quite embarrassing, unhealthy, even deviant.

At first the writer shared this attitude, but he overcame his Anglo-Saxon reserve and got used to the Provençal delight in physical contact. Now he actually enjoys it.

But more than that, the writer has developed a fascination for the codes of social behaviour, the little rituals that go with every meeting: the different kinds of handshake, embracings, and whether to kiss twice or three times. We can see this from the amount of detail he goes into. Indeed he finds it all a bit perplexing, as he doesn't seem to have mastered the code himself.

His attitude is also one of amusement at times. We gather this from his very graphic and exaggerated description of an over-friendly greeting. 'When a Provençal man is truly pleased to see you, there is a real possibility of coming away from his clutches with superficial bruising.' Does this indicate a little of the superior English attitude towards the rough peasant? Perhaps he is not all that different from his friend after all.

But on the surface at least, the attitude of the writer towards the French seems to be much more relaxed and accepting than that of his friend the London lawyer.

(iii) Yes, the writer has a very keen eye for observation. He has logged in detail the various types of handshake, from little finger to forearm, that you will be offered. He describes exactly the various movements of the embrace: 'squeeze shoulders, slap backs, pummel kidneys, pinch cheeks.' Indeed, he needs to use his powers of observation every day: he must pay close attention to the movement of the female head if he is to give the correct number of kisses.

The writer certainly has a sense of fun, and this comes out in his description and his very amusing similes, such as when he describes 'a Provençal welcome, as thorough and searching as being frisked by airport security guards.' It comes across also in the exaggeration of his description, such as 'the superficial bruising' of a friendly embrace and in the repeated embarrassment at getting the kissing code wrong.

Now answer the 1993 reading question for yourself.

Section 1: Reading [40 marks]

Read carefully the following passage and then answer the questions that follow it. [Junior Certificate examination, 1993]

Victoria White asks, Do uniforms broadcast the right messages?
The following feature article, in abbreviated form, is taken from *Image* magazine.

READING 5

ls': that's what uniforms are all about, according to one expert. ' changes the significance of an action. A smile, for instance, h a playful punch from one delivered in earnest. Similarly, the n transforms a simple finger-wag into a warning. Put a per- y young man, with negligible body-personality, into a police- n, and his every act becomes immediately more authoritative, laden. He becomes identified with the Law, and people as a respond to his actions.

s where authority is stressed, like schools, prisons and armies, uniforms. There are lots of practical reasons for this—such as wn clothes—but most researchers would agree that uniforms ress the individuality of the wearer. One researcher claims that all to do with the power of the employer. 'A uniform stan- workers and keeps them in line,' he says. Higher up in the e workers have more authority and their status is partly heir right to dress whatever way they like.

r I spoke to in a fast food restaurant detested her uniform pre- she felt it demeaned her, took away from her individuality. 'I e a human being in this thing,' she said. 'And that's exactly nt, because if I wore my normal clothes I don't think I'd do ake me do.' She said she would be 'mortified' if any of her er and certainly her tunic and trousers were pretty revolting.

men, however, seem to like the division a uniform makes k and 'real life'. One woman, who was fortunate enough to onderful uniform that she said it made her much more posi- r work and employers, nevertheless declared: 'But I do not orm in the same wardrobe as my "real" clothes. The uniform totally separate work and spare time. It means that my work nothing to do with my individuality.'

icial institutions have a uniform for women but not for men. women I spoke to seemed bothered or perplexed by this. The n blithely unaware that there is anything strange in the fact nen wear uniform. One man says: 'It's the norm and nobody has objected. Anyway, I do like a uniform on ladies in the office—I think they look attractive. It would look strange if the men wore one—with the name of the financial institution printed on it, and a cap …' 'Like a fast-food restaurant?' I interjected. 'Exactly.'

6. Surely this distinction between what men and women are obliged to wear has to be worrying, if it is accepted that wearing a uniform keeps you in line and is not usually associated with top management positions? There may be deeper reasons still. Perhaps it's because women are all different, and making women wear a uniform pins down what men tend to see as their unpredictability. Men see themselves as the rational ones.

7. Feminists may ask why women should have to wear uniforms when naturally their taste in clothes seems to run for colour and variety. Perhaps it is that many women putting on a uniform every morning echo the glad words of one financial female employee: 'It means I don't have to think!'

Answer ALL the questions which follow.
1. What, in your own words, is the principal point being made about uniforms in paragraph 2 above? Briefly, do you agree with this point of view? Give one reason for your answer. (10)

2. What do you think of the *male* attitude to uniforms for women, as found in paragraph 5 above? (10)

3. How many different *female* attitudes to uniforms for women can you detect in the passage above? Briefly state each, and say which one of them you are most inclined to agree with. Explain your choice. (20)

Section 2 — Personal writing

Overview of grammar, style and spelling

In order to write well it is necessary to have some awareness of the function of words in a sentence and how they combine to form phrases and longer sentences. If you have some knowledge of the mechanics of a sentence, then you should find it easier to build efficient and elegant sentences of your own.

Even though this does not form a separate and distinct examination question, your ability to recognise and construct sophisticated sentences and paragraphs will gain you merit throughout the entire written exam, but most particularly in this 'personal writing' section.

So, before we go on to study and practise the many different categories of prose writing, there follows a brief overview of grammar, style, and spelling. Some of this will be revision of concepts you have already learnt.

Words—recognition

Words are categorised or classified into **parts of speech**: noun, pronoun, adjective, verb, adverb, preposition, conjunction, interjection, and the article (definite and indefinite).

A word is classified as a certain part of speech depending on how it is used in the sentence. For example, consider the sentence:

'Oh, dear, the boring teacher will have explained the simple problem slowly and carefully to the bright students and confused them.'

Oh, dear—**interjections.**
the—**definite article,** refers to a particular thing. 'A' is the indefinite article.
boring—**adjective,** a descriptive word used to tell us more about (modify) a noun—in this case 'teacher'.
teacher—**noun,** a word that tells us the name of a person, place, or thing or abstraction, such as John, Dublin, school, horror.
will have—**auxiliary verb,** a helping verb.
explained—**verb,** usually an action word, describing the action made by the subject of the sentence.

8 Grammar, Style and Spelling

Note 1. The verb 'to be' is also a full verb: is, was, etc.

Note 2. Verbs can be 'finite' or 'non-finite'. When a verb has a subject—i.e. someone or something doing the action—we consider that it is attached or limited to one subject and so it is a 'finite' verb (finite means 'limited'). For example: 'the cat sniggered' (finite verb); 'the sniggering cat' (non-finite verb). A sentence needs a finite verb in order to make complete sense on its own.

the—*definite article*
simple—*adjective* (describes or modifies the noun 'problem')
problem—*noun*
slowly—**adverb** another 'colour' word used to describe or tell us more about the activity in question. Most adverbs end in *ly*. Technically we say an adverb 'modifies' the verb, in this case 'explained'.
and—**conjunction** a word that joins words, phrases, or clauses. Common conjunctions are 'and', 'but', 'or', 'neither', 'nor', 'for', 'whereas', 'accordingly', 'consequently', 'nevertheless', etc.
carefully—*adverb*

to—**preposition** shows the relation of a noun or pronoun to some other word in the sentence. Much-used prepositions are 'above', 'across', 'after', 'at', 'beside', 'between', 'during', 'for', 'from', 'in', 'near', 'off', 'on', 'over', 'to', 'under', 'up', 'with', etc.
the—*definite article*
bright—*adjective*
students—*noun*
and—*conjunction*
confused—*verb*
them—*pronoun* a word that is used instead of a noun. Examples: 'I', 'me', 'we', 'you', 'she', 'it', 'they', etc.; 'mine', 'yours', 'ours', etc.; 'this', 'that', 'these', 'those', 'who', 'whose', etc.; 'which', 'that', 'someone', 'anyone', etc.

▬ The sentence—syntax

A sentence is a group of words expressing a complete thought.

There are two essential parts of a sentence: the SUBJECT and the PREDICATE.

The subject is what the sentence is all about: the part of the sentence making the statement, or doing the action, or asking the question.

The predicate is the statement made about the subject, or what follows from the subject.

Subject	Predicate
The fat cat	greedily devoured the famous singing canary.
Simple subject: cat	**Verb**: devoured

Within the full subject there is always a word (usually a noun or pronoun) that carries the essential notion of that subject—the SIMPLE SUBJECT—here 'cat'.

Within the predicate there is always a word that carries the essence of the predicate—the VERB—here 'devoured'.

Many verbs have someone or something at the receiving end of the activity. This is the OBJECT—here 'canary'.

Subject	Predicate/verb	Object
cat	devoured	canary

Some verbs can take two objects—a DIRECT OBJECT and INDIRECT OBJECT. The thing towards which the action of the verb is directed is called the direct object. The person to whom or for whom the action is done is the indirect object. The indirect object usually comes immediately after the verb. **Example**:

'The canary teaches	me	singing.'
	indirect object	**direct object**

Some verbs need a word or group of words to complete the meaning partially expressed by the verb. This is called a COMPLEMENT. **Example**: 'The student declared the cat to be innocent.'

The student declared the cat	to be innocent
	complement

10 Grammar, Style and Spelling

Sometimes the sentence also carries an addition or extension called an ADJUNCT.

Subject	Predicate	Indirect object	Object	Adjunct
The fat cat	told	the singing canary	lies	of the greatest magnitude.

The structure or flow of a simple English sentence usually follows the pattern *subject—predicate—object—adjunct* (SPOA). But, as we will see, it can be varied to APOS or ASPO, etc.

So perhaps we can redefine a sentence as A GROUP OF WORDS, CONTAINING AT LEAST A SUBJECT AND A PREDICATE, THAT MAKES COMPLETE SENSE ON ITS OWN.

Sentences can be long or short. Longer sentences are subdivided into phrases and clauses.

Phrase: A group of words lacking a subject and a verb, for example 'of the greatest magnitude'.

Clause: A group of words with a subject and a predicate that is part of a longer sentence.

If the clause makes complete sense on its own it is called a MAIN CLAUSE. If it does not make complete sense on its own it is a SUBORDINATE CLAUSE. For example:

Main clause	Subordinate clause
'The cat finally knocked out the canary,	after she had fought valiantly for two hours.'

There are three types of subordinate clause: ADJECTIVAL, ADVERBIAL and NOUN clause.

An adjectival clause modifies or tells us more about a noun in another clause. **Example**: 'The cat <u>that belonged to the sleepy student</u> finally finished off the canary, after she had fought valiantly for two hours.' The underlined adjectival clause modifies the noun 'cat'.

An adverbial clause does the work of an adverb and modifies a verb, adjective or adverb in some other clause. **Example**: 'The cat that belonged to the sleepy student finally finished off the canary, <u>after she had fought valiantly for two hours</u>.' This adverbial clause tells us when the action happened.

A noun clause does the work of a noun, so it can be the subject, object etc. of the sentence. **Example**: 'I should like to know <u>what you feed that cat</u>.'

Remember, arrange your phrases and clauses in the sentence so that the statement makes sense. Avoid ambiguity.

Exercise

Restructure the following sentences to clear up any ambiguity:

(a) Now that you watched me use the rifle, would you like to try shooting yourself?

(b) I relaxed in my chair, watching the cat playing and puffing away at my pipe.

(c) Write your ideas about keeping canaries on a postcard.

(d) You won't catch butterflies resting on your bed.

Construction of elegant sentences

When you have mastered the habit of structuring your sentences so that the meaning is clear, then you can progress to the construction of more elegant and sophisticated sentences. These are the main types of sentence you will find:

SIMPLE

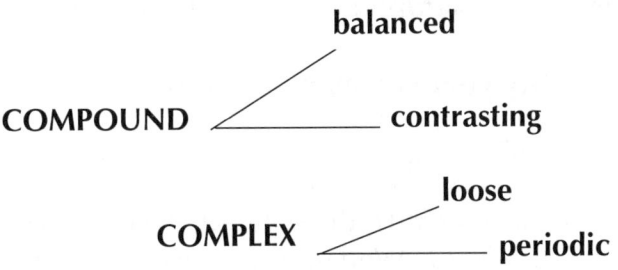

COMPOUND-COMPLEX

SIMPLE SENTENCE: consists of one main clause. **Example**: 'That cat needs a psychiatrist.'

COMPOUND SENTENCE: consists of two or more main clauses. **Example**: 'That cat needs a psychiatrist and we can help him find one, but he won't listen to reason.'

A compound sentence can be BALANCED or ANTITHETICAL (contrasting). A balanced sentence is one where the clauses support each other in structure and meaning. **Example**: 'The cat came, he saw, and he conquered.'

A contrasting (antithetical) sentence is one where the clauses balance each other but are opposite in meaning and so provide a contrast. **Examples**: 'The cat arrived and the canary departed.' 'Man proposes, God disposes.'

A COMPLEX sentence has one main clause and one or more subordinate clauses. **Example**: 'That cat resents the canary, instead of welcoming her, as they are both strays.'

There are two types of complex sentence: LOOSE and PERIODIC. A loose sentence has the main idea or clause at the beginning. It is a top-heavy sentence, but it is easy to understand, as you get the main part first. **For example**: 'The student was terrified that the neighbours would report him to the ISPCA after the terrific din involving the cat and the canary had resulted in a broken window and numerous phone calls to the Gardaí.'

A periodic sentence keeps the main idea to the end. This is a good form to use if you want to build up the tension. **For example**: 'Instead of welcoming him, as they were both strays, that cat resents the canary.'

A COMPOUND-COMPLEX sentence has two or more main clauses and at least one subordinate clause. **For example**: 'That cat needs a psychiatrist, and we must help him to find one who will listen to his tales of unhappy kittenhood.'

A SENTENCE FRAGMENT or phrase can be effective in a proper context, if not over-used. **Example**: 'That cat looks twenty years old. Perhaps older.'

¶ For elegant writing, **vary your sentence structures**.

Exercises

Study, and as far as possible identify, the sentence structures used by that master of English prose P. G. Wodehouse in each of the following extracts.

(a) The summer day was drawing to a close and dusk had fallen on Blandings Castle, shrouding from view the ancient battlements, dulling the silver surface of the lake and causing Lord Emsworth's supreme Berkshire sow Empress of Blandings to leave the open air portion of her sty and withdraw into the covered shed where she did her sleeping. A dedicated believer in the maxim of early to bed and early to rise, she always turned in at about this time. Only by getting its regular eight hours can a pig keep up to the mark and preserve that schoolgirl complexion.

Deprived of her society, which he had been enjoying since shortly after lunch, Clarence, ninth Earl of Emsworth, the seigneur of this favoured realm, pottered dreamily back to the house, pottered dreamily to the great library which was one of its features, and had just pottered dreamily to his favourite chair, when Beach, his butler, entered bearing a laden tray. He gave it the vague stare which had so often incurred the censure—'Oh, for goodness' sake, Clarence, don't stand there looking like a goldfish'—of his sisters Constance, Dora, Charlotte, Julia and Hermione.

'Eh?' he said. 'What?' he added.

'Your dinner, m'lord.'

Lord Emsworth's face cleared. He was telling himself that he might have known that there would be some simple explanation for that tray. Trust Beach to have everything under control.

(b) A thouroughly misspent life had left the Hon. Galahad Threepwood, contrary to the most elementary justice, in what appeared to be perfect, even exuberantly perfect physical condition. How a man who ought to have had the liver of the century could look and behave as he did was a constant mystery to his associates. His eye was not dimmed nor his natural force abated. And when, skipping blithely across the turf, he tripped over the spaniel, so graceful was the agility with which he recovered his balance that he did not spill a drop of the whiskey-and-soda in his hand. He continued to bear the glass aloft like some brave banner beneath which he had often fought and won. Instead of the blot on the proud family, he might have been a teetotal acrobat.

(c) *[Ronald Fish found his girl-friend with a strange man in a restaurant and proceeded to wreck the place before he was evicted by a posse of waiters.]*

The Law of Great Britain is a remorseless machine, which, once set in motion, ignores first causes and takes into account only results. It will not accept shattered dreams as an excuse for shattering glassware: nor will you get far by pleading a broken heart in extenuation of your behaviour in breaking waiters. Haled on the morrow before the awful majesty of Justice at Bosher Street Police Court and charged with disorderly conduct in a public place—to wit, Mario's Restaurant, and resisting an officer—to wit, P.C. Murgatroyd, in the execution of his duties, Ronald Fish made no impassioned speeches. He did not raise clenched fists aloft and call upon Heaven to witness that he was a good man wronged. Experience, dearly bought in the days of his residence at the University, had taught him that when the Law gripped you with its talons the only thing to do was to give a false name, say nothing and hope for the best.

14 Grammar, Style and Spelling

Paragraphs

> **HINTS**
>
> **1.** One main theme or topic per paragraph. The kernel of this idea is usually found in a sentence called the TOPIC SENTENCE.
>
> **2.** Be aware of the shape or the structure of each paragraph. Some paragraphs have the topic idea at the start and the remainder of the paragraph explains, fills out or gives examples of that theme.

Exercise

Read and explain the structure of this opening paragraph from an essay by George Orwell.

Shooting an elephant (extract)

In Moulmein, in Lower Burma, I was hated by large numbers of people—the only time in my life that I have been important enough for this to happen to me. I was subdivisional police officer of the town, and in an aimless, petty kind of way anti-European feeling was very bitter. No one had the guts to raise a riot, but if a European woman went through the bazaars alone somebody would probably spit betel juice over her dress. As a police officer I was an obvious target and was baited whenever it seemed safe to do so. When a nimble Burman tripped me up on the football field and the referee (another Burman) looked the other way, the crowd yelled with hideous laughter. This happened more than once. In the end the sneering yellow face of the young men that met me everywhere, the insults hooted after me when I was at a safe distance, got badly on my nerves. The young Buddhist priests were the worst of all. There were several thousand of them in the town and none of them seemed to have anything to do except stand on street corners and jeer at Europeans.

> **HINTS**
>
> **3.** Some paragraphs build up to a climax, where each sentence is a carefully constructed rung on the ladder leading up to the final punch-line. Examine this paragraph by P. G. Wodehouse and explain the structure.

Ronnie Fish in the course of his life had had many ambitions. As a child, he had yearned some day to become an engine-driver. At school, it had seemed to him that the most attractive career the world had to offer was that of the professional cricketer. Later, he had hoped to run a prosperous night-club. But now, in his twenty-sixth year, all these desires were cast aside and forgotten. The only thing in life that seemed really worth while was to massacre waiters; and to this task he addressed himself with all the energy and strength at his disposal.

> **HINTS** **4.** Paragraphs need to be LINKED to each other, so linking sentences are important. **HINTS**

Exercise

Examine the following piece and explain how the ideas are linked, i.e. how each paragraph follows from the previous one.

Energy

Despite what certain advertisements may try to tell you, lost energy cannot be replaced. Energy is never really lost in the first place, merely transformed from a usable form to a non-usable form. Unfortunately, the non-usable form of energy is often a form of pollution.

The laws of physics tell us that energy cannot be created or destroyed but only transformed from one state to another. This means that the amount of energy in the universe today is exactly the same as the amount of energy present when the universe was first created. It is the constant which connects us to the billions of years of evolution of this planet. How long human beings continue to live in this universe depends very much on our future use of energy resources.

The more conventional view of energy is energy which can be harnessed to perform 'work'. Seen in this sense, the energy on Planet Earth is derived from the sun and can be divided into two categories, renewable and non-renewable.

Renewable energy sources—those most favoured by the Green Movement—include solar, wind, tidal and wave energy. As long as the sun exists these energy resources will be with us. According to reliable scientific predictions, the sun will continue to produce heat for many billions of years.

On the other hand, non-renewable resources such as coal, oil and gas, which are in effect forms of stored solar energy, will run out much sooner. Recoverable oil deposits are expected to last another 60 years. The world is still rich in coal and the resources may last as long as two hundred years.

It is, however, our overuse of these fuels which has led to some of the worst environmental problems, among them acid rain and urban smog. But the problem which is of most concern to governments, scientists and environmentalists is the 'Greenhouse Effect'. Carbon dioxide released when fossil fuels are burnt is one of the main greenhouse gases. What is perhaps even more alarming is the way in which the nuclear industry is using the 'Greenhouse Effect' as a way of promoting nuclear power as an environmentally safe energy source!

> **HINTS** **5.** Opening paragraphs are particularly important. They need to grab attention and set the tone. They can be descriptive, explanatory, dramatic, formal, conversational—the choice is yours, and it is wide. **HINTS**

16 Grammar, Style and Spelling

Exercise

Here are some opening paragraphs from novels. **(a)** Which ones do you think most effective and why? **(b)** What kind of book do you think is likely to develop from each?

(i) There were no curtains up. The window was a hard edged block the colour of the night sky. Inside the bedroom the darkness was of a gritty texture. The wardrobe and bed were blurred shapes in the darkness. Silence.

(ii) 'Now, what I want is, Facts. Teach these boys and girls nothing but Facts. Facts alone are wanted in life. Plant nothing else, and root out everything else. You can only form the minds of reasoning animals upon Facts: nothing else will ever be of any service to them. This is the principle on which I bring up my own children, and this is the principle on which I bring up these children. Stick to Facts, sir!'

(iii) 'You keep away from the Birdman, Gracie,' my father had warned me often enough. 'Keep well clear of him, you hear me now?' And we never would have gone anywhere near him, Daniel and I, had the swans not driven us away from the pool under Gweal Hill where we always went to sail our boats.

(iv) When he was nearly thirteen, my brother Jem got his arm badly broken at the elbow. When it healed, and Jem's fears of never being able to play football were assuaged, he was seldom self-conscious about his injury. His left arm was somewhat shorter than his right; when he stood or walked, the back of his hand was at right-angles to his body, his thumb parallel to his thigh. He couldn't have cared less, so long as he could pass and punt.

(v) Once upon a time and a very good time it was there was a moocow coming down along the road and this moocow that was coming down along the road met a nicens little boy named baby tuckoo ... His father told him that story: his father looked at him through a glass: he had a hairy face.

Style

Most literary criticism tends to focus on two aspects of writing: content and style.

STYLE is generally taken to mean **THE DISTINCTIVE TRAITS OF A PARTICULAR WRITER**. The style is linked to the content. For the style to be effective it must communicate the content clearly, suit the subject matter, and fulfil the author's purpose in writing.

When examining a writer's style, ask yourself:
(a) Is the writing clear and effective?
(b) Does it fulfil the author's purpose? (What is the author's purpose in writing—to inform us of facts? to persuade or move us? to give directions or orders? to entertain us? etc.)
(c) What is the **TONE** of the piece? (For tone, think of tone of voice. Is the author being objective or emotional? happy or sad? gentle? abrasive? angry? humorous? ironic? etc.)
(d) What particular language features does the author use? Consider:
VOCABULARY—simpler or sophisticated? Obscure old-fashioned (archaic) dialect? slang? etc.
TYPES OF SENTENCES—Refer back to simple, complex, compound sentences etc. What is the effect of these: variety? humour? serious tone? or what?
FIGURES OF SPEECH—such as:

Alliteration: when words following each other begin with the same letter or sound. *Example*: 'When weeds in wheels shoot long and lovely and lush.' This device can be used for sound effects or to emphasise a point.

Antithesis: contrasting ideas set opposite each other in balanced phrases or clauses. *Example*: 'Man proposes, God disposes.'

Assonance: repetition of the same sound in consecutive words. *Example*: 'No go for Coe.' Again this device is used for musical effect or to draw attention.

Euphemism: an inoffensive-sounding expression used to conceal the grim reality. *Example*: 'being economical with the truth'—lying! This can be used for humorous effect.

Hyperbole: exaggeration in order to draw attention to something. *Example*: 'I could eat a horse.'

Irony: saying one thing but meaning another. *Example*: 'That was a good day's work. We only lost our major contract!' This device is usually used when one wants to be sarcastic or cutting. So it might be an important element in the tone of a piece of writing.

Metaphor: an image that describes one thing in terms of another. *Examples*: 'He was a rock of a full-back.' 'She sailed out the door in disgust.' This is used to add colour to the writing: to paint pictures for the reader.

Onomatopoeia: when the sound of the word suggests the meaning. *Examples*: 'lash', 'crunch', 'sizzle', 'echo', etc. This is used to create musical sound effects and also to evoke realism in a piece.

18 GRAMMAR, STYLE AND SPELLING

Paradox: a statement that appears at first reading to be contradictory. *Examples*: 'the wisest fool in Christendom'; 'a sweet unrest'.

Pathetic fallacy: giving human characteristics to inanimate objects. *Example*: 'The skies wept at the sight.'

Rhetorical question: a question asked for effect, a question that you do not expect to be answered. *Example*: 'Why should I blame her that she filled my days with misery!'

Simile: when two unlike things or ideas are compared, using the words 'like', 'as', or 'than'. *Examples*: 'as daft as a coot'; 'kisses like wine'. This device is used to add colour to writing.

■ Spelling: some rules

Plural of nouns

For most nouns add *s*:
  girl—girls
  boy—boys
  stone—stones
  book—books

Add **es** to some words where it would be difficult to pronounce them just as an **s**:
  bus—buses
  buzz—buzzes
  six—sixes
  church—churches
  thrush—thrushes
Note: These are words ending in s, z, x, ch, and sh.

Nouns ending in *f* or *fe*: change to *ves*:
  half—halves
  loaf—loaves
  calf—calves
  wife—wives

Exceptions:
  chief—chiefs
  grief—griefs
  roof—roofs
  cliff—cliffs

Nouns ending in *y*
(a) ending in a vowel + **y**: add **s**:
  boy—boys
  bay—bays
  donkey—donkeys
  abbey—abbeys
  monkey—monkeys
(b) ending in a consonant + **y**: change **y** to **i** and add **es**:
  baby—babies
  daisy—daisies
  lorry—lorries
  fly—flies
  sky—skies

Nouns ending in *o*
(a) ending in a vowel + **o**: add **s**:
  radio—radios
  stereo—stereos
  video—videos

(b) consonant + **o**: add **es**:
cargo—cargoes
echo—echoes
hero—heroes
potato—potatoes
tomato—tomatoes
This rule has many exceptions:
  grotto—grottos
  halo—halos
  piano—pianos
  solo—solos
Can you think of others?

Unusual plurals

foot—feet
man—men
woman—women
mouse—mice
ox—oxen
child—children
sheep—sheep
salmon—salmon
deer—deer
Can you think of others?

ie or ei

Usually *i* before *e* except after *c*:
brief   ceiling
grief   deceive
niece   perceive
priest   receive
shield
siege

How many more can you think of?

Exceptions
(a) where there is an '**ay**' sound:
  eight
  reign
  sleigh
  neighbour

(b) odd ones!
  either
  neither
  foreigner
  seize
  weird
Can you think of others?

Adding a suffix

1. If the word ends in a silent **e**, drop the **e** before adding a suffix beginning with a vowel:
  argue—arguing
  come—coming
  cure—curable
  fame—famous
  have—having
  refuse—refusal
Some exceptions:
  canoe—canoeing
  courage—courageous
  advantage—advantageous
  notice—noticeable
  knowledge—knowledgeable

2. If the word ends in a consonant + **y**, change the **y** to **i** before any suffix except **ing**:
  marry—married (but marrying)
  try—tried (but trying)
  beauty—beautiful
  mystery—mysterious

empty—emptiness
study—studied (but studying)
Some exceptions
dry—dryness
shy—shyness
day—daily } vowel + **y**,
pay—paid   } yet it changes
say—said   } nevertheless

Exception:
limit—limited

4. Adding **ful** to nouns: note that there is only one **l**:
beauty—beautiful
success—successful
hope—hopeful

Doubling the final letter

3. A word ending in a single consonant that is preceded by a single vowel doubles the consonant when you add an ending that begins with a vowel:
drop—dropped—dropping
hum—hummed—humming
rob—robbed—robbing
run—runner—running
begin—beginner—beginning
commit—committed—committing
permit—permitted—permitting
occur—occurred—occurring

5. Most words don't change when **ly** is added:
bold—boldly
warm—warmly
If the word ends in **y**, change it to **i** before **ly**:
happy—happily

6. Adding **'ally'**
To make adverbs, add **ally** to adjectives ending in **ic**, even though the **al** is not sounded:
basic—basically
realistic—realistically
Exception:
public—publicly

List of words frequently misspelt

(i) Check each one, and underline any that give you trouble. **(ii)** Add words that you yourself frequently misspell.

absence	appearance	
accidentally	appoint	beautifully
accommodation	arctic	beginning
achieve	arguing	believing
acknowledge	argument	beneficial
aerial	ascend	benefited
agreeable	athletics	breathe
all right	awful	budgeted
amateur	awkward	business

ceiling
cemetery
changeable
character
cloth
clothes
college
coming
committed
committee
competent
conscience
conscientious
conscious
consistent
coolly
courageous
courtesy

deceive
definitely
develop
disappearance
disappointment
dissatisfied
drunkenness

eerie
eight
eliminated
embarrassed
emigrate
emphasise
enthusiasm
equipped
essential
exaggerate
excellent
exhausted

existence
experience
explanation
extremely

February
financial
forehead
foreigner
friend
fulfil
fulfilled

gauge
glamorous
glamour
grammar
grievance
guard

handkerchief
handkerchiefs
height
humorous
humour
hurriedly
hypocrisy

imaginatively
immediately
immigrate
independence
indispensable
intelligence
irresistible

knowledge
knowledgeable

leisure

liaison
likeable/likable
literature
loneliness
lonely
lose
loveable/lovable

maintain
maintenance
manageable
marriage
medicine
Mediterranean
miniature
minutes
mischief
mischievous

necessary
negotiate
niece
noticeable

occasionally
occur
occurred
occurrence
omit
omitted
organiser
originally

panic
panicked
parallel
paralysis
parliament
permanent
permissible

perseverance
personnel
physical
planning
pleasant
poem
poetry
possesses
preceding
preference
prejudice
preliminary
prestige
privilege
procedure
proprietary
prosecutor
psychology
pursue

quarrel
quarrelling
queue
queuing
quiet

receipt
received
recipe

recognise
recommend
referred
relieved
repetition
restaurant
rhyme
rhythm
rhythmic
ridiculous

scene
science
secretaries
seize
sense
sentence
separate
siege
similar
sincerely
skilful
skilfully
solemnly
statutory
successfully
supersede
suppression
surprise

synonym
synonymous
taught
tendency
thorough
thought
tragedy
tranquil
truly
twelfth
tyranny
unconscious
undoubtedly
unnecessary
until
usually

valuable
vicious
view

Wednesday
weird
whole
wholly
wilful
wilfully
wool
woollen

Common confusions

These words are often mistakenly used in the wrong context. For each one construct a sentence that demonstrates its correct usage.

their	to	were
there	too	we're
they're	two	where

quite	eminent	pedal
quiet	imminent	peddle
	immanent	
its		lightening
it's	draft	lightning
	draught	
taught		brooch
thought	principle	broach
	principal	
of		canvass
off	accept	canvas
	except	
course		steak
coarse	board	stake
	bored	
waist		advice
waste	cue	advise
	queue	
lose		practice
loose	plain	practise
	plane	
immigrant		stationary
emigrant	council	stationery
	counsel	

Add your own common confusions to this list.

Categories of prose writing

The personal writing question offers you a wide choice of titles and writing format. In the section you get an opportunity to examine and to practise different categories and styles of prose writing, in particular: descriptive writing, autobiographical writing, the short story, diary writing, and an essay. As a result you should be in a position to choose a form of writing that suits you best and shows off your literary skills.

Descriptive prose—characterisation

Perhaps the easiest way into descriptive writing is to begin with character descriptions. Who better to launch us than Dylan Thomas, with his delightfully eccentric yet poetic caricatures of his uncle and aunt? His particular technique involves the use of simile, metaphor (comparisons), and hyperbole (exaggeration).

Uncle
Dylan Thomas

I was staying at the time with my uncle and his wife. Although she was my aunt, I never thought of her as anything but the wife of my uncle, partly because he was so big and trumpeting and red-hairy and used to fill every inch of the hot little house like an old buffalo squeezed into an airing cupboard, and partly because she was so small and silk and quick and made no noise at all as she whisked about on padded paws dusting china dogs, feeding the buffalo, setting the mousetraps that never caught her; and once she sleaked out of the room, to squeak in a nook or nibble in a hay loft, you forgot she had ever been there. But there he was, always, a steaming hulk of an uncle, his braces straining like hawsers, crammed behind the counter of the tiny shop at the front of the house, and breathing like a brass band, or guzzling and blustery in the kitchen over his gutsy supper, too big for everything except the great black boats of his boots. As he ate, the house grew smaller, he billowed out over the furniture, the loud check meadow of his waistcoat littered as though after a picnic, with cigarette ends, peelings, cabbage stalks, birds' bones, gravy; and the forest fire of his hair crackled among the crooked beams on the ceiling.

Exercises

1. What picture of the uncle do you get from this description? Examine how this picture is created through the connotations or suggestions of the many similes and metaphors used; for example, 'like an old buffalo squeezed into an airing cupboard' carries suggestions of a huge, shaggy, unkempt creature, totally out of place in a tiny little house.

   Now examine the other descriptive metaphors and similes and say what picture of the uncle emerges.

2. What picture of the aunt do you get? Examine the images used to describe her.
3. Do you think the hyperbole is effective in this case?
4. Make a list of any words or phrases you thought particularly effective and that you might use in your own writing.

HOME BEFORE NIGHT (EXTRACT)
Hugh Leonard

My grandmother made dying her life's work. I remember her as a vast malevolent old woman, so obese that she was unable to wander beyond the paved yard outside her front door. Her pink-washed cottage had two rooms and she agonized her way through and around them, clutching at the furniture for support and emitting heart-scalding gasps, as if death was no further off than the dresser or the settle bed where my uncle Sonny slept himself sober. In those days people confused old age with valour; they called her a great old warrior. This had the effect of inspiring her to gasp even more distressingly by way of proving them right and herself indomitable. In case her respiratory noises should come to be as taken for granted as the ticking of the clock (which at least stopped now and then), she provided a contrapuntal accompaniment by kicking the chairs, using the milk jugs as cymbals and percussing the kettle and frying pan.

To be fair, it was her only diversion. The rent-man, peering in over the half door, would suffer like a damned soul as she counted out three shillings and ninepence in coppers, threepenny bits and sixpences, wheezing a goodbye to each coin, and then began her tortured via dolorosa towards him, determined to pay her debts before dropping dead at his feet, a martyr to landlordism. Even Dr Enright was intimidated. When he had listened to her heartbeats it was not his stethoscope but her doomed slaughterhouse eyes imploring the worst which caused him to tell her: 'Sure we've all got to go some day, ma'am.' That pleased her. Privately, she saw no reason why she should go at any time, but she liked to nod submissively, essay a practice death-rattle and resignedly endorse the will of the Almighty.

She dressed in shiny black and wore a brooch inscribed 'Mother'. Her girth almost exceeded her stature, and her prodigious appetite amazed me, for her cooking verged on the poisonous: in fact, I have known no other woman who could make fried eggs taste like perished rubber. On the occasions when my mother deposited me at Rosanna Cottage for the day, the midday meal consisted unvaryingly of fried eggs and potatoes. I was too afraid of her baleful eyes to refuse to eat, so would get rid of the accursed egg by balancing it on the blade of my knife and swallowing it whole. This she came to interpret as a tribute to her culinary powers and, as my eyes steamed and gorge rose, would set about frying me another egg.

Her husband, a casual labourer, had died suddenly in 1926 after cleaning out a cesspit. They had four children: Sonny, Mary, Christine and Margaret, my mother. Sonny, who lived at home, courted a laundress named Kate Fortune for more than thirty years and finally married her when the will of God at last prevailed over that of my grandmother. By then the lovers were in their mid-fifties. Kate Fortune was sheep-faced, bony and as tall—above six feet—as Sonny was short. She exuded a perpetual dampness, which I always ascribed to her labours in the Dargle Laundry, and was permitted to cross my grandmother's threshold only at Christmas. She would sit, dumbly miserable, the heiress presumptive to the cottage and on that account hated, trying to find a hiding place for the marzipan from the home-baked Christmas cake. Even Sonny came to ignore her, for she grew plainer and bonier each year. Once, such was her hurry to be off and catch the Bray bus home that she forgot to stoop and banged her head against the lintel. She cried out and slid to the ground, folding at the joints this way and that like an anchor chain and clutching her forehead. When Sonny pulled her hand away to examine the injury, a viscous grey slime oozed down between her eyes, and at first we thought that she had dashed her brains out. Then we realised it was squashed marzipan which she had been concealing in her fist.

Less from choice than necessity, Kate went on toiling in the laundry after she and Sonny were married. His life had always been encompassed by the labour exchange, Dowling's betting office and Larkin's public house and it seemed only commonsense to him that for Kate to cease work and for him to commence would be a case of robbing Peter to pay Paul. Also, as he pointed out, to disrupt the balance of nature so late in life could be injurious to their systems. He had dark, disappointed eyes. He stood in Gilbey's doorway which commanded a view of Castle Street and nodded curtly at passers-by, knowing that every one of them would do him down if given the chance. His shortness was aggravated by a hoppity limp which obliged him to stand to attention with one leg and at ease with the other, and was caused, so my father told me—perhaps apocryphally—by Sonny having fallen asleep in the lavatory for six hours when the worse for drink. There was a long narrow lane leading to Rosanna Cottage, and there I found him once, standing erect but unconscious, his head embedded in the depths of a prickly hedge. The smell of stale porter constantly enveloped him like a caul, and, in common with the other Doyles, in drink or out of it he was a ready enemy. Forget to salute him in the town, and your name was scrawled indelibly in the black book of his brain. When he limped out of the betting office and tore up his docket, there was a smell of anger as well as of porter. He would smile, biding his hour against the hidden beings who had denied him a fair crack of life's whip.

Writing style

1. The writer avoids the more predictable approach to character description—i.e. going through a list of facial features: hair, eyes, nose, teeth, etc., and so down the body. Instead he focuses on certain outstanding features or qualities: her obesity; her walk or waddle; her health and impressions of dying; her cooking; and her sheer power and dominance over people.

2. The description is strikingly visual: he makes pictures for the readers. Examine, for instance, the memorable account of her walking. He uses unusual and graphic verbs to communicate the laborious: 'she agonised her way ... clutching at the furniture ... emitting heart-scalding gasps ...' And later 'she provided a contrapuntal accompaniment by kicking the chairs, using the milk jugs as cymbals and percussing the kettle and frying pan.' This image of a grotesque one-woman orchestra might be wildly exaggerated but is surely memorable.

3. There is a great variety of sentence length and structures, which is essential in any good writing. For example, the piece opens with a simple sentence, short, striking, witty in its paradox (apparent contradiction)—a catchy opening. This is followed by two more involved, complex sentences. Then the fourth sentence is a fine example of a symmetrical, balanced sentence, the second half complementing the first, like a folded newspaper. 'In those days people confused old age with valour: they called her a great old warrior.'

28 Descriptive Prose—Characterisation

Exercises

1. What picture of his grandmother does the writer want us to remember? Refer to the text to support your views.
2. In his description of her, what image do you find most effective, and why?
3. 'His description of Kate Fortune is equally memorable.' Comment on this statement.
4. How does the writer approach the characterisation of Uncle Sonny? Do you think it is effective?
5. 'The use of striking and unusual similes is one of Hugh Leonard's most effective techniques.' Comment on the truth of this.
6. Do you think humour plays any part in the effective characterisation here?
7. How would you describe the writer's attitude to the characters he portrays? What words and images best convey this attitude?
8. Make a list of any words and phrases you thought effective.

MOTHER
From *Cider with Rosie* by Laurie Lee

Deserted, debt-ridden, flurried, bewildered, doomed by ambitions that never came off, yet our Mother possessed an indestructible gaiety which welled up like a thermal spring. Her laughing, like her weeping, was instantaneous and childlike, and switched without warning—or memory. Her emotions were entirely without reserve; she clouted you one moment and hugged you the next—to the ruin of one's ragged nerves. If she knocked over a pot, or cut her finger she let out a blood-chilling scream—then forgot about it immediately in a hop and skip or a song. I can still seem to hear her blundering about the kitchen: shrieks and howls of alarm, an occasional oath, a gasp of wonder, a sharp command to things to stay still. A falling coal would set her hair on end, a loud knock made her leap and yell, her world was a maze of small traps and snares acknowledged always by cries of dismay. One couldn't help jumping in sympathy with her, though one learned to ignore these alarms. They were, after all, no more than formal salutes to the devils that dogged her heels.

Often, when working and not actually screaming, Mother kept up an interior monologue. Or she would absent-mindedly pick up your last remark and sing it back at you in doggerel. 'Give me some tart,' you might say, for instance. 'Give you some tart? Of course … Give me some tart! O give me your heart! Give me your heart to keep! I'll guard it well, my pretty Nell, As the shepherd doth guard his sheep, tra-la …'

Whenever there was a pause in the smashing of crockery, and Mother was in the mood, she would make up snap verses about local characters that could stab like a three-pronged fork:

Mrs Okey
Makes me choky:
Hit her with a mallet!—croquet.

This was typical of their edge, economy, and freedom. Mrs Okey was our local postmistress and an amiable, friendly woman; but my mother would sacrifice anybody for a rhyme.

Mother, like Gran Trill, lived by no clocks, and unpunctuality was bred in her bones. She was particularly offhand where buses were concerned and missed more than she ever caught. In the free-going days when only carrier-carts ran to Stroud she would often hold them up for an hour, but when the motor-bus started she saw no difference and carried on in the same old way. Not till she heard the horn winding down from the Sheepscombe did she ever begin to get ready. Then she would cram on her hat and fly round the kitchen with habitual cries and howls.

'Where's my gloves? Where's my handbag? Damn and cuss—where's my shoes? You can't find a thing in this hole! Help me, you idiots—don't just jangle and jarl—you'll all make me miss it, I know. Scream! There it comes!—Laurie, run up and stop it. Tell them I won't be a minute ...'

So I'd tear up the bank, just in time as usual, while the packed bus came to a halt.

'... Just coming, she says. Got to find her shoes. Won't be a minute, she says ...'

Misery for me; I stood there blushing; the driver honked his horn, while all the passengers leaned out of the windows and shook their umbrellas crossly.

'Mother Lee again. Lost 'er shoes again. Come on, put a jerk in it there!'

Then sweet and gay from down the bank would come Mother's placating voice.

'I'm coming—yoo-hoo! Just mislaid my gloves. Wait a second! I'm coming, my dears.'

Puffing and smiling, hat crooked, scarf dangling, clutching her baskets and bags, she'd come hobbling at last through the stinging-nettles and climb hiccuping into her seat ...

When neither bus nor carrier-cart were running, Mother walked the four miles to the shops, trudging back home with her baskets or groceries and scattering packets of tea in the mud. When she tired of this, she'd borrow Dorothy's bicycle, though she never quite mastered the machine. Happy enough when the thing was in motion, it was stopping and starting that puzzled her. She had to be launched on her way by running parties of villagers; and to stop she rode into a hedge. With the Stroud Co-op Stores, where she was a registered customer, she had come to a special arrangement. This depended for its success upon a quick ear and timing, and was a beautiful operation to watch. As she coasted downhill towards the shop's main entrance she would let out one of her screams; an assistant, specially briefed, would tear through the shop, out the side door, and catch her in his arms. He had to be both young and nimble, for if he missed her she piled up by the police-station.

Our mother was a buffoon, extravagant and romantic, and was never wholly taken seriously. Yet within her she nourished a delicacy of taste, a sensibility, a brightness of spirit, which though continuously bludgeoned by the cruelties of her luck remained uncrushed and unembittered to the end. Wherever she got it from, God knows—or how she managed to preserve it. But she loved this world and saw it fresh with hopes that never clouded. She was an artist, a light-giver, and an original, and she never for a moment knew it ...

Exercises

1. From the first paragraph, what impression of the writer's mother do you get? What details reinforce this impression?
2. Do you think the simile in the first sentence catches the essential character of the woman? Explain.
3. What do the interior monologue and the rhyming verses of paragraphs 2 and 3 suggest about the character of the woman? Explain.
4. Punctuality is not one of her strong points and she gets into a right muddle at the arrival of the bus. (*a*) Explain how the dialogue at this point catches the atmosphere. (*b*) Study the graphic description of her entry to the bus. What effect is created?
5. What do you think were the author's feelings towards his mother (*a*) at the time of the story and (*b*) now as he remembers? Support your views with reference to the extract.
6. Contrast the tone of the piece with the tone of the previous extract.

    TONE refers to the writer's feelings and attitude towards the subject matter, as reflected in the choice of words, images, etc. Think of **TONE OF VOICE**. Would you consider the writer in each case to be savagely critical or satirical; gently critical; unsympathetic; amused; indifferent; sad; humorous; nostalgic? Support your views with reference to the text.
7. What elements of the writing style make this a memorable characterisation? Consider such techniques as descriptive writing, imagery, realistic dialogue, and tone.
8. Make a list of any new vocabulary you encountered or phrases you thought interesting and might use again.

Writing

1. Compose three descriptive paragraphs on a grandmother, grandfather, uncle or aunt you know or remember.

2. Choose any one of these photographs and compose an imaginative characterisation of five paragraphs on the person of your choice. It may help you to think up a name, occupation, age, interests, family situation, house details, patterns of speech, etc. Place the character in some contexts such as at work, leisure, home, shopping, etc. Choose significant details and locations.

DESCRIPTIVE PROSE—CHARACTERISATION 31

32 Descriptive Prose—Characterisation

Descriptive Prose—Characterisation

34 Descriptive Prose—Characterisation

Descriptive Prose 35

Characterisation

> **EXAM HINTS**
> 1. Make **pictures** for the reader.
> 2. Choose significant or **interesting details** or characteristics that reveal the character.
> 3. Place your character in **contexts** or situations that help bring him or her alive.

Other descriptive prose
Travel, places, etc.

What do you need to aim at?
(What does the reader want?)

WRITING AND EXAM HINTS

| 1. DETAILS— the *w* questions: who, where, what, when, why? etc. But details can be boring to read, so —MAKE PICTURES CREATE COLOUR Use similes metaphors adjectives adverbs etc. | 2. ATMOSPHERE— the feelings of people present; the general mood of the event, whether relaxed or tense, etc. State of mind of the writer. —ESTABLISH MOOD Adopt a tone of voice | 3. STRUCTURE— needs to be logical and easily understood, so it must be paragraphed, but not tedious to read, so —VARIETY in sentences and paragraphs. |

WRITING AND EXAM HINTS

Read this description of a meal from Peter Mayle's *A Year in Provence* and discuss how it measures up to the criteria above. First do your own analysis, then see if you can agree with the analysis underneath.

A Year in Provence (extract)

1. The cold weather cuisine of Provence is peasant food. It is made to stick to your ribs, keep you warm, give you strength and send you off to bed with a full belly. It is not pretty, in the way that the tiny and artistically garnished portions served in fashionable restaurants

are pretty, but on a freezing night with the Mistral coming at you like a razor there is nothing to beat it. And on the night one of our neighbours invited us to dinner it was cold enough to turn the short walk to their house into a short run.

2. We came through the door and my glasses steamed up in the heat from the fireplace that occupied most of the far wall of the room. As the mist cleared I saw that the big table, covered in checked oilcloth, was laid for ten; friends and relations were coming to examine us. A television set chattered in the corner, the radio chattered back from the kitchen, and assorted dogs and cats where shooed out of the door as one guest arrived, only to sidle back in with the next. A tray of drinks was brought out, with pastis for the men and chilled, sweet muscat wine for the women, and we were caught in a crossfire of noisy complaints about the weather. Was it as bad as this in England? Only in the summer, I said. For a moment they took me seriously before someone saved me from embarrassment by laughing. With a great deal of jockeying for position—whether to sit next to us or as far away as possible, I wasn't sure—we settled ourselves at the table.

3. It was a meal that we shall never forget; more accurately, it was several meals that we shall never forget, because it went beyond the gastronomic frontiers of anything we had ever experienced, both in quantity and length.

4. It started with home-made pizza—not one, but three: anchovy, mushroom and cheese, and it was obligatory to have a slice of each. Plates were then wiped with pieces torn from the two-foot loaves in the middle of the table, and the next course came out. There were pâtés of rabbit, boar and thrush. There was a chunky, pork-based terrine laced with *marc*. There were *saucissons* spotted with peppercorns. There were tiny onions marinated in a fresh tomato sauce. Plates were wiped once more and duck was brought in. The slivers of *magret* that appear, arranged in fan formation and lapped by an elegant smear of sauce on the refined tables of nouvelle cuisine—these were nowhere to be seen. We had entire breasts, entire legs, covered in a dark, savoury gravy and surrounded by wild mushrooms.

5. We sat back, thankful that we had been able to finish, and watched with something close to panic as plates were wiped yet again and a huge, steaming casserole was placed on the table. This was the speciality of Madame our hostess—a rabbit *civet* of the richest, deepest brown—and our feeble requests for small portions were smilingly ignored. We ate it. We ate the green salad with knuckles of bread fried in garlic and olive oil, we ate the plump round *crottins* of goat's cheese, we ate the almond and cream gâteau that the daughter of the house had prepared. That night, we ate for England.

6. With coffee, a number of deformed bottles were produced which contained a selection of locally-made *digestifs*. My heart would have sunk had there been any space left for it to sink to, but there was no denying my host's insistence. I must try one particular concoction, made from an eleventh-century recipe by an alcoholic order of monks in the Basses-Alpes. I was asked to close my eyes while it was poured, and when I opened them a tumbler of viscous yellow fluid had been put in front of me. I looked in despair round the table. Everyone was watching me; there was no chance of giving whatever it was to the dog, or letting it dribble discreetly into one of my shoes. Clutching the table for support with one hand, I took the tumbler with the other, closed my eyes, prayed to the patron saint of indigestion, and threw it back.

7. Nothing came out. I had been expecting at best a scalded tongue, at worst permanently cauterised taste buds, but I took in nothing but air. It was a trick glass, and for the

first time in my adult life I was deeply relieved not to have a drink. As the laughter of the guests died away, genuine drinks were threatened, but we were saved by the cat. From her headquarters on top of a large *armoire*, she took a flying leap in pursuit of a moth and crash-landed among the coffee cups and bottles on the table. It seemed like an appropriate moment to leave. We walked home pushing our stomachs before us, oblivious of the cold, incapable of speech, and slept like the dead.

Notes
marc: white brandy   *digestifs*: liqueur   *armoire*: cupboard
magret: slices of duck   *saucissons*: salami-type sausages
civet: stew   *crottins*: slices

Analysis
Paragraph 1: A good introductory paragraph with a variety of sentence structure. The first sentence is a simple one, makes a statement, and is the key sentence or topic sentence of the whole paragraph, as it carries the main idea. This is followed by a complex sentence in a loose form. The third sentence is shaped symmetrically, with a fine balance between the two contrasting halves—'it is not pretty … but …' The fourth and final sentence rounds off the general discussion by bringing it down to the matter in hand, the particular meal.

Paragraph 2: This creates the atmosphere: the heat; full table; slight unease at being examined by all; the variety of noise—television, radio, cats and dogs, general talk of the weather, etc. The writer establishes a sort of mocking, humorous tone with reference to the seating arrangements.

This paragraph is shaped so as to come to a conclusion at the end. And it finishes with a good complex periodic sentence (i.e. main clause kept to the end) to reach the main point: settling down at the table.

Paragraph 3: For variety here is a short paragraph, of one complex sentence, with the main clause situated in the opening phrase.

Paragraph 4: In this paragraph the writer uses similar sentence shapes and repeated phrases to convey the notion of abundance: 'there were … there was … there were …' etc. In another context this might be poor writing and unimaginative structuring, but here it suggests the relentless procession of courses, which the writer is unable for. The repetition of phrases 'plates were then wiped' and 'plates were wiped once more' adds to this atmosphere.

Paragraph 5: Again the repetition of phrase; this time 'we ate' is very effective in conveying abundance and building up the tension. The climax is reached with a good concluding sentence, still carrying the key phrase. 'That night, we ate for England.' Notice the shape of this paragraph. It builds to a climax.

Paragraph 6: Another paragraph full of tension, which builds up to the end. Indeed the last sentence too is structured in phrases that all lean towards that last phrase 'and threw it back.' Good dramatic building.

Paragraph 7: This has a lovely opening sentence, just three words, which make a perfect contrast to all that complex structuring that went before and is a perfect anti-climax. Notice the variety of sentence openers here: 'Nothing came ... I had ... It was ... As the ... From her ... It seemed ... We walked ...' And the last sentence, a loose format of complex sentence, forms a good round-up and a nice cadence effect (or fall-off of the voice) at the end. It is structured so as to encourage this natural fall-off of the voice at the last phrase and so concludes or wraps up effectively.

You might also notice the colour of the writing: similes such as 'the Mistral coming at you like a razor'; colourful phrases such as 'an elegant smear of sauce'; graphic verbs such as 'dogs and cats *were shooed* out of the door ... only *to sidle* back in ...'; adjectives such as '*dark savoury* gravy ... *wild* mushrooms ... *huge steaming* casserole ... *deformed* bottles ... *viscous yellow* fluid', etc.

What tone does the writer establish? Examine his attitude to the French and their food. Is it respectful; overawed; amused; sneering; or what? Examine also his attitude to himself. Is it very serious or self-deprecating or what? What words and images best convey this tone?

Writing

Think in paragraphs

Write a description of a family meal you remember. It could be for a celebration such as Christmas, birthday, anniversary, other;

or a meal at which you helped to cook or serve;

or a description of an invitation to a friend's house for food;

or a party to which you were invited.

THE HEDGE SCHOOL

This extract is from Traits and Stories of the Irish Peasantry *by William Carleton (1794–1869), novelist and writer of short stories. He was born in Prillisk, Co. Tyrone, one of the large bilingual family of a small farmer. His works especially reflect the conditions and speech of the Irish peasantry.*

THE HEDGE SCHOOL

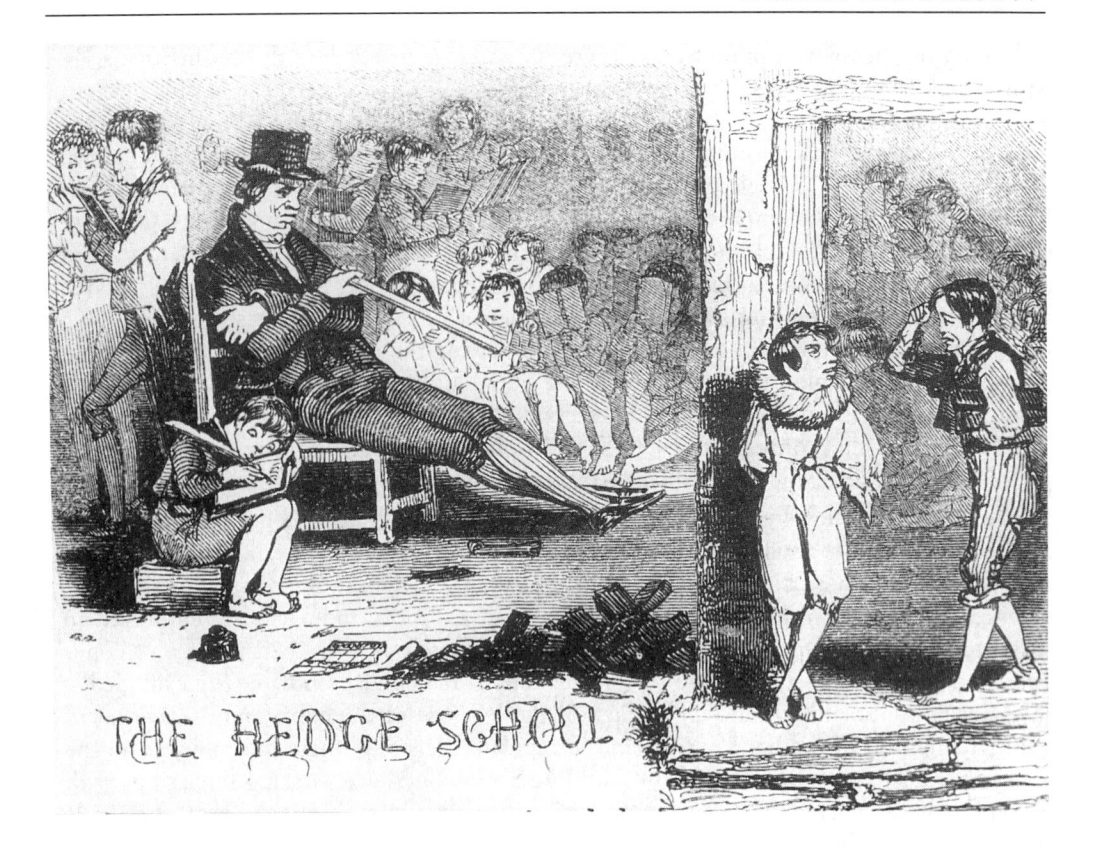

The reader will then be pleased to picture to himself a house in a line with the hedge; the eave of the back roof within a foot of the ground behind it; a large hole exactly in the middle of the 'riggin',' as a chimney; immediately under which is an excavation in the floor, burned away by a large fire of turf, loosely heaped together. This is surrounded by a circle of urchins, sitting on the bare earth, stones, and hassocks, and exhibiting a series of speckled shins, all radiating towards the fire like sausages on a Poloni dish. There they are—wedged as close as they can sit; one with half a thigh off his breeches—another with half an arm off his tattered coat—a fifth, with a cap on him, because he has got a scald, from having sat under the juice of fresh hung bacon—a sixth with a black eye—a seventh, two rags about his heels to keep his kibes clean—an eighth crying to get home, because he has got a headache, though it may be as well to hint that there is a drag-hunt to start from beside his father's in the course of the day.

In this ring, with his legs stretched in a most lordly manner, sits, upon a deal chair, Mat himself, with his hat on, basking in the enjoyment of unlimited authority. His dress consists of a black coat, considerably in want of repair, transferred to his shoulders through means of a clothes-broker in the country-town; a white cravat, round a large stuffing, having that part which comes in contact with the chin somewhat streaked with brown—a black waistcoat, with one or two 'tooth-an'-egg' metal buttons sewed on where the original had fallen off—black corduroy inexpressibles, twice dyed, and sheep's-gray stockings. In his hand is a large, broad ruler, the emblem of his power, the woeful instrument of executive justice, and the signal of terror to all within his jurisdiction.

In a corner below is a pile of turf, where on entering, every boy throws his two sods, with a hitch from under his left arm. He then comes up to the master, catches his forelock with finger and thumb, and bobs down his head, by way of making him a bow, and goes to his seat. Along the walls on the ground is a series of round stones, some of them capped with a straw collar or hassock, on which the boys sit; others have bosses, and many of them have hobs—a light but compact kind of boggy substance found in the mountains. On these several of them sit; the greater number of them, however, have no seats whatever, but squat themselves down, without compunction, on the hard floor. Hung about, on wooden pegs driven into the walls, are the shapeless 'caubeens' of such as can boast the luxury of a hat, or caps made of goat or hare's skin, the latter having the ears of the animal rising ludicrously over the temples, or cocked out at the sides, and the scut either before or behind, according to the taste or humour of the wearer.

The floor, which is only swept every Saturday, is strewed over with tops of quills, pens, pieces of broken slate, and tattered leaves of *Reading Made Easy*, or fragments of old copies. In one corner is a knot engaged at 'Fox and Geese', or the 'Walls of Troy' on their slates; in another, a pair of them are 'fighting bottles', which consists in striking the bottoms together, and he whose bottle breaks first, of course, loses. Behind the master is a third set, playing 'heads and points'—a game of pins. Some are more industriously employed in writing their copies, which they perform seated on the ground, with their paper on a copy-board—a piece of planed deal, the size of the copy, an appendage now nearly exploded—their cheek-bones laid within half an inch of the left side of the copy, and the eye set to guide the motion of the hand across, and to regulate the straightness of the lines and the forms of the letters. Others, again, of the more grown boys, are working their sums with becoming industry. In a dark corner are a pair of urchins thumping each other, their eyes steadily fixed on the master, lest he might happen to glance in that direction. Near the master himself are the larger boys, from twenty-two to fifteen—shaggy-headed slips, with loose-breasted shirts lying open upon them, that never knew a razor; strong stockings on their legs; heavy brogues, with broad, nail-paved soles; and breeches open at the knees. Nor is the establishment without a competent number of females. <u>These were, for the most part, the daughters of wealthy farmers, who considered it necessary to their respectability, that they should not be altogether illiterate; such a circumstance being a considerable drawback, in the opinion of an admirer, from the character of a young woman for whom he was about to propose—a drawback, too, which was always weighty in proportion to her wealth or respectability.</u>

Reading

1. In your own words and using not more than two sentences, express the main idea of the first paragraph.
2. What impression of the character and circumstances of Mat, the hedge school master, is conveyed through the details of the second paragraph?
3. 'The full variety of life was to be found even in the primitive hedge school.' Do you consider this statement a true reflection of Carleton's hedge school as it is described above? Illustrate your answers with references.
4. In your own words explain the underlined sentence.

Writing style

1. Examine the structure of the piece: four paragraphs, a different scene in each paragraph. (*a*) In your own words, briefly describe each scene. (*b*) Mention two details of each scene that make it graphic or vivid and say why you think this is so.

2. Notice the long complex sentences and the formal phrasing, which give it a rather grand style. For example, in paragraph 2 'His dress consists of a black coat, considerably in want of repair, transferred to his shoulders through the means of a clothes-broker in the country-town' could be translated as 'He wore a ragged black coat, which he got in a swap shop in town.' But has it the same elegant ring to it?

(*a*) Select four other rather grand or formal expressions that catch your eye and translate each into modern conversational idiom (style of speaking).

(*b*) Using this formal or grand style of writing, construct a description of this classroom scene or a typical classroom scene in your own school—five paragraphs.

3. Remembering the need for structure and graphic details, write a description of the scene in a train carriage or a bus or car in which you travelled recently. Or compose a description of a church service or meeting you attended—five paragraphs.

JOURNAL OF BORDERLINE CASES
From *A Place Apart* by Dervla Murphy

Today I left Cavan town soon after eight o'clock—a sunny morning with a strong cool wind and swift white clouds. In Belturbet post office advice about cross-border routes was offered by a friendly clerk and a tall old farmer with a leathery face. They thought a cyclist might be able to get across, if the water was low, where the bridge used to be. 'It was blown up twice,' explained the clerk, 'so now they'll leave it that way.' When I asked who had blown it up, and why, they obviously thought I was 'leading them on' and changed the subject. But I genuinely wanted to know. I have a very limited understanding of these matters.

Beyond Belturbet the hilly third-class road passed a few poor little farms and presented two crossroads without sign-posts. Uncertain of the way, I approached a depressed-looking farm dwelling. As I crossed the untidy yard I called out 'Anybody at home?'—not realizing (stupidly) the effect an unknown voice would have a quarter of a mile from the border. As I stood at the open door the whole family faced me silently like figures in a tableau, eyes full of fear, everybody motionless. A thin bent granddad stood in the centre of the kitchen floor leaning on an ash-plant, his hat pushed back off his forehead. A woman of about my own age, with unkempt foxy hair and a torn pink jersey, had been making bread and stood with floury hands held over a basin. A young woman with impetigo, a ragged skirt and sandals not matching was just inside the door holding an empty pail. A skinny, freckled little boy had been pulling a cardboard carton full of turf sods across the floor and he it was who broke the silence by beginning to cry. It is many years since I last saw that degree of slovenly poverty in my own part of rural Ireland. (Yet the inevitable television set stood in one corner.) But it was the fear, not the poverty, that shook me; that instant of pure terror before my harmlessness was recognized. Then everybody relaxed—except the child—and the women came out to the road to give me precise instructions. They didn't think the stepping-stones would be above water today—and they were right.

Round the next corner a concrete roadblock supported a *No road* sign. Then I saw a river lined with willows and alders. Its fast brown water was swirling and glinting in the sun below the trees' fresh green, and it seemed incongruous—yet obscurely reassuring—to find such a troublesome border taking such a lovely form. Standing on the remains of the old narrow bridge (it must have been very attractive) I looked at a newish county council cottage twenty yards away—deserted, all its windows blown in, yet a framed photograph of a County Cavan football team still hanging on the inside wall. Across the border was a thatched cottage half-hidden by trees: probably it was empty, too. I could see not a sign of life anywhere and suddenly I remembered the Turkish-Soviet border at Ani. Though there are no watch-towers here one gets the same feeling of animation artificially suspended by politics. I looked down at the rusty carcass of a bus filled with boulders; the locals' attempt—plus these submerged stepping stones—to replace the bridge. How much more efficiently the Baltis or Nepalese would have coped, with so many boulders and trees available!

Back on the road I was nearly run down by two Irish Army Land-Rovers going towards the non-bridge at top speed. As I turned off on to another by-road they raced back towards Belturbet. Pedalling slowly along a deserted hilly road parallel with the border, I looked north when the high hedges permitted. Fermanagh was a long ridge of wooded or cultivated land with little houses that even from a distance were perceptibly neater than most Co. Cavan homesteads. Within only a few miles, I passed several abandoned farmhouses, cottages and hovels; it must be easy to go to ground hereabouts. Most gates had been improvised from old bedsteads, tar-barrels and/or bundles of thorn. I surmounted one bedstead to attend to my morning duty, leaving Roz in the ditch and paying no attention to an approaching vehicle. But it stopped beside Roz with a squeal of brakes and three young soldiers clutching rifles came over the 'gate' so quickly that it collapsed. As my activities were at a crucial stage I could do nothing but squat on, causing the Irish Army to retreat in such confusion that one youth tripped over his rifle.

Reading

1. What evidence is there from the first two paragraphs to show that the writer is not fully sensitive to the problems of the border area?
2. 'Above all else the writer is conscious of houses.' What is her impression of the houses she notices on her journey?
3. What would you say this extract reveals about the personality of the writer? Support your views with examples from the text.

Writing style

Notice 1

The opening sentence is simple and economical yet sufficiently descriptive to make the reader visualise the scene: 'a sunny morning with a strong cool wind and swift clouds.' Small graphic details really bring the picture alive; for example 'a tall old farmer with a leathery face.'

Exercise

Which descriptive details from the second paragraph do you find most striking, and why? What is the overall effect suggested about the lifestyle of the people?

Notice 2

Interspersed with the description of people and places the writer analyses and reflects on what she sees. For example, in paragraph 2 'it is many years since I last saw that degree of slovenly poverty in my own part of rural Ireland.'

Exercises

1. Where else in the extract does the writer analyse and make comparisons on what she sees, and what is the effect of this?
2. List any phrases you thought particularly effective.

Not all descriptive writing tries to create a realistic picture. Sometimes the writer may try a more imaginative, even surreal style and still remain true to the essence of the scene. (Surrealism is a movement in twentieth-century art and literature that tries to express the unconscious. Hence strange images and dream-like happenings appear in the paintings and writings.)

A PROSPECT OF THE SEA
Dylan Thomas

It was high summer, and the boy was lying in the corn. He was happy because he had no work to do and the weather was hot. He heard the corn sway from side to side above him, and the noise of the birds who whistled from the branches of the trees that hid the house. Lying flat on his back, he stared up into the unbrokenly blue sky falling over the edge of the corn. The wind, after the warm rain before noon, smelt of rabbits and cattle. He stretched himself like a cat, and put his arms behind his head. Now he was riding on the sea, swimming through the golden corn waves, gliding along the heavens like a bird: in seven-league boots he was springing over the fields; he was building a nest in the sixth of the seven trees that waved their hands from a bright, green hill. Now he was a boy with tousled hair, rising lazily to his feet, wandering out of the corn to the strip of river by the hillside. He put his fingers in the water, making a mock sea-wave to roll the stones over and shake the weeds; his fingers stood up like ten tower pillars in the magnifying water, and a fish with a wise head and a lashing tail swam in and out of the tower gates. He made up a story as the fish swam through the gates into the pebbles and the moving bed. There was a drowned princess from a Christmas book, with her shoulders broken and her two red pigtails stretched like the strings of a fiddle over her broken throat; she was caught in a fisherman's net, and the fish plucked her hair. He forgot how the story ended, if ever there were an end to a story that had no beginning. Did the princess live again, rising like a mermaid from the net, or did a prince from another story tauten the tails of her hair and bend her shoulder-bone into a harp and pluck the dead, black tunes for ever in the courts of the royal country? The boy sent a stone skidding over the green water. He saw a rabbit scuttle, and threw a stone at its tail. A fish leaped at the gnats, and a lark darted out of the green earth. This was the best summer since the first seasons of the world. He did not believe in God, but God had made this summer full of blue winds and heat and pigeons in the house wood. There were no chimneys on the hills with no name in the distance, only the trees which stood like women and men enjoying the sun; there were no cranes or coal-tips, only the nameless distance and the hill with seven trees. He could think of no words to say how wonderful the summer was, or the noise of the wood-pigeon, or the lazy corn blowing in the half wind from the sea at the river's end. There were no words for the sky and the sun and the summer country: the birds were nice, and the corn was nice.

Writing style

1. In the first six sentences the writer tries to make the scene appeal to our different senses. Which senses are appealed to? Do you think this is an effective way of describing the scene?
2. After the introductory sentences his imagination takes over and he visualises himself as a swimmer, a bird, and a giant. Examine this technique. Does he still manage to convey something of the scene he is describing, which is, after all, a cornfield? Explain your views.
3. 'Now he was a boy with tousled hair ...' What exactly is Dylan Thomas trying to convey about the boy's experience of the scene? Do you think this is effective?
4. The writer uses metaphors and similes in order to paint pictures for the reader. Examine any two of these, and in each case (*a*) say what suggestions are conveyed by the image and (*b*) comment on how effective you think it is.
5. Comment on the style of the last sentence.
6. List any words, phrases or images you might like to use in your own writing.

Writing

Using a surrealistic or similarly poetic style, compose three or four paragraphs on any scene or location with which you are familiar.

Both the following extracts deal with the same topic: a funeral. Yet the styles of writing are very different. The first extract, from The Aran Islands *by J. M. Synge, describes the customs and ritual of an island burial. The second extract is an episode from James Joyce's novel* Ulysses, *where the central character, Leopold Bloom, attends a funeral.*

THE ARAN ISLANDS (EXTRACT)
John Millington Synge

After Mass this morning an old woman was buried. She lived in the cottage next mine, and more than once before noon I heard a faint echo of the keen. I did not go to the wake for fear my presence might jar upon the mourners, but all last evening I could hear the strokes of a hammer in the yard, where, in the middle of a little crowd of idlers, the next of kin laboured slowly at the coffin. Today, before the hour for the funeral, poteen was served to a number of men who stood about upon the road, and a portion was brought to me in my room. Then the coffin was carried out sewn loosely in sailcloth, and held near the ground by three cross-poles lashed upon the top. As we moved down to the low eastern portion of the island, nearly all the men, and all the older women, wearing petticoats over their heads, came out and joined in the procession.

While the grave was being opened the women sat down among the flat tombstones, bordered with a pale fringe of early bracken, and began the wild keen, or crying for the dead. Each old woman, as she took her turn in the leading recitative, seemed possessed for the moment with a profound ecstasy of grief, swaying to and fro, and bending her forehead to the stone before her, while she called out to the dead with a perpetually recurring chant of sobs.

All round the graveyard other wrinkled women, looking out from under the deep red petticoats that cloaked them, rocked themselves with the same rhythm, and intoned the inarticulate chant that is sustained by all as an accompaniment.

The morning had been beautifully fine, but as they lowered the coffin into the grave, thunder rumbled overhead and hail-stones hissed among the bracken.

In Inishmaan one is forced to believe in a sympathy between man and nature, and at this moment when the thunder sounded a death-peal of extraordinary grandeur above the voices of the women, I could see the faces near me stiff and drawn with emotion. When the coffin was in the grave, and the thunder had rolled away across the hills of Clare, the keen broke out again more passionately than before.

This grief of the keen is no personal complaint for the death of one woman over eighty years, but seems to contain the whole passionate rage that lurked somewhere in every native of the island. In this cry of pain the inner consciousness of the people seems to lay itself bare for an instant, and to reveal the mood of beings who feel their isolation in the face of a universe that wars on them with winds and seas. They are usually silent, but in the presence of death all outward show of indifference or patience is forgotten, and they shriek with pitiable despair before the horror of the fate to which they all are doomed.

Before they covered the coffin an old man kneeled down by the grave and repeated a simple prayer for the dead.

There was an irony in these words of atonement and Catholic belief spoken by voices that were still hoarse with the cries of pagan desperation.

A little beyond the grave I saw a line of old women who had recited in the keen sitting in the shadow of a wall beside the roofless shell of the church. They were still sobbing and shaken with grief, yet they were beginning to talk again of the daily trifles that veil from them the terror of the world.

When we had all come out of the graveyard, and two men had rebuilt the hole in the wall through which the coffin had been carried in, we walked back to the village, talking of anything, and joking of anything, as if merely coming from the boat-slip, or the pier.

One man told me of the poteen drinking that takes place at some funerals.

'A while since,' he said, 'there were two men fell down in the graveyard while the drink was on them. The sea was rough that day, the way no one could go to bring the doctor, and one of the men never woke again, and found death that night.'

Reading

1. This a very logical piece of writing, which goes step by step through the progress of the funeral. In you own words, trace the steps.
2. Do you find anything unusual about the customs? Explain.

Writing style

1. The writing style is a mixture of description and analysis. In your own words, how does Synge describe the 'keen' and how does he explain or rationalise it?
2. Do you think he has evoked the atmosphere of a funeral? Explain your opinions.
3. *Tone*: The writer recounts this episode from the point of view of an observer. Is he at all touched by the occasion? Does he reveal feelings and attitudes? How would you describe the tone of the piece? Justify your opinion with reference to the vocabulary used, the imagery chosen, and the writer's actual involvement.

ULYSSES (EXTRACT)
James Joyce

Gentle sweet air blew round the bared heads in a whisper. Whisper. The boy by the gravehead held his wreath with both hands staring quietly in the black open space. Mr Bloom moved behind the portly kindly caretaker. Well cut frockcoat. Weighing them up perhaps to see which will go next. Well it is a long rest. Feel no more. It's the moment you feel. Must be damned unpleasant. Can't believe it at first. Mistake must be: someone else. Try the house opposite. Wait, I wanted to. I haven't yet. Then darkened deathchamber. Light they want. Whispering around you. Would you like to see a priest? Then rambling and wandering. Delirium all you hid all your life. The death struggle. His sleep is not natural. Press his lower eyelid. Watching is his nose pointed is his jaw sinking are the soles of his feet yellow. Pull the pillow away and finish it off on the floor since he's doomed. Devil in that picture of sinner's death showing him a woman. Dying to embrace in his shirt. Last act of *Lucia. Shall I never behold thee*? Bam! expires. Gone at last. People talk about you a bit: forget you. Don't forget to pray for him. Remember him in your prayers. Even Parnell. Ivy Day dying out. Then they follow: dropping into a hole one after the other.

We are praying now for the repose of his soul. Hoping you're well and not in hell. Nice change of air. Out of the fryingpan of life into the fire of purgatory.

Does he ever think of the hole waiting for himself? They say you do when you shiver in the sun. Someone walking over it. Callboy's warning. Near you. Mine over there towards Finglas, the plot I bought. Mamma poor mamma, and little Rudy.

The gravediggers took up their spades and flung heavy clods of clay in on the coffin. Mr Bloom turned his face. And if he was alive all the time? Whew! By Jingo, that would be awful! No, no: he is dead, of course. Of course he is dead. Monday he died. They ought to have some law to pierce the heart and make sure or an electric clock or a telephone in the coffin and some kind of a canvas airhole. Flag of distress. Three days. Rather long to keep them in summer. Just as well to be shut of them as soon as you are sure there's no.

The clay fell softer. Begin to be forgotten. Out of sight, out of mind.

The caretaker moved away a few paces and put on his hat. Had enough of it. The mourners took heart of grace, one by one, covering themselves without show. Mr Bloom put on his hat and saw the portly figure making its way deftly through the maze of graves. Quietly, sure of his ground, he traversed the dismal fields.

Hynes jotting down something in his notebook. Ah, the names. But he knows them all. No: coming to me.

—I am just taking the names, Hynes said below his breath. What is your christian name? I'm not sure.

—L, Mr Bloom said. Leopold.

Writing style

The 'stream of consciousness' technique used here can be described as seemingly uncontrolled and scattered thoughts passing through a character's mind, thoughts that are unlikely to be voiced. It is a sort of intellectual daydreaming!

1. Do you think this technique allows the writer to react more personally and more deeply to his subject?
To answer this, first consider what Mr Bloom has to say about death and burial. List his ideas on the subject. Then compare them with Synge's reflections on the same subject.
2. Consider the tones of voice used by Bloom. Is he always grave and serious? Is he frightened or courageous, disgusted, awed? How many different tones can you discover? Support your views with reference to the text.
3. Note the lack of punctuation in the sentences. What effect does this technique have? Do you think it works well?
4. Which extract do you think you are more likely to remember in six months' time, and why?

Writing

Using the stream of consciousness technique, write a piece expressing the thoughts and feelings of one of the following characters:
—an old person sitting on a park bench
—a shy young person at a disco
—a person waiting in a doctor's surgery
—a teacher trying to control a disorderly class.

SUBTERRANEAN GOTHIC (EXTRACT)
Paul Theroux

When people say the subway frightens them, they are not being silly or irrational. It is no good saying how cheap or how fast it is. The subway is frightening. It is also very easy to get lost on the subway, and the person who is lost in New York City has a serious problem. New Yorkers make it their business to avoid getting lost.

It is the stranger who gets lost. It is the stranger who follows people hurrying into the stair-well: subway entrances are just dark holes in the sidewalk—the stations are below ground. There is nearly always a bus-stop near the subway entrance. People waiting at a bus-stop have a special pitying gaze for people entering the subway. It is sometimes not pity, but fear, bewilderment, curiosity, or fatalism; often they look like miners' wives watching their menfolk going down the pit.

The stranger's sense of disorientation down below is immediate. The station is all tile and iron and dampness; it has bars and turnstiles and steel grates. It has the look of an old prison or a monkey cage.

Buying a token, the stranger may ask directions, but the token booth—reinforced, burglar-proof, bullet-proof—renders the reply incoherent. And subway directions are a special language: 'A-train ... Downtown ... Express to the Shuttle ... Change at Ninety-sixth for the two ... Uptown ... The Lex ... CC ... LL ... The Local ...'

Most New Yorkers refer to the subway by the now-obsolete forms of 'IND', 'IRT', 'BMT'. No one intentionally tries to confuse the stranger; it is just that, where the subway is concerned, precise directions are very hard to convey.

Verbal directions are incomprehensible, written ones are defaced. The signboards and subway maps are indiscernible beneath layers of graffiti. That Andy Warhol, the stylish philistine, has said, 'I love graffiti' is almost reason enough to hate it. One is warier still of Norman Mailer, who naively encouraged this scrawling in his book *The Faith of Graffiti*. 'Misguided' seems about the kindest way of describing Mailer who, like Warhol, limps after the latest fashions in the hope of discovering youthfulness or celebrity in colourful outrage. That Mailer's judgement is appalling is clear from his bluster in the cause of the murderer and liar Jack Abbot, who brought about a brief, bloody New York run of *Mr Loveday's Little Outing*. Mailer admires graffiti.

Graffiti is destructive; it is anti-art; it is an act of violence, and it can be deeply menacing. It has displaced the subway signs and maps, blacked-out the windows of the trains and obliterated the instructions. *In case of emergency* is cross-hatched with a felt-tip. *These seats are for the elderly and disabled*—a yard-long signature obscures it. *The subway tracks are very dangerous: if the train should stop, do not*—the rest is black and unreadable. The stranger cannot rely on printed instructions or warnings and there are few cars out of the six thousand on the system in which the maps have not been torn out. Assuming the stranger had boarded the train, he or she can feel only panic when, searching for a clue to his route, he sees in the map frame the message—*Guzmán—Ladrón, Maricón y Asesino*.

Panic: and so he gets off the train, and then his troubles really begin.

He may be in the South Bronx or the upper reaches of Broadway on the Number 1 line, or on any of a dozen lines that traverse Brooklyn. He gets off the train, which is covered in graffiti, and steps on to a station platform which is covered in graffiti. It is possible (this is true of many stations) that none of the signs will be legible. Not only will the stranger not know where he is, but the stairways will be splotched and stinking—no *Uptown*, no *Downtown*, no *Exit*. It is also possible that not a single soul will be around, and the most dangerous stations—ask any police officer—are the emptiest. Of course, the passenger might just want to sit on a broken bench and, taking Mailer's word for it, contemplate the macho qualities of the graffiti; on the other hand, he is more likely to want to get the hell out of there.

This is the story that most people tell of subways fear. In every detail it is like a nightmare, complete with rats and mice and a tunnel and a low ceiling. It is manifest suffocation, straight out of Poe. Those who tell this story seldom have a crime to report. They have experienced fear. It is completely understandable—what is worse than being trapped underground?—but it has been a private horror. In most cases, the person will have come to no harm. He will, however, remember his fear on that empty station for the rest of his life.

Notes

token: metal disc allowing entry to the subway.
Andy Warhol: controversial modern painter of unusual subjects, for example soup tins.
Norman Mailer: twentieth-century American writer and journalist and winner of the Pulitzer Prize.

Reading

1. Why, according to Theroux, is it the stranger who is most at risk on the subway?
2. What is the writer's attitude to graffiti? Refer to the text to support the points you make.
3. What is the key idea that ties this whole piece together? Can you express it in two or three sentences?

Writing style

1. Notice how paragraphs are structured around a key phrase or sentence. For example, in paragraph 1 the key phrase is 'The subway is frightening.' Paragraph 2: 'It is the stranger who gets lost.' Paragraph 3: 'Disorientation down below is immediate.'

Exercise

What, in your opinion, is the key phrase or sentence in each of the other paragraphs? Justify your choice.

2. Each paragraph is linked to the following one.
For example, in paragraph 1 the main idea is that the subway is frightening, so 'New Yorkers make it their business to *avoid getting lost.*'

52 Descriptive Prose

Paragraph 2 immediately takes up the notion of being lost. 'It is the *stranger who gets lost*.' Then it goes on to talk of strangers hurrying below ground, and ends with a reference to 'wives watching their menfolk going *down the pit*.'

Paragraph 3 takes up this notion of underground depths: ' ... disorientation *down below* is immediate.'

Exercise
Explain how the remaining paragraphs are linked.

3. In the second paragraph Theroux uses a simile to describe the attitude of people waiting at a bus stop towards those entering the subway. Do you think this is appropriate?

4. 'The shortest paragraph of this piece is probably the most effective.' Comment.

5. Make a list of any words or phrases or images you thought effective and might use in your own writing.

Writing
1. Write a descriptive piece on losing your way, at home or abroad, in this world or any other.
2. Write an imaginative description of the scene in any one of these photographs.

Descriptive Prose 53

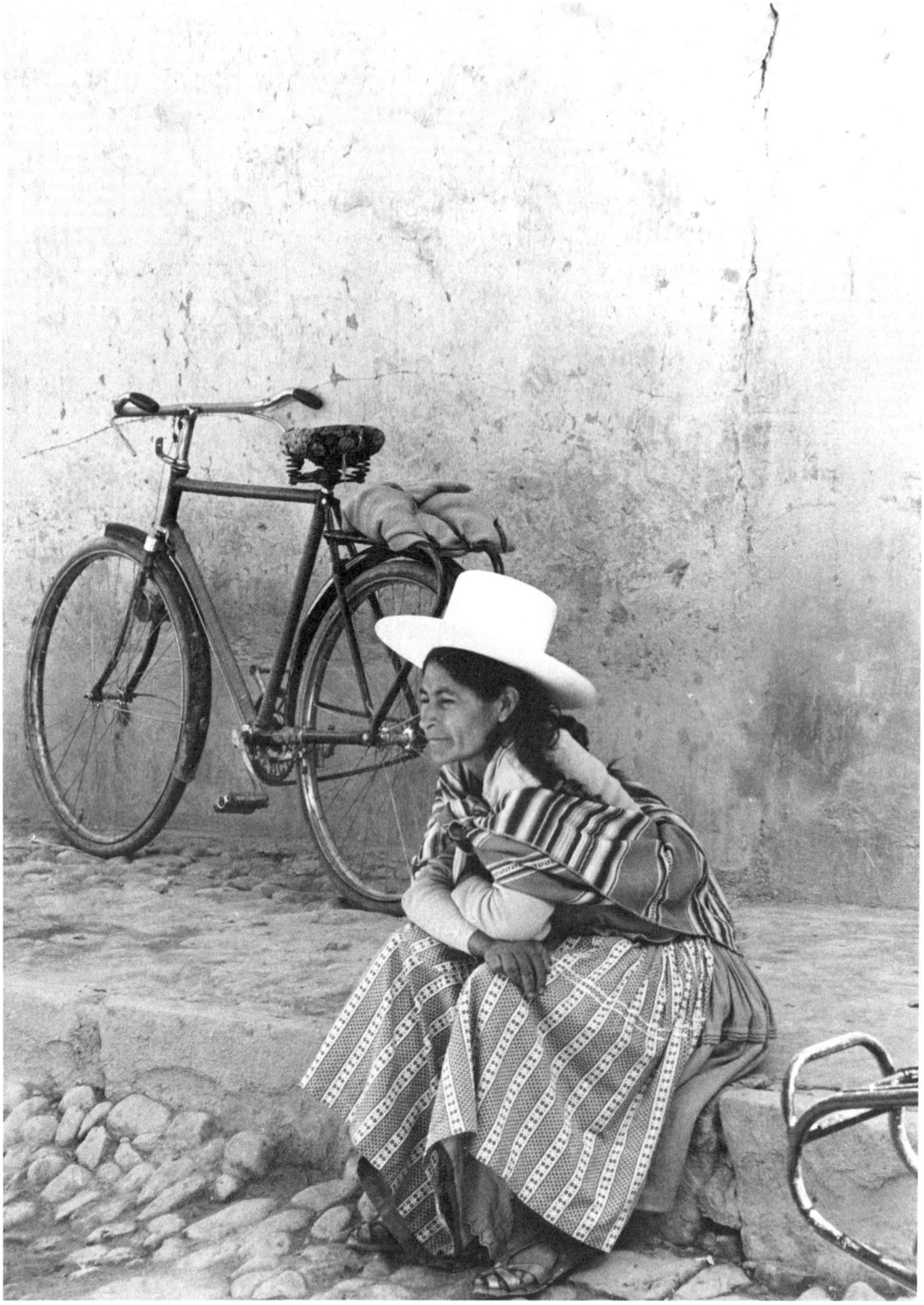

Autobiography

> **WRITING AND EXAM HINTS**
>
> 1. *First-person narration*. You are writing as yourself, about yourself. Autobiography is about self-revelation.
>
> 2. *Clear, logical structure or sequence of events*. When talking about ourselves we have a tendency to flit from one incident to another with no thought of time or context. The listener or reader is merely confused.
>
> 3. *Draw pictures*. The reader has never seen your family, house, garden, surroundings, etc. Describe them: make verbal pictures.
>
> 4. *Comment on past events from your present standpoint*. Attempt to analyse some of the events and memories. One of the more interesting features of autobiographical writing is seeing the author analyse past happenings and commenting on himself or herself as a young person.

A PORTRAIT OF THE ARTIST AS A YOUNG GIRL (EXTRACT)
Edna O'Brien

I am always astonished by people who tell me that they don't remember their childhood, or who think there is something ridiculous or perhaps shameful about the memory. We are our memories. Memory and one's dreams constitute such a bulk of what we are, because as human beings, we live very much internally.

My earliest memory is of an inability, or perhaps a fear, of getting down steps—possibly a parable for life! There were two blue stone steps leading from our back kitchen, as we called it, outside; and, as they were quite steep and I always did—indeed always do—have a longing to be out of doors, I imagine that I kept falling and having this great anxiety about having to climb to different levels.

My early memory is connected with the outdoors. It is of trees: always of trees blowing in the wind. I remember, in particular, the lustre and comfort of a copper beech behind our house. I also have an indoor memory—which I think most children have—of the bedroom being a long way from where one's parents were. There was, if you like, a sense of banishment, of being cut off. It is a memory that goes back quite a long way: I remember being in my cot and feeling stranded in it. I am told, and it is something that I believe, that the earlier you remember, the better for yourself, the more you are in touch with yourself.

I know that when I start to write, my memories come to me unsummoned and I remember things—a piece of wallpaper, a stain in a flower in the wallpaper, the way the sun came in on the linoleum, the dust in the room—and once I start remembering I can't stop.

Home was in Tuamgraney, Co. Clare. I was the youngest of four children (I had one brother and two sisters) although there had been a child before me that had died, so I was the fifth child really. I was a good deal younger than the sister who was next to me so that when my brother and sisters went away to school for much of the time I was the only child at home with my parents.

My relationship with my father wasn't very serene. It got better, of course, as he got older and as I grew older and understood him more; but he was a very restless man. He had been married very young, at twenty-three, or four, which is young—even though people do get married nowadays at that age. I didn't feel easy with him. I was afraid of him; and really, I think chemically we were not elective creatures. I read once in Herzen's memoirs that the relationships we form with people—whether we love or don't love them—are always chemical; but the fact that people happen to be your parents or your brother or sisters doesn't necessarily mean that they are people in the world to whom you're closest. It would be humbug to pretend that. If you are close to them, then it's an extra bonus from God. I was afraid of my father, and I would be a hypocrite if I said that it had been an easy or a loving relationship.

I miss very much not having had a tender relationship with him, but you have to measure the blessings as much as the curses; I feel that to a great extent it was obviously that tension and that fear that were the sources of my becoming a writer. I don't think happy people become writers. They wouldn't bother, because writing by necessity is a very gruelling and very lonely and very anxious occupation—that's if you take it seriously. I have also to thank my father for something else which I remember very clearly: that is a great sense of story-telling. He was a hypnotic story-teller, and I was very aware of that, but he was an egotistical man and he didn't want any interruptions in his stories. He loved it when visitors came because then he could tell again the stories that he had told before.

He was also a gambler. He loved playing cards, he liked greyhounds and he loved horses. My mother was not approving of horses, but even so there always seemed to be very restless unwieldy thoroughbreds—usually roan-coloured—in the fields. I was quite afraid of them: I remember them being broken in—and quite a violent thing. But my father loved these horses.

He also loved a drink and he was unlucky in that he couldn't drink very much without it having a disastrous effect on him, and on us.

I was very close to my mother. I have written about her in a story called 'A Rose in the Heart', in which the child describes her mother as being *everything*—the tabernacle with the host in it, the altar with the flowers, the bog with the bog lakes, the cupboard with the linen. My mother was someone to whom I felt umbilically and osmotically attached. I remember that when I was going to school each morning, I was terrified that she would not be there when I came home. It was very childish, I suppose; but it was a question of distance—the school was only one and a half miles away, but to a fearful child it was almost eternity.

We lived in a big house—or so it seemed to me as a child—with about five bedrooms. There was a long avenue up from the roadside gate, then a second gate that led into the front of the house; and when the sun shone I used to think that it was a kind of heaven. It was a very beautiful place.

Standing on the stone step to look across the fields I felt, as I always did, that rush of freedom and pleasure when I looked at all the various trees and outer stone buildings set far away from the house, and at the fields very green and very peaceful. Outside the paling wire was a walnut tree, and under its shade there were bluebells, tall and intensely blue, a grotto of heaven—blue flowers among the limestone boulders. And my swing was swaying in the wind, and all the leaves on the treetops were stirring lightly.

—The Country Girls

My mother was extremely house-proud. In a sense, the house was done up like a doll's house. My mother had a wonderful collection of china objects. I remember in particular a pair of large busts of ladies, called Iris and Gala. My mother would dust them, put an artificial flower in the hand of one of them—and paint their finger nails! She was also very keen on furniture. Whenever she had any money, she would go to auctions and buy something new; and as a result the rooms were crammed with furniture.

Oddly enough, the room I remember best was called the 'vacant room'—because it was still relatively devoid of furniture. It had a huge long oak table, which in autumn was laden down with ripening apples. There are two things I connect with that room—the smell of slightly rotting apples and the fact that the wallpaper was hung upside down! The latter event happened many, many years ago on a day when my mother had gone to Limerick. She had a penchant for fortune tellers, and when she visited one in Limerick she was told that there was a job being done in her house that day and it would be done wrong. She came home to discover that the wallpaper motif was cockeyed. It had been hung upside down. She was furious.

Reading

1. This piece has quite a logical structure. Can you trace the line of thought through it?—i.e. what is the main idea in each paragraph? Try to express the essence of each paragraph in one sentence.

2. If you had the opportunity, what questions about her childhood would you like to ask the author?

3. How did the author assess her own relationship with her father? Were there any positive aspects to it?

4. Autobiography is about self-revelation. What do we discover about the author as a person in this piece? Quote or refer to the text to substantiate your points.

5. Comment on the effectiveness of any two descriptions or images that the author uses.

6. Compare her present memory of the house and grounds with her fictional re-creation of it in *The Country Girls*, from which she quotes. Does this indicate anything abut the relationship between life and art?

7. List any phrases or images you find effective.

Writing

1. What is your earliest memory? Write three or four paragraphs about it or about any poignant memory you can recall.
2. Looking back, describe your home and family as they were a number of years ago, say when you were in second or third class of primary school.
3. Compose three or four paragraphs on your grandparents or any older relatives or neighbours as you remember them when you yourself were younger.

CROSSING THE LISBURN ROAD
Michael Longley
From *Poetry Review*, January 1985.

Because of our reduced circumstances my parents could not afford to send Peter and me to one of the posher preparatory schools. (They were both old-fashioned Tories.) We attended the local Public Elementary School where, out of a large class of nearly forty pupils, we were almost the only middle-class children. Most of the others lived on 'the wrong side' of the Lisburn Road. Their clothes were different from ours—woollen balaclavas, laced boots with studs in the soles. Alongside them Peter and I must have appeared chubby and well-scrubbed. I noticed at once the skinny knees and snotty noses, but most of all the accent, abrasive and raucous as a football rattle. This I soon acquired in order to make myself less unacceptable. 'Len' us a mey-ek'—'Lend me a make' (a ha'penny). At home I would try to remember to ask for a 'slice of cake' and not 'a slice a' cey-ek', to refer to the 'door' and the 'floor' rather than 'doo-er' and floo-er'. By the age of six or seven I was beginning to lead a double life, learning how to re-create myself twice daily.

I made friends with the other pupils and started to explore the Lisburn Road. Belfast's more prosperous citizens have usually been careful to separate themselves safely from the ghettoes of the bellicose working classes. An odd exception is the Lisburn Road which runs south from the city centre. Intermittently for about three miles workers' tiny two-up-and-two-down houses squint across the road at the drawing-rooms of dentists, doctors, solicitors: on the right, as you drive towards Lisburn gardenless shadowy streets, on the right rhododendrons and rose bushes. Belfast laid bare, an exposed artery.

I spent much of my childhood drifting from one side to the other, visiting the homes of my new friends: the lavatory outside in the yard, stairs ascending steeply as you entered, low ceilings and no elbow-room at all. My first tea at Herbie Smith's was fried bread sprinkled with salt. Herbie came to our house and gasped when he saw the size of our back garden. For the first time I felt ashamed of our relative affluence. Our separate drawing and dining-rooms, the hall with its wooden panelling, the lavatory upstairs were all novelties to Herbie. He seemed curious rather then envious. Every corner of the home I had taken for granted was illuminated by his gaze as by wintry sunlight.

Another pupil John McCluskey was often caned for being late. He delivered papers for Younger the newsagent. If the *Belfast News Letter* was delayed, John without complaint or explanation would be standing at 9.30 in front of the class, his hand presented to the whistling cane and then hugged under his armpit as he stumbled over schoolbags to his desk. Should I have told the teacher that he delivered papers to our house? Sometimes, as though to drown his sorrows, John would swig the blue-grey sludge from one of the small white inkwells. Every December my father gave me a half-crown as a Christmas box for the paper boy, as he called him. I never told my father that the paper boy was in my class. On the doorstep John McCluskey and I behaved like strangers and avoided each other's eyes as the half-crown changed hands. Later in class the transaction would not be mentioned.

John and Herbie shared with me their mythology which was mostly concerned with Roman Catholics. Did I know why Taigs crossed themselves? What dark practices lurked behind confession and Mass? Didn't the nuns kidnap little girls and imprison them behind the suspiciously high walls of the big convent at the top of the Ormeau Road? The Orange Order and the B-Specials marched through our conversations. The son of English parents, I was, at nine, less politically aware than my classmates. A photograph at home of Grandpa George lording it in his Mason's apron prompted me once to speak with snooty disparagement of the less dignified Orangemen. I was sent to Coventry until I apologised. To secure the conversion two friends smuggled to me under the desk pamphlets which purported to describe Catholic atrocities from the twenties to the thirties. Every page carried blurred photographs of victims, who, it was claimed, had been tortured and mutilated, their brains or hearts cut out, their genitals chopped off. Forgeries? Adaptations of photographs of road accidents from forensic files? Or real victims? This vitriolic propaganda burned deep into my mind, and I perused those grim pages with the same obsessiveness that I was later to devote to *The Red Light* and nudist magazines. I craved the bond of shared fears and superstitions.

At primary school (and later at grammar school) there was little on the curriculum to suggest that we were living in Ireland: no Irish history except when it impinged on the grand parade of English monarchs; no Irish literature; no Irish art; no Irish music. When we sang in music classes we mouthed English songs. One inspector criticised our accents and forced us to sing, 'Each with his bonny lawss/a-dawncing on the grawss.' Our teacher in Form Three, an affable man who coaxed us through the Three Rs with care and skill, became tense when for one term we were joined by a boy from Dublin—a Protestant but still a focus for our suspicions. <u>Having flirted for a while with the unfortunate nine-year-old's political ignorance and his own paranoia, the teacher eventually decided to confront this embodiment of menace and treachery.</u> It was a crude question.

'Niall, who owns Belfast?'

'Dublin, sir.'

'Who? Who?' This was much more than he had hoped for. 'To the front of the class, boy.'

'Who owns Belfast?'

'Dublin, sir.' A slap in the face.

'Who told you that?' Another slap. A spittly crescendo of hatred.

'My granny, sir.' More slaps. And Niall in tears.

We were invited to correct the error, to put down the rebellion. We did so and felt frightened and exhilarated.

With its dozens of little shops and the Regal Cinema where entrance to the front stalls cost threepence, the Lisburn Road became my hinterland. The cinema was demolished not so long ago, and many of the shops have now been transformed into Chinese restaurants and fast food takeaways. But the rows of back-to-back houses remain, the homes of Herbie Smith, John McCluskey, Norman Hamilton, Sally Patterson, John Boland, Alan Gray, Helen Ferguson, Norma Gamble.

Reading

1. Michael Longley begins by making points of analysis or commenting on the social circumstances of the family and the school. What are these?
2. He uses images to convey the differences between himself and the other boys. What are these images, and do you think they are effective?
3. 'Belfast's more prosperous citizens have usually been careful to separate themselves safely from the ghettoes of the bellicose working classes.'
(*a*) What does the author mean by this statement?
(*b*) Was the truth of this illustrated in his own area? Explain.
(*c*) The author describes the Lisburn Road vista as 'Belfast laid bare, an exposed artery.' Do you find this an effective image?
4. The author really only notices the features of his own house when he takes his new friend, Herbie Smith, round to visit. Examine the simile he uses to describe Herbie's reaction. Do you think it is effective?
5. What particular problems do the class differences create for the author?
6. 'The vitriolic propaganda burned deep into my mind.' Describe what the author is referring to in this statement.
7. Does the author, on reflection, feel that there was anything unusual or ironic about the education curriculum in his primary school? Explain.
8. Do his experiences differ in any way from your own experience of primary school?
9. Would you agree that there was considerable tension in the author's life as a young boy? Examine the whole article for evidence to support your assertions.
10. In your own words explain the underlined sentence ('Having flirted for a while ...').
11. Make a list of any words, phrases or images you thought particularly effective and that you might use in your own writing.

Writing

Using this memoir to stimulate your thinking, compose a mature reflection on your own primary school days. Attempt to combine descriptive passages with points of analysis and comment. For example, think about your first impressions of the place, teachers and pupils; particular incidents; special friends; the books you enjoyed; the games you played; etc.

   Analyse, if you can, what effect the school had on you.

MEMORIES OF CHRISTMAS
Dylan Thomas

One Christmas was so much like another, in those years, around the sea-town corner now, and out of all sound except the distant speaking of the voices I sometimes hear a moment before sleep, that I can never remember whether it snowed for six days and six nights when I was twelve or whether it snowed for twelve days and twelve nights when I was six; or whether the ice broke and the skating grocer vanished like a snowman through a white trap-door on that same Christmas Day that the mince-pies finished Uncle Arnold and we tobogganed down the seaward hill all the afternoon, on the best tea-tray, and Mrs Griffiths complained, and we threw a snowball at her niece, and my hands burned so, with the heat and cold, when I held them in front of the fire, that I cried for twenty minutes and then had some jelly.

All the Christmases roll down the hill towards the Welsh-speaking sea, like a snowball growing whiter and bigger and rounder, like a cold and headlong moon bundling down the sky that was our street; and they stop at the rim of the ice-edged, fish-freezing waves, and I plunge my hands in the snow and bring out whatever I can find; holly or robins or pudding, squabbles and carols and oranges and tin whistles, and the fire in the front room, and bang go the crackers, and holy, holy, holy, ring the bells, and the glass bells shaking on the tree, and Mother Goose, and Struwelpeter—oh! the baby-burning flames and the cracking scissorman!—Billy Bunter and Black Beauty, Little Women and boys who have three helpings, Alice and Mrs Potter's badgers, penknives, teddy-bears—named after a Mr Theodore Bear, their inventor, or father, who died recently in the United States—mouth-organs, tin-soldiers, and blancmange, and Auntie Bessie playing 'Pop Goes the Weasel' and 'Nuts in May' and 'Oranges and Lemons' on the untuned piano in the parlour all through the thimble-hiding musical-chairing blind-man's-buffing party at the end of the never-to-be-forgotten day at the end of the unremembered year.

In goes my hand into that wool-white bell-tongued ball of holidays resting at the margin of the carol-singing sea, and out came Mrs Prothero and the firemen.

It was on the afternoon of the day of Christmas Eve, and I was in Mrs Prothero's garden, waiting for cats, with her son Jim. It was snowing. It was always snowing at Christmas; December, in my memory, is white as Lapland, though there were no reindeers. But there were cats. Patient, cold, and callous, our hands wrapped in socks, we waited to snowball the cats. Sleek and long as jaguars and terrible-whiskered spitting and snarling they would slink and sidle over the white back-garden walls, and the lynx-eyed hunters, Jim and I, fur-capped and moccasined trappers from Hudson's Bay of Eversley Road, would hurl our deadly snowballs at the green of their eyes. The wise cats never appeared. We were so still, Eskimo-footed arctic marksmen in the muffling silence of the eternal snows—eternal, ever since Wednesday—that we never heard Mrs Prothero's first cry from her igloo at the bottom of the garden. Or, if we heard it at all, it was, to us, like the far-off challenge of our enemy and prey, the neighbour's Polar Cat. But soon the voice grew louder. 'Fire!' cried Mrs Prothero, and she beat the dinner-gong. And we ran down the garden, with the snowballs in our arm, towards the house, and smoke, indeed, was pouring out of the dining-room and the gong was bombilating, and Mrs Prothero was announcing ruin like a town-crier in Pompeii. This was better than all the cats in Wales standing on the wall in a row. We bounded into the house, laden with snowballs, and stopped at the open door of the smoke-filled room. Something was burning all right; perhaps it was Mr Prothero, who always slept there after midday dinner with a newspaper over his face; but he was standing in the middle of the room, saying 'A fine Christmas!' and smacking at the smoke with a slipper.

'Call the fire-brigade,' cried Mrs Prothero as she beat the gong.

'They won't be there,' said Mr Prothero, 'it's Christmas.'

There was no fire to be seen, only clouds of smoke and Mr Prothero standing in the middle of them, waving his slipper as though he were conducting.

'Do something,' he said.

And we threw all our snowballs into the smoke—I think we missed Mr Prothero—and ran out of the house to the telephone-box.

'Let's call the police as well,' Jim said.

'And the ambulance.'

'And Emie Jenkins, he likes fires.'

But we only called the fire-brigade, and soon the fire-engine came and three tall men in helmets brought a hose into the house and Mr Prothero got out just in time before they turned it on. Nobody could have had a noisier Christmas Eve. And when the firemen turned off the hose and were standing in the wet and smoky room, Jim's aunt, Miss Prothero, came downstairs and peered in at them. Jim and I waited, very quietly, to hear what she would say to them. She said the right thing, always. She looked at the three tall firemen in their shining helmets, standing among the smoke and cinders and dissolving snowballs, and she said: 'Would you like something to read?'

Now out of that bright white snowball of Christmas gone comes the stocking, the stocking of stockings, that hung at the foot of the bed with the arm of a golliwog dangling over the top and small bells ringing in the toes. There was a company, gallant and scarlet but never nice to taste though I always tried when very young, of belted and busbied and musketed lead soldiers so soon to lose their heads and legs in the wars on the kitchen table after the tea-things, the mince-pies, and the cakes that I helped to make by stoning the raisins and eating them, had been cleared away; and a bag of moist and many-coloured jelly-babies and a folded flag and a false nose and a tram-conductor's cap and a machine that punched tickets and rang a bell; never a catapult; once, by mistake that no one could explain, a little hatchet; and a rubber buffalo, or it may have been a horse, with a yellow head and haphazard legs; and a celluloid duck that made, when you pressed it, a most ducklike noise, a mewing moo that an ambitious cat might make who wishes to be a cow; and a painting-book in which I could make the grass, the trees, the sea, and the animals any colour I pleased: and still the dazzling sky-blue sheep are grazing in the red field under a flight of rainbow-beaked and pea-green birds.

Christmas morning was always over before you could say Jack Frost. And look! suddenly the pudding was burning! Bang the gong and call the fire-brigade and the book-loving firemen! Someone found the silver three-penny-bit with a currant on it; and the someone was always Uncle Arnold. The motto in my cracker read:

Let's all have fun this Christmas Day,

Let's play and sing and shout hooray!

and grown-ups turned their eyes towards the ceiling, and Auntie Bessie, who had already been frightened, twice, by a clockwork mouse, whimpered at the sideboard and had some elderberry wine. And someone put a glass bowl full of nuts on the littered table, and my uncle said, as he said once every year: 'I've got a shoe-nut here. Fetch me a shoe-horn to open it, boy.'

And dinner was ended.

And I remember that on the afternoon of Christmas Day, when the others sat around the fire and told each other that this was nothing, no, nothing, to the great snowbound and turkey-proud yule-log-crackling holly-berry-bedizoned and kissing-under-the-mistletoe Christmas when they were children, I would go out, school-capped and gloved and muffled, with my bright new boots squeaking, into the white world on to the seaward hill, to call on Jim and Dan and Jack and to walk with them through the silent snowscape of our town.

We went padding through the streets, leaving huge deep footprints in the snow, on the hidden pavements.

'I bet people'll think there's been hippoes.'

'What would you do if you saw a hippo coming down Terrace Road?'

'I'd go like this, bang! I'd throw him over the railings and roll him down the hill and then I'd tickle him under the ear and he'd wag his tail ...'

'What would you do if you saw *two* hippoes?'

Iron-flanked and bellowing he-hippoes clanked and blundered and battered through the scudding snow towards us as we passed by Mr Daniel's house.

'Let's post Mr Daniel a snowball through his letterbox.'
'Let's write things in the snow.'
'Let's write "Mr Daniel looked like a spaniel" all over his lawn.'
'Look', Jack said, 'I'm eating snow-pie.'
'What's it taste like?'
'Like snow-pie,' Jack said.
Or we walked on the white shore.
'Can the fishes see it's snowing?'
'They think it's the sky falling down.'
The silent one-clouded heavens drifted on to the sea.
'All the old dogs have gone.'

Dogs of a hundred mingled makes yapped in the summer at the sea-rim and yelped at the trespassing mountains of the waves.

'I bet St Bernards would like it now.'

And we were snowblind travellers lost on the north hills, and the great dewlapped dogs, with brandy-flasks round their necks, ambled and shambled up to us, baying 'Excelsior.'

We returned home through the desolate poor sea-facing streets where only a few children fumbled with bare red fingers in the thick wheel-rutted snow and cat-called after us, their voices fading away, as we trudged uphill, into the cries of the dock-birds and the hooters of ships out in the white and whirling bay.

Bring out the tall tales now that we told by the fire as we roasted chestnuts and the gaslight bubbled low. Ghosts with their heads under their arms trailed their chains and said 'whooo' like owls in the long nights when I dared not look over my shoulders; wild beasts lurked in the cubby-hole under the stairs where the gas-meter ticked. 'Once upon a time,' Jim said, 'there were three boys, just like us, who got lost in the dark in the snow, near Bethesda Chapel, and this is what happened to them ...' It was the most dreadful happening I had ever heard.

And I remember that we went singing carols once, a night or two before Christmas Eve, when there wasn't the shaving of a moon to light the secret, white-flying streets. At the end of a long road was a drive that led to a large house, and we stumbled up the darkness of the drive that night, each one of us afraid, each one holding a stone in his hand in case, and all of us too brave to say a word. The wind made through the drive-trees noises as of old and unpleasant maybe web-footed men wheezing in caves. We reached the black bulk of the house.

'What shall we give them?' Dan whispered.

'"Hark the Herald"? "Christmas Comes But Once a Year"?'

'No,' Jack said: 'We'll sing "Good King Wenceslas." I'll count to three.'

One, two, three, and we began to sing, our voices high and seemingly distant in the snow-felted darkness round the house that was occupied by nobody we knew. We stood close together, near the dark door.

> Good King Wenceslas looked out
> On the Feast of Stephen.

And then a small, dry voice, like the voice of someone who has not spoken for a long time, suddenly joined our singing: a small, dry voice, through the keyhole. And when we stopped running we were outside our house; the front room was lovely and bright; the gramophone was playing; we saw the red and white balloons hanging from the gas bracket; uncles and aunts sat by the fire; I thought I smelt our supper being fried in the kitchen. Everything was good again, and Christmas shone through all the familiar town.

'Perhaps it was a ghost,' Jim said.

'Perhaps it was trolls,' Dan said, who was always reading.

'Let's go in and see if there's any jelly left,' Jack said.

And we did that.

Writing style

1. *Notice*: DRAMATIC QUALITY. Dylan Thomas tries to communicate the excitement of Christmas by piling up phrase upon phrase, without pause. For instance, the opening paragraph is all one sentence!

2. *Notice*: COLOURFUL WRITING. (*a*) He uses unusual and striking adjectives and adjectival phrases, for example the *sea-town* corner, the *seaward* hill. In paragraph 2: the *ice-edged, fish-freezing* waves, or the *thimble-hiding, musical-chairing, blind-man's-buffing* party at the end of the *never-to-be-forgotten* day. In paragraph 3: the *carol-singing* sea.

(*b*) Examine the description of the imaginary cats, and notice how he uses the sounds of words to create the atmosphere: 'sleek and long as jaguars and terrible-whiskered, spitting and snarling they would slink and sidle over the white back garden wall.' The alliteration of the *s* sounds suggests the hissing enmity and danger of the cats.

(*c*) Notice the repeated metaphor of the snowball of memories. List all the instances where we find this employed. Do you think it is effective?

3. *Notice*: CAMEO CHARACTERS. He succeeds in creating cameo characters (who make a single brief appearance) almost with a stroke of the pen—just a phrase of description or a reference to a peculiarity. For example, who could forget Mrs Prothero, 'announcing ruin like a town crier in Pompeii.' This brief description instantly conjures up the panic-stricken, hysterical figure warning of imminent and terrible catastrophe—a fire that turns out to be just a lot of smoke.

Exercises

1. Explain what is suggested about each of the characters: Miss Prothero, Uncle Arnold, and Auntie Bessie.
2. List any words, phrases or images from this piece that you would like to use in your own writing.

Writing

1. (*a*) Concentrating on exciting and appropriate adjectives and images, write a description of a holiday you remember, or a place you visited, or a particular time of year you like or hate.

(*b*) Introduce a few cameo characters of your acquaintance.

(*c*) Add some drama and see where it goes!

2. Write a personal autobiographical composition, timing yourself to about one hour as if under exam conditions. Remember:
—a good opening
—logical structure
—make pictures
—a few points of reflection or analysis of events you consider significant in your development
—the tone can be serious or humorous
—a good ending to balance the opening.

The short story

Mrs Pulaska
Christopher Burns

No one knew where she came from, or why she had sought refuge among us. Perhaps she yearned for the tiny villages and small farms of her childhood, now denied to her for ever by the forces of history; perhaps she merely sought escape.

For people such as us she was an emissary from an unknown world, a bizarre and oddly self-absorbed stranger with a heavy accent. The very planes and set of her face were different to the ones we were used to. She was angular, with bony features and protuberant eyes and long black hair like a witch's. For my schoolfriends and me she was a figure of both fear and scorn; we even imagined that she might be German, and to us all Germans were still enemies.

But her name was Mrs Pulaska, and she was Polish. Of Mr Pulaska or of a wedding ring, there was no sign. For the time she was with us she lived in a tiny room at the back of the butcher's shop in the village. It must have been narrow and damp, but from the solitary window she could look out across the fields and towards the hills. Because she always looked cold and undernourished the shopkeepers gave her scraps of meat or the occasional vegetables, despite rationing. She wore black clothes even in summer, always with gloves; in winter she wore mittens, boots, and what looked like an outsize greatcoat scavenged from the remains of an unidentified army.

When she began to come to our farm I felt both threatened and guilty. There had been no need for me to think such terrible things about Mrs Pulaska, I decided, for I feared that in some obscure way she had come to take revenge.

Instead she ignored me. She spent most of her time in the old barn my father rented her. She wanted to work in there, she explained.

I couldn't imagine what kind of work she would be doing in that cavernous and gloomy interior. The barn was no longer used; it was a relic from earlier days. My father always said that when better times came he would buy a prefabricated building, one that would cost little and be easy to maintain. As soon as they had agreed the arrangement she painted the door a vivid fiery crimson.

So Mrs Pulaska, a bag slung over her shoulder, came down the muddy track into the barn, closing the door firmly behind her. Often, too, I would see her scouring the hillsides, turning over stones as if she expected to find something hidden underneath them, or splashing calf-deep in water while she prodded at the streambed with a stick. Usually she would bring home a prize from these foraging missions, and return to the bank cradling a piece of limestone or quartz as if it was a precious object. Once she returned with a roll of discarded barbed wire. From within the secrecy of Mrs Pulaska's barn there came a series of noises which, although identifiable, only helped to create further mystery—a liquid slap and dribble, the rough scrape of heavy objects dragged along the floor, the wooden bangs of ladders or planking.

I asked my father what she was building. He told me that she was not a builder, but an artist. We were eating a meal. He spoke the word *artist* as if it was both a puzzle and an affront, and licked his fingers free of chicken fat.

'An artist?' I asked. For me, an artist was someone who drew the pictures in the *Beano* or the *Wizard*.

'If that's what she wants to call herself,' my mother said, 'then let her.'

'She's no more of an artist than I am,' my father said. 'She's just a crazy Polish woman, that's all.' Finished with his part of the bird, he threw the bones into the fire.

'But she's harmless,' my mother said. 'Just let her do what she wants to do. Why worry about what she is?'

My father grunted. He could tolerate only a little disagreement, and if my mother persisted he flew into a rage. I had often watched her abandon an argument because she hated his anger: usually I wished that she would stand up to him. The chicken bones, rich with fat, blazed and cracked.

Mrs Pulaska ignored me for months. I saw her in freezing slush, in sudden bright sunshine, in ceaseless rain, and always she had the same intent, preoccupied expression, as if the only things that mattered were held captive within her own imagination.

One day, however, she caught me spying on her.

My parents had agreed that we would leave her alone, and that we would not enter the barn. This made no difference to my father; he had no use for the building, and no interest in what she was doing. He only knew that it must be both temporary and irrelevant. But I was consumed with curiosity.

I had looked at some books in the tiny public library—books by artists. Inside their pages I found rich and luxurious images, lingering studies of disported flesh, sumptuous textures of limbs, shadow, and hair. Quite suddenly I associated Mrs Pulaska with a kind of sensual comfort, and with nudity. It did not matter to me that I found her old, unattractive, bony, spare. Without warning she had become unnervingly physical, and I realised that her body must possess its own secret history, about which I knew nothing.

There was a slight gap in the barn door where the planking had shrunk. Furtive and eager, I pressed my eye to it.

I don't know what I expected to see; in the event, I saw nothing. A hessian bag had been fastened over the inside of the gap, blocking even a partial view.

As I stood back, crestfallen, Mrs Pulaska came round the side of the barn and bore down on me across the farmyard. The chickens scattered across the cobblestones.

I froze with guilt. She was wearing her greatcoat, which was torn and shabby by now, and her long hair trailed behind her like a sign of wickedness.

She put one hand on my shoulder—not hard, but my imagination turned it into a fierce grip. At several places her mittens had unravelled, and white skin showed through. She bent to look into my eyes. I thought she was going to hit me, and flinched. But instead she merely stared at me, as if I was an example of a species she had not noticed before. Then she let go and her mouth opened in a sad, lopsided smile. There was blood on her teeth.

She said something I could not understand, and her breath smelled of dandelions and earth.

'What?' I asked, my voice shaking.

She pointed at the barn and spoke again, but the vowels were hobbled and I could only pick out what I thought was the word 'wreck'. I nodded rapidly as if I understood, took a few steps to one side, then turned on my heel and raced away.

Now I began to notice that Mrs Pulaska was returning with other kinds of booty—shards of tile, the ribs and horns from sheep. She began to pester my mother for unwanted cutlery or broken glass. Or she would come up the lane with a borrowed wheelbarrow containing a hundredweight bag of plaster and a gallon tin of paint. When my father's friends arrived to slaughter our pig she watched with nervous dismay, and scurried out across the fields in a dismal, saturating rain rather than hear the animal killed. When it began to squeal she was a long way away, a scarecrow in a distant field, but I could see her raise her hands to cover her ears. Afterwards, however, she asked if she could be given the bones and skull.

Later that year a neighbour visited our farm with her small baby, and, in halting English, Mrs Pulaska asked to see it. My father was wary—the Polish woman coughed and spat a lot, he claimed. But the neighbour could see no reason to refuse. When Mrs Pulaska saw the child she reached out to hold it, and withdrew as if all her nerve had unexpectedly vanished. She ran to her barn and secured the door behind her.

Afterwards, I heard the sound of a hacksaw grating through metal behind the red door. But in the pauses I could hear a high, stifled sound, only slightly more human. I walked away, not realising for some time that Mrs Pulaska was weeping.

Winter came early that year. Sleet drove from the skies for days on end; the rivers burst their banks and the lanes lay beneath water. Inside the farmhouse the fire burned constantly, and my father grumbled that the chimney should have been swept long before the weather had turned. We put log after log on the fire; even then, the walls dripped with condensation and the rooms all smelled damp.

My mother took pity on Mrs Pulaska. One morning she wanted to invite her to eat with us, but my father objected. The villagers had put an end to their charity, he told us. They all agreed that Mrs Pulaska might be poor, but that she could afford to feed herself. Instead of that she squandered her money on ridiculous things—builders' things. If she no longer had free food, then perhaps she would see sense.

Of course my father agreed with them.

'But she's ill,' my mother protested. 'Anyone can see that. All you have to do is look at her.'

'So let her feed herself and then go to a doctor,' my father said.

'Don't be heartless,' my mother said. 'The poor woman probably doesn't know what to do. Would *you* know what to do if you were ill in Poland?'

But my father was stubborn and bitter. 'It's not our fault that she's here. We're not to blame for what's gone on in Europe. Anyways, it's time she moved on from here. I told her she could only have the barn temporarily.'

My mother, colouring with anger, asked what he meant. There was an envelope on the table where he did his paperwork. He tipped the contents—several brochures with plans and photographs of prefabricated buildings. 'That's what we need,' he said triumphantly. 'I always said it. Let's move with the times.'

'But Mrs Pulaska won't understand this,' my mother said. 'She probably didn't even know what "temporarily" meant. And she's still working in there.'

My father, angered at having his judgement questioned, strode to the door. 'I don't care if she's working. I don't care what she's doing. Because whatever it is she'll have to stop. And I'll make sure she knows exactly what "temporarily" means.'

I sat looking at the fire because I did not want to look at my mother's face as she paced the floor.

After a few minutes she went out our front door. I followed, still not daring to look at her.

The farmyard lay under pools of water. My father, his face rigid with shock, was backing away from Mrs Pulaska, who was on her knees in front of him. Her black dress was spattered with mud and animal dirt, and her hands were held high in supplication. It was the first time I had seen her with bare hands; they were covered with white paint.

As we watched, my father took several steps backwards, and Mrs Pulaska pitched forward and sprawled across the muddy cobblestones like someone no longer able to walk. Suddenly she began to cough harshly and repetitively, as if she could not stop. From her lips there came a trickle of blood, bright as the paint on the barn door.

My mother ran across to the sprawled body. 'She needs an ambulance,' she told my father grimly and he walked to the telephone as if under protest.

We carried Mrs Pulaska into the house and sat her in a chair in the warmest part of the room. I put another log on the fire while my mother wrapped her in a blanket. Mrs Pulaska had quietened now. She gazed ahead unseeingly, but her face twitched when the log's bark cracked as the flames took it. My mother wiped the blood from her chin, but as soon as she had done it a little more dribbled out of her mouth.

Mrs Pulaska's hands stuck out from under the blanket, and I saw that one of her wrists had something tattooed on it, a number that stood out in vivid purple lines against the bloodless skin. My mother reached forward and pulled the blanket across, as if she was covering something shameful. As she did we began to hear a muffled roaring noise; the soot in the chimney had caught fire.

My father looked outside. The wind had dropped, and smoke covered the farmyard in a greasy, swirling cloud.

We hardly spoke until the ambulance arrived. Mrs Pulaska did nothing as she was carried into it, but merely stared at a horizon that was out of sight of the rest of us.

We followed my father across the farmyard and paused before the red door. 'She'll not need this any more,' my father said in a voice of a man finally proved right. He pushed the door open.

In the middle of the barn was a trestle-table, littered with implements—chisel, paintbrushes, a heavy hammer. Half-opened bags of plaster and tins of paint were scattered around the table-legs. But it was the walls which had altered beyond recognition.

On them were figures, some of them painted, some of them built in relief, all of them naked. Skeins of barbed wire threaded across through them, and there was subdued, ghostly glitter where the light caught tiny reflective fragments fixed into the vertical surfaces.

I was horrified and fascinated, and walked slowly round the walls. The more I looked, the more detailed and terrifying the work seemed. Here was a face with stones for eyes and teeth of rusted metal; here were children, their bodies dissected by hooks and claws. And here were tortured men with hearts of shattered tile, beaten women with skins of glass. The ribs of animals protruded from their chests, the skulls of beasts showed beneath the faces. A hundred or more tiny bones had been set into plaster to look like the shadow of an infant. One figure reached out, its fingernails delicately fashioned from filed portions of horn, but its face was a mere daub of black paint in a white circle. Here there was no luxury, no pleasure; these people had no dignity, not even rest. If I had ever had doubts about their fate, these walls would have told me what it had been.

I came back to the door and stepped outside. I was trembling, and the smell of fire was in my nostrils.

'I don't understand this,' my father said.

Glowing flakes of soot drifted around me. 'It's a record,' I said.

He turned to my mother. 'I told you it would be worthless. The sooner we get rid of it, the better.'

He walked to the table and picked up a hammer.

My mother took him by the arm. I could see the force of her grip.

'Don't you dare,' she said.

The Short Story 71

Writing style—characterisation

1. Notice the very fine opening paragraph. We are drawn immediately into the life of the main character. This character is interesting or different because of her obscure background or origins. Her strangeness is established in the first two paragraphs. 'An emissary from an unknown world' sticks in the memory.

2. The PHYSICAL DESCRIPTIONS reinforce this notion of strangeness: 'She was angular with bony features and protuberant eyes and long black hair like a witch's.' The simile plants her in our minds. Her clothes too suggest oddness: 'she wore black clothes even in summer, always with gloves.'

Exercise
What other physical details are used by the author as the story progresses, and what do they suggest about the character of Mrs Pulaska?

3. Notice that there is a GRADUAL REVELATION OF THE CHARACTER of Mrs Pulaska as the story unfolds. We get to know her really through the cumulative effect of the many little pen pictures of her activities, such as 'splashing calf-deep in water while she prodded at the streambed with a stick.' Also the noises in the barn, her reaction to the pig killing, and others.

Exercises
(*a*) Examine two or three pen pictures of her activities and say what each adds to our understanding of the character. Which made the greatest impression on you, and why?
(*b*) What do we learn about the mother and father in this story? Examine the characterisation of both by studying such details as physical description; habits; attitude; actions and relationships.

4. *Narrator*: Notice that the story is told in the first person (I, we) by a narrator who also features as a character in the story.

Exercises
(*a*) What kind of person is the narrator? Examine the narrator's relationship with the other characters. Refer to details in the story to substantiate your views.
(*b*) Do you like the idea of telling a story with a first-person narrator? What are the advantages and disadvantages of this technique?

5. Relationships

Exercises

(*a*) Examine the relationship between Mrs Pulaska and each of the other characters. How does each one view her? Refer to details.

(*b*) Nothing much happens, yet this is a story filled with tension. Explain where this occurs and how it is built up.

6. *Themes and issues*: This is a powerful story about war and suffering. It is unusual in that it deals with war from an unexpected point of view: the effect of war on a human being who managed to survive it, for a time. The suffering humanity, felt in her soul, is given expression in her art work. Her horrific vision of humanity is reflected in that wall: 'Here was a face with stones for eyes and teeth of rusted metal; here were children, their bodies dissected by hooks and claws …'

This broken woman, so upset by the sight of an innocent newborn child, can only give birth now to images of torture and suffering. The war still haunts her. And this nightmare she must carry in secret, because she does not speak the language and only finds expression behind the locked door of her sanctuary barn.

Perhaps this story is saying that there are really no survivors from a war: all participants emerge crippled for whatever life is left to them.

Another issue this story confronts is that of the artist: the nature of artistic creativity, a solitary compulsion; how all-absorbing the drive is; the artist will work rather than eat; how the artist is not always appreciated or even understood; art communicated in a non-verbal way. Indeed Mrs Pulaska's wall cries out to us more eloquently than words.

Exercise

Explore the other themes that this story confronts. What does it say about family, about life in a small town, about the meaning of life, etc.?

7. *The plot*.

Exercise

Recount the plot of this story.

8. *The setting*.

Exercise

Do you think this is an appropriate setting for this story? Explain your view, referring to the text for support.

9. *Summary of techniques*:
—first-person narrative
—unusual character; vivid characterisation
—gradual revelation of the story
—dramatic climax
—powerful pictures and descriptions.

Writing

1. Retell this story or a part of it from the point of view of either Mrs Pulaska or the father.
2. Rewrite a section of it in the third person (he/she/they), omitting the narrator altogether. What effect has this on the story?

SECRETS
Bernard MacLaverty

He had been called to be there at the end. His Great Aunt Mary had been dying for some days now and the house was full of relatives. He had just left his girlfriend home—they had been studying for 'A' levels together—and had come back to the house to find all the lights spilling onto the lawn and a sense of purpose which had been absent from the last few days.

He knelt at the bedroom door to join in the prayers. His knees were on the wooden threshold and he edged them forward onto the carpet. They had tried to wrap her fingers round a crucifix but they kept loosening. She twisted her head from side to side, her eyes closed. The prayers chorused on, trying to cover the sound she was making deep in her throat. Someone said about her teeth and his mother leaned over her and said, 'That's the pet', and took her dentures from her mouth. The lower half of her face seemed to collapse. She half opened her eyes but could not raise her eyelids enough and showed only crescents of white.

'Hail Mary full of grace ...' the prayers went on. He closed his hands over his face so that he would not have to look but smelt the trace of his girlfriend's handcream from his hands. The noise, deep and guttural, that his aunt was making became intolerable to him. It was as if she were drowning. She had lost all the dignity he knew her to have. He got up from the floor and stepped between the others who were kneeling and went into her sitting-room off the same landing.

He was trembling with anger or sorrow, he didn't know which. He sat in the brightness of her sitting-room at the oval table and waited for something to happen. On the table was a cut-glass vase of irises, dying because she had been in bed for over a week. He sat staring at them. They were withering from the tips inward, scrolling themselves delicately, brown and neat. Clearing up after themselves. He stared at them for a long time until he heard the sounds of women weeping from the next room . . .

His aunt had been small—her head on a level with his when she sat at her table—and she seemed to get smaller each year. He skin fresh, her hair white and waved and always well washed. She wore no jewellery except a cameo ring on the third finger of her right hand and, round her neck, a gold locket on a chain. The white classical profile on the ring was almost worn through and had become translucent and indistinct. The boy had noticed the ring when she had read to him as a child. In the beginning fairy tales, then as he got older extracts from famous novels, *Lorna Doone*, *Persuasion*, *Wuthering Heights* and her favourite extract, because she read it so often, Pip's meeting with Miss Haversham from *Great Expectations*. She would sit with him on her knee, her arms around him and holding the page flat with her hand. When he was bored he would interrupt her and ask about the ring. He loved hearing her tell of how her grandmother had given it to her as a brooch and she had had a ring made from it. He would try to count back to see how old it was. Had her grandmother got it from *her* grandmother? And if so what had she turned it into? She would nod her head from side to side and say, 'How would I know a thing like that?' keeping her place in the closed book with her finger.

'Don't be so inquisitive,' she'd day. 'Let's see what happens next in the story.'

One day she was sitting copying figures into a long narrow book with a dip pen when he came into her room. She didn't look up but when he asked her a question she just said, 'Mm?' and went on writing. The vase of irises on an oval table vibrated slightly as she wrote.

'What is it?' She wiped the nib on blotting paper and looked up at him over her reading glasses.

'I've started collecting stamps and Mamma says you might have some.'

'Does she now—?'

She got up from the table and went to the tall walnut bureau-bookcase standing in the alcove. From the shelf of the bookcase she took a small wallet of keys and selected one for the lock. There was a harsh metal shearing sound as she pulled the desk flap down. The writing area was covered with green leather which had dog-eared at the corners. The inner part was divided into pigeon holes, all bulging with papers. Some of them, envelopes, were gathered in batches nipped at the waist with elastic bands. There were postcards and bills and cashbooks. She pointed to the postcards.

'You may have the stamps on those,' she said. 'But don't tear them. Steam them off.'

She went back to the oval table and continued writing. He sat on the arm of the chair looking through the picture post-cards—torchlight processions at Lourdes, brown photographs of town centres, dull black and whites of beaches backed by faded hotels. Then he turned them over and began to sort the stamps. Spanish, with a bald man, French with a rooster, German with funny jerky print, some Italian with what looked like a chimney-sweep's bundle and a hatchet.

'These are great,' he said. 'I haven't got any of them.'

'Just be careful how you take them off.'

'Can I take them downstairs?'

'Is your mother there?'

'Yes.'

'Then perhaps it's best if you bring the kettle up here.'

He went down to the kitchen. His mother was in the morning room polishing silver. He took the kettle and the flex upstairs. Except for the dipping and scratching of his Aunt's pen the room was silent. It was at the back of the house overlooking the orchard and the sound of traffic from the main road was distant and muted. A tiny rattle began as the kettle warmed up, then it bubbled and steam gushed quietly from its spout. The cards began to curl slightly in the jet of steam but she didn't seem to be watching. The stamps peeled moistly off and he put them in a saucer of water to flatten them.

'Who is Brother Benignus?' he asked. She seemed not to hear. He asked again and she looked over her glasses.

'He was a friend.'

His flourishing signature appeared again and again. Sometimes Bro Benignus, sometimes Benignus and once Iggy.

'Is he alive?'

'No, he's dead now. Watch the kettle doesn't run dry.'

When he had all the stamps off he put the postcards together and replaced them in the pigeon-hole. He reached over towards the letters but before his hand touched them his aunt's voice, harsh for once, warned.

'A-A-A,' she moved her pen from side to side.' Do-not-touch,' she said and smiled. 'Anything else, yes! That section, no!' She resumed her writing.

The boy went through some other papers and found some photographs. One was of a beautiful girl. It was very old-fashioned but he could see that she was beautiful. The picture was a pale brown oval set on a white square of card. The edges of the oval were misty. The girl in the photograph was young and had dark, dark hair scraped severely back and tied like a knotted rope on the top of her head—high arched eyebrows, her nose straight and thin, her mouth slightly smiling, yet not smiling—the way a mouth is after smiling. Her eyes looked out at him dark and knowing and beautiful.

'Who is that?' he asked.

'Why? What do you think of her?'

'She's all right.'

'Do you think she is beautiful?' The boy nodded.

'That's me,' she said. The boy was glad he had pleased her in return for the stamps.

Other photographs were there, not posed ones like Aunt Mary's but Brownie snaps of laughing groups of girls in bucket hats like German helmets and coats to the ankles. They seemed tiny faces covered in clothes. There was a photograph of a young man smoking a cigarette, his hair combed one way by the wind against a background of sea.

'Who is that in the uniform?" the boy asked.

'He was a friend of mine before you were born,' she said. Then added, 'Do I smell something cooking? Take your stamps and off you go. That's the boy.'

The boy looked at the back of the picture of the man and saw in black spidery ink 'John, Aug '15 Ballintoye'.

'I thought maybe it was Brother Benignus,' he said. She looked at him, not answering.

'Was your friend killed in the war?'

At first she said no, but then changed her mind.

'Perhaps he was,' she said, then smiled. 'You are far too inquisitive. Put it to use and go and see what is for tea. Your mother will need the kettle.' She came over to the bureau and helped tidy the photographs away. Then she locked it and put the keys on the shelf.

'Will you bring me up my tray?'

The boy nodded and left.

It was a Sunday evening, bright and summery. He was doing his homework and his mother was sitting on the carpet in one of her periodic fits of tidying out the drawers of the mahogany sideboard. On one side of her was a heap of paper scraps torn in quarters and bits of rubbish, on the other the useful items that had to be kept. The boy heard the bottom stair creak under Aunt Mary's light footstep. She knocked and put her head round the door and said that she was walking to Devotions. She was dressed in her good coat and hat and was just easing her fingers into her second glove. The boy saw her stop and pat her hair into place before the mirror in the hallway. He mother stretched over and slammed the door shut. It vibrated, then he heard the deeper sound of the outside door closing and her first few steps on the gravelled driveway. He sat for a long time wondering if he would have time or not. Devotions could take anything from twenty minutes to three quarters of an hour, depending on who was saying it.

Ten minutes must have passed, then the boy left his homework and went upstairs and into his aunt's sitting room. He stood in front of the bureau wondering, then he reached for the keys. He tried several before he got the right one. The desk flap screeched as he pulled it down. He pretended to look at the postcards again in case there were any stamps he had missed. Then he put them away and reached for the bundle of letters. The elastic band was thick and old, brittle almost and when he took it off its track remained on the wad of letters. He carefully opened one and took out the letter and unfolded it, frail, khaki-coloured.

> My dearest Mary, it began. I am so tired I can hardly write to you. I have spent what seems like all day censoring letters (there is a howitzer about 100 yds away firing every 2 minutes). The letters are heart-rending in their attempt to express what they cannot. Some of the men are illiterate, others almost so. I know that they feel as much as we do, yet they do not have the words to express it. That is your job in the schoolroom, to give us generations who can read and write well. They have …

The boy's eye skipped down and over the next. He read the last paragraph.

> Mary I love you as much as ever—more so that we cannot be together. I do not know which is worse, the hurt of this war or being separated from you. Give all my love to Brendan and all at home.

It was signed, scribbled with what he took to be John. He folded the paper carefully into its original creases and put it in the envelope. He opened another.

> My love, it is thinking of you that keeps me sane. When I get a moment I open my memories of you as if I were reading. Your long dark hair—I always imagine you wearing the blouse with the tiny roses, the white one that opened down the back—your eyes that said so much without words, the way you lowered your head when I said anything that embarrassed you, and the clean nape of your neck.
>
> The day I think about most was the day we climbed the head at Ballycastle. In a hollow, out of the wind, the air full of pollen and the sound of insects, the grass warm and dry and you lying beside me your hair undone, between me and the sun. You remember that that was where I first kissed you and the look of disbelief in your eyes that made me laugh afterwards.
>
> It makes me laugh now to see myself savouring these memories standing alone up to my thighs in muck. It is everywhere, two, three feet deep. To walk ten yards leaves

you quite breathless.

I haven't time to write more today so I leave you with my feet in the clay and my head in the clouds.

I love you, John.

He did not bother to put the letter back into the envelope but opened another.

My dearest, I am so cold that I find it difficult to keep my hands steady enough to write. You remember when we swam the last two fingers of your hand went the colour and texture of candles with the cold. Well that is how I am all over. It is almost four days since I had any real sensation in my feet or legs. Everything is frozen. The ground is like steel.

Forgive me telling you this but I feel I have to say it to someone. The worst thing is the dead. They sit or lie frozen in the position they died. You can distinguish them from the living because their faces are the colour of slate. God help us when the thaw comes … This war is beginning to have an effect on me. I have lost all sense of feeling. The only emotion I have experienced lately is one of anger. Sheer white trembling anger. I have no pity or sorrow for the dead or injured. I thank God it is not me but I am enraged that it had to be them. If I live through this experience I will be a different person.

The only thing that remains constant is my love for you.

Today a man died beside me. A piece of shrapnel had pierced his neck as we were moving under fire. I pulled him into a crater and stayed with him until he died. I watched him choke and then drown in his blood.

I am full of anger which has no direction.

He sorted through the pile and read half of some, all of others. The sun had fallen low in the sky and shone directly into the room onto the pages he was reading making the paper glare. He selected a letter from the back of the pile and shaded it with his hand as he read.

Dearest Mary, I am writing this to you from my hospital bed. I hope that you were not too worried about not hearing from me. I have been thinking a lot as I lie here about the war and about myself and about you. I do not know how to say this but I feel deeply that I must do something to make up for the horror of the past year. In some strange way Christ has spoken to me through the carnage …

Suddenly the boy heard the creak of the stair and he frantically tried to slip the letter back into its envelope but it crumpled and would not fit. He bundled them all together. He could hear his aunt's familiar puffing on the short stairs to her room. He spread the elastic band wide with his fingers. It snapped and the letters scattered. He pushed them into their pigeon hole and quickly closed the desk flap. The brass screeched loudly and clicked shut. At that moment his aunt came into the room.

'What are you doing boy?' she snapped.

'Nothing.' He stood with the keys in his hand. She walked to the bureau and opened it. The letters sprung out in an untidy heap.

'You have been reading my letters,' she said quietly. Her mouth was tight with the words and her eyes blazed. The boy could say nothing. She struck him across the side of the face.

'Get out,' she said. 'Get out of my room.'

The boy, the side of his face stinging and red, put the keys on the table on his way out. When he reached the door she called him. He stopped, his hand on the handle.

'You are dirt,' she hissed, 'and always will be dirt. I shall remember this till the day I die.'. . .

Even though it was a warm evening there was a fire in the large fireplace. His mother had asked him to light it so that she could clear out Aunt Mary's stuff. The room could then be his study, she said. She came in and seeing him at the table said, 'I hope I'm not disturbing you.'

'No.'

She took the keys from her pocket, opened the bureau and began burning papers and cards. She glanced quickly at each one before she flicked it onto the fire.

'Who was Brother Benignus?' he asked.

His mother stopped sorting and said, 'I don't know. Your aunt kept herself very much to herself. She got books from him through the post occasionally. That much I do know.'

She went on burning the cards. They built into strata, glowing red and black. Now and again she broke up the pile with the poker, sending showers of sparks up the chimney. He saw her come to the letters. She took off the elastic band and put it on one side with the useful things and began dealing the envelopes into the fire. She opened one and read quickly through it, then threw it on top of the burning pile.

'Mama,' he said.

'Yes?'

'Did Aunt Mary say anything about me?'

'What do you mean?'

'Before she died—did she say anything?'

'Not that I know of—the poor thing was too far gone to speak, God rest her.' She went on burning, lifting the corners of the letters with the poker to let the flames underneath them.

When he felt a hardness in his throat he put his head down on his books. Tears came into his eyes for the first time since she had died and he cried silently into the crook of his arm for the woman who had been his maiden aunt, his teller of tales, that she might forgive him.

Writing style
1. Plot

Exercise
Retell the plot of the story. Is it an unusual structure?

2. Characterisation

The characterisation is gradual and natural. We get to know the characters as the story unfolds. We get to know them in an indirect way: we need to pick up the hints ourselves.

The boy:
—He is an ordinary senior student, and has a girl-friend—all in the first paragraph.
—We find that he is carrying a sense of guilt, for a deed done long ago: a childhood fault of unbridled curiosity. See the end of the story: 'Tears came into his eyes … that she might forgive him.'
—So he is a sensitive boy, to carry this sense of sin. He is unable to face the death of his aunt: 'The noise, deep and guttural, that his aunt was making became intolerable to him.'
—He is a caring, loving boy. He cries for his aunt, 'his teller of tales'.
—He was the usual, curious, imaginative young child: 'Don't be so inquisitive,' she'd say. 'Let's see what happens next in the story.'
—What else do you notice about him?

The aunt:
—A small, neat person, who wears no jewellery except one cameo ring.
—A schoolteacher with a taste for classical novels.
—There is evidence that she had a good sense of discipline. She only had to say 'A-A-A,' and moved her pen from side to side. 'Do not touch', she said, and smiled.
—A very private person, her reaction to the boy's intrusion is quite unbalanced, over the top: '"You are dirt," she hissed, "and always will be dirt. I shall remember this to the day I die."'
—There are hints of a very poor relationship with the boy's mother. Where are these?
—What else do you notice about the aunt?

The mother:
This is quite an interesting cameo portrayal, mainly because of what is hinted at rather than actually said or demonstrated. What do we learn of this character?

3. **Relationships**: Examine all the relationships in this story. Are they all unsatisfactory in some way or other?

4. **Themes**: The story explores, among other things:
—UNSATISFACTORY RELATIONSHIPS, a theme you have examined already.
—DIFFERENT TYPES OF LOVE. Examine, for instance, the devotion

of the young boy for his teller of tales. Notice the *romantic love* between the aunt and her soldier, a love that turns into *friendship. Family love* between the boy and his mother. *Love of God* also features in the soldier's vocation.

Write about the story's treatment of each of these.

WAR: The story deals with the usual face of war, the savagery, carnage, indignity of it; it was a wrecker of lives and loves. But there is a positive note too in that love and beauty survive in the midst of war.

Where are these ideas found in the story? Write about this theme.

GUILT: How important is this theme in this story?

DEATH: The story shows many different circumstances of death: in bed from old age; in war; the death of a relationship, etc. Write about this, with exact reference to the text.

COMMUNICATION: or rather the need for it. It is ironic that despite the difficulties of wartime, communications are kept up; yet there is very poor communication in one house. Examine this theme in detail.

5. *Conflict*: Write about the conflicts in this story.

6. *Techniques*: These refer to the technicalities employed by the writer.

—UNDERSTATEMENT: One of the beauties of this particular story is the practice of hinting at things rather than explicitly stating them. What unanswered questions do you find in this story? Do you like this approach?

—IRONY: Irony is a good technique for illustrating contradictions. We already noticed one irony: communications are good in war but poor in the home. Look also at the burning of the letters—all that guilt and turmoil the boy experienced because he wanted to read them, yet here is his mother burning them unread. Also the aunt while alive protects those letters from the boy's mother. Now the mother has total freedom with them, and she's not interested.

Are there any other ironies in the story?

—DESCRIPTIVE DETAILS: Which descriptions do you find most effective, and why? Are there any symbolic details, and what do they suggest?

—ATMOSPHERE: Is the author good at creating atmosphere? Examine the opening scene, the war letter, and any other dramatic scene you choose.

Exercise

Write a short story on one of the following titles:
—The unfairness of life
—Youth is wasted on the young

—A severe disappointment
—Falling in love again.
—I squirm to think
—Some people have all the luck
—Memories
—The things I feel but never say

Writing short stories

EXAM HINTS

1. It is a SHORT story, i.e. a limited piece of fiction: limited in time, setting, and characters. You cannot cover the Second World War in one short story. So FOCUS IN ON A LITTLE CORNER OF LIFE. There is also a time limit: one hour.

2. It is a STORY, which involves some plot, happening or progression of some sort. This will usually mean some tension or conflict and a resolution of that conflict.

3. It reveals CHARACTERS, through:
description
dialogue
actions
- Go for a little depth and difference.
- Make the characters credible.
- Try basing one of your characters around an interesting or odd character you know. Then add on.

4. LOCATION: Create the atmosphere:
Feel it
See it
Smell it
- Try basing a story in a location you saw and found striking.

5. MAKE PICTURES: Let the reader *see* the locations and characters, so go for *colour*, i.e.
descriptions
images
similes, metaphors
adjectives
adverbs, etc.

6. RELEVANT TO THE TITLE.
- Don't wander off and then try to force it round at the very end.
- Beware of over-long introductions.

Diary writing

Diary writing used to be one of the most widely practised forms of literary creativity. It wasn't just writers, politicians and allied globetrotters who kept diaries but ordinary people: housewives, students, bank officials, gardeners—anyone who could write and was willing to create some spare time in order to record, for personal satisfaction, the passing debris of the day.

Diary writing is a unique form of literary creativity. There are no rules, no standards to be reached, no public to please. Anything goes—from the briefest of notes to the most ornate of sophisticated prose; from mundane observations about food or weather to the complicated secrets of the human heart. You create your own diary in your own style.

Because most diaries are not for publication, the content is usually composed of personal observations of everyday events, while the style is informal and intimate.

One of the most famous diaries of the twentieth century is that of Anne Frank, a Dutch Jewish girl who hid with her family and another family, the van Daans, in a concealed attic annexe above Mr Frank's office in Amsterdam, from 1942 to 1944, in an attempt to escape the Nazi death camps.

The first two entries from Anne Frank's diary printed below deal with their lives before they went into hiding.

THE DIARY OF ANNE FRANK (EXTRACTS)
Saturday 20 June 1942

I haven't written for a few days, because I wanted first of all to think about my diary. It's an odd idea for someone like me to keep a diary; not only because I have never done so before, but because it seems to me that neither I—nor for that matter anyone else—will be interested in the unbosomings of a thirteen-year-old schoolgirl. Still, what does that matter: I want to write, but more than that I want to bring out all kinds of things that lie buried deep in my heart.

There is a saying that 'paper is more patient than man'; it came back to me on one of my slightly melancholy days, while I sat chin in hand, feeling too bored and limp even to make up my mind whether to go out or to stay at home. Yes, there is no doubt that paper is patient and as I don't intend to show this cardboard-covered notebook, bearing the proud name of 'diary', to anyone, unless I find a real friend, boy or girl, probably nobody cares. And now I come to the root of the matter, the reason for my starting a diary: it is that I have no such real friend.

Let me put it more clearly, since no one will believe that a girl of thirteen feels herself quite alone in the world, nor is it so. I have darling parents and a sister of sixteen. I know about thirty people whom one might call friends—I have strings of boy friends, anxious to catch a glimpse of me and who, failing that, peep at me through mirrors in class. I have relations, aunts and uncles, who are darlings too, a good home, no—I don't seem to lack anything. But it's the same with all my friends, just fun and games, nothing more. I can never bring myself to talk of anything outside the common round. We don't seem to be able to get any closer, that is the root of the trouble. Perhaps I lack confidence, but anyway, there it is, a stubborn fact and I don't seem to be able to do anything about it.

Hence, this diary. In order to enhance in my mind's eye the picture of the friend for whom I have waited so long, I don't want to set down a series of bald facts in a diary like most people do, but I want this diary itself to be my friend, and I shall call my friend Kitty. No one will grasp what I'm talking about if I begin my letters to Kitty just out of the blue, so, albeit unwillingly, I will start by sketching in brief the story of my life.

My father was 36 when he married my mother, who was then 25. My sister Margot was born in 1926 in Frankfort-on-Main. I followed on 12th June 1929, and, as we are Jewish, we emigrated to Holland in 1933, where my father was appointed Managing Director of Travies, N.V. This firm is in close relationship with the firm of Kolen & Co. in the same building, of which my father is a partner.

The rest of our family, however, felt the full impact of Hitler's anti-Jewish laws, so life was filled with anxiety. In 1938 after the pogroms, my two uncles (my mother's brothers) escaped to the USA. My old grandmother came to us, she was then 73. After May, 1940, good times rapidly fled: first the war, then the capitulation, followed by the arrival of the Germans. That is when the sufferings of us Jews really began. Anti-Jewish decrees followed each other in quick succession. Jews must wear a yellow star, Jews must hand in their bicycles, Jews are banned from trams and are forbidden to drive. Jews are only allowed to do their shopping between three and five o'clock and then only in shops which bear the placard 'Jewish shop.' Jews must be indoors by eight o'clock and cannot even sit in their own gardens after that hour. Jews are forbidden to visit theatres, cinemas, and other places of entertainment. Jews may not take part in public sports. Swimming baths, tennis courts, hockey fields, and other sports grounds are all prohibited to them. Jews may not visit Christians. Jews must go to Jewish schools, and many more restrictions of a similar kind.

So we could not do this and were forbidden to do that. But life went on in spite of it all. Jopie used to say to me: 'You're scared to do anything, because it may be forbidden.' Our freedom was strictly limited. Yet things were still bearable.

Granny died in January, 1942; no one will ever know how much she is present in my thoughts and how much I love her still.

In 1934 I went to school at the Montessori Kindergarten and continued there. It was at the end of the school year, I was in form 6B, when I had to say good-bye to Mrs. K. We both wept, it was very sad. In 1941 I went, with my sister Margot, to the Jewish Secondary School, she into the fourth form and I into the first.

So far everything is all right with the four of us and here I come to the present day.

Sunday 21 June 1942

Dear Kitty,

Our whole class B1 is trembling: the reason is that the teachers' meeting is to be held soon. There is much speculation as to who will move up and who will stay put. Meip de Jong and I are highly amused at Wim and Jacques, the two boys behind us. They won't have a bean left for the holidays, it will all be gone on betting 'You'll move up,' 'Shan't,'

'Shall,' from morning till night. Even Meip pleads for silence and my angry outbursts don't calm them.

According to me, a quarter of the class should stay where they are: there are some absolute cuckoos, but teachers are the greatest freaks on earth, so perhaps they will be freakish and in the *right* way for once.

I'm not afraid about my girl friends and myself, we'll squeeze through somehow, though I'm not too certain about my maths. Still we can but wait patiently. Till then, we cheer each other along.

I get along quite well with all my teachers, nine in all, seven masters and two mistresses. Mr Keptor, the old maths master, was very much annoyed with me for a long time because I chatter so much. So I had to write a composition with 'A Chatterbox' as the subject. A chatterbox! Whatever could one write? However, deciding I would puzzle that out later, I wrote it in my notebook, and tried to keep quiet.

That evening, when I'd finished my other homework, my eyes fell on the title in my notebook. I pondered, whilst chewing the end of my fountain-pen, that anyone can scribble some nonsense in large letters with the words well spaced but the difficulty was to prove beyond doubt the necessity of talking. I thought and thought and then, suddenly having an idea, filled my three allotted sides and felt completely satisfied. My arguments were that talking is a feminine characteristic and that I would do my best to keep it under control, but I should never be cured, for my mother talked as much as I, probably more, and what can one do about inherited qualities? Mr. Keptor had to laugh at my arguments, but when I continued to hold forth in the next lesson, another composition followed. This time it was 'Incurable Chatterbox.'

Saturday 11 July 1942
Dear Kitty,
Daddy, Mummy, and Margot can't get used to the sound of the Westertoren clock yet, which tells us the time every quarter of an hour. I can. I loved it from the start, and especially in the night it's like a faithful friend. I expect you will be interested to hear what it feels like to 'disappear'; well, all I have to say is that I don't know myself yet. I don't think I shall ever feel really at home in this house, but that does not mean that I loathe it here, it is more like being on holiday in a very peculiar boarding-house. Rather a mad idea, perhaps, but that is how it strikes me. The 'Secret Annexe' is an ideal hiding-place. Although it leans to one side and is damp, you'd never find such a comfortable hiding-place anywhere in Amsterdam; no, perhaps not even in the whole of Holland. Our little room looked very bare at first with nothing on the walls; but thanks to Daddy who had brought my film-star collection and picture postcards on beforehand, and with the aid of paste-pot and brush, I have transformed the wall into one gigantic picture. This makes it look much more cheerful, and, when the van Daans come, we'll get some wood from the attic and make a few little cupboards for the walls and other odds and ends to make it look more lively.

Margot and Mummy are a little bit better now. Mummy felt well enough to cook some soup for the first time yesterday, but then forgot all about it, while she was downstairs talking, so the peas were burnt to a cinder and utterly refused to leave the pan. Mr. Koophuis has brought me a book called *Young People's Annual*. The four of us went to the private office yesterday evening and turned on the radio. I was terribly frightened that someone might hear it that I simply begged Daddy to come upstairs with me. Mummy understood how I felt and came too. We are very nervous in other ways, too, that the neighbours might hear us or see something going on. We made curtains straight away on the first day. Really one can hardly call them curtains, they are just light, loose strips of material, all different shapes, quality, and pattern, which Daddy and I sewed together in a most unprofessional way. These works of art are fixed in position with drawing-pins, not to come down until we emerge from here.

There are some business premises on the right of us, and on the left a furniture workshop; there is no one there after working hours but, even so, sounds could travel through the walls. We have forbidden Margot to cough at night, although she has a bad cold, and make her swallow large doses of codeine. I am longing for Tuesday when the van Daans arrive: it will be much more fun and not so quiet. It is the silence that frightens me so in the evenings and at night. I wish like anything that one of our protectors could sleep here at night. I can't tell you how oppressive it is never to be able to go outdoors, also I'm scared to death that we shall be discovered and be shot. That is not exactly a pleasant prospect. We have to whisper and tread lightly during the day, otherwise, the people in the warehouse might hear us.

Someone is calling me.

Yours, Anne.

Tuesday 1 August 1944
Dear Kitty,
'Little bundle of contradictions.' That's how I ended my last letter and that's how I'm going to begin this one. 'A little bundle of contradictions,' can you tell me exactly what it is? What does contradictions mean? Like so many words, it can mean two things, contradiction from without and contradiction from within.

The first in the ordinary 'not giving in easily, always knowing best, getting in the last word,' *enfin*, all the unpleasant qualities for which I'm renowned. The second nobody knows about, that's my own secret.

I've already told you before that I have, as it were, a dual personality. One half embodies my exuberant cheerfulness, making fun of everything, my high-spiritedness, and above all, the way I take everything lightly. This includes not taking offence at a flirtation, a kiss, an embrace, a dirty joke. This side is usually lying in wait and pushes away the other, which is much better, deeper and purer. You must realise that no one knows Anne's better side and that's why most people find me so insufferable.

Certainly, I'm a giddy clown for one afternoon, but then everyone's had enough of me for another month. Really, it's just the same as a love film is for deep-thinking people, simply a diversion, amusing just for once, something which is soon forgotten, not bad, but certainly not good. I loathe having to tell you this, but why shouldn't I, if I know it's true anyway? My lighter superficial side will always be too quick for the deeper side of me and that's why it will always win. You can't imagine how often I've already tried to push this Anne away, to cripple her, to hide her, because after all, she's only half of what's called Anne: but it doesn't work and I know too why it doesn't work. I'm awfully scared that everyone who knows me as I always am will discover that I have another side, a finer and better side. I'm afraid they'll laugh at me, think I'm ridiculous and sentimental, not take it seriously. I'm used to not being taken seriously but it's only the 'light-hearted' Anne that's used to it and can bear it; the 'deeper' Anne is too frail for it. Sometimes, if I really compel the good Anne to take the stage for a quarter of an hour, she simply shrivels up as soon as she has to speak, and lets Anne number one take over, and before I realise it, she has disappeared.

Therefore, the nice Anne is never present in company, has not appeared one single time so far, but almost always predominates when we're alone. I know exactly how I'd like to be, how I am too ... inside. But, alas, I'm only like that for myself. And perhaps that's why, no, I'm sure it's the reason why I say I've got a happy nature within and why other people think I've got a happy nature without. I am guided by the pure Anne within, but outside I'm nothing but a frolicsome little goat who's broken loose.

As I've already said, I never utter my real feelings about anything and that's how I've acquired the reputation of being boy-crazy, a flirt, know-all, reader of love stores. The cheerful Anne laughs about it, gives cheeky answers, shrugs her shoulders indifferently, behaves as if she doesn't care, but, oh dearie me, the quiet Anne's reactions are just the opposite. If I'm to be quite honest, then I must admit that it does hurt me, that I try terribly hard to change myself, but that I'm always fighting a more powerful enemy.

A voice sobs within me: 'There you are, that's what's become of you: you're uncharitable, you look supercilious and peevish, people dislike you and all because you won't listen to the advice given you by your own better half.' Oh, I would like to listen, but it doesn't work; if I'm quiet and serious, everyone thinks it's a new comedy and then I have to get out of it by turning it into a joke, not to mention my own family, who are sure to think I'm ill, make me swallow pills for headaches and nerves, feel my neck and my head to see whether I'm running a temperature, ask if I'm constipated and criticise me for being in a bad mood. I can't keep that up: if I'm watched to that extent, I start by getting snappy, then unhappy, and finally I twist my heart round again, so that the bad is on the outside and the good is on the inside, and keep on trying to find a way of becoming what I would so like to be, and what I could be, if ... there weren't any other people living in the world.

Yours, Anne.

[Anne's diary ended here]

Reading
Extract 1

1. Why does Anne Frank want to keep a diary?

2. What does the extract reveal about the character of Anne Frank? Refer to the text to support your observations.

Extract 2

3. Comment on the atmosphere in the school, as revealed by this diary extract.

Extract 3

4. In your own words, describe the conditions and atmosphere in the secret annexe, as described by Anne.

Extract 4

5. What does this extract reveal about the writer?
6. What are your own reactions to Anne's secret feelings, as revealed here?
7. Comment on the style of writing in these extracts. You might include comments on: ability to describe aptly and colourfully; the honesty and intimacy of the writing; the tone of the pieces; or anything else you notice.

Writing

1. Compose three entries for the imaginary diary of any one of the following: a rock musician; a gardener; a prisoner; a Junior Cert student; a snob; a nobody.
2. Write the diary for a day in the life of one of these characters.

Speech writing

When composing a speech, remember you are now writing for a different medium. As with radio, you are now *writing for the ear*. The speaker gets only *one shot* at communicating ideas. The listener, unlike the reader, cannot check back to clarify a point. So bear in mind the following hints.

1. POINTS EXPRESSED CLEARLY: Is any point open to another interpretation? If so, clarify.
2. LOGICAL STRUCTURE: Ideas should follow logically. Link them in some way.
3. 'COLOUR OF SAYING': Make pictures for your listeners. Help them *see* what you mean. Use examples and illustrations. Sometimes humour helps.
4. VARY THE VOICE: Avoid a boring monotone. Write for variety.
5. BE CONVINCING: This is the key purpose of your effort: to convince the audience to support your position.
6. FORM OF ADDRESS: This will vary depending on the audience. It could be 'Fellow-students,' 'Ladies and gentlemen,' even 'Young people of Ireland.' A debating speech is usually begun 'Mr/Madam chairperson, adjudicators, members of the proposition/opposition, ladies, and gentlemen.'
7. A DEBATING SPEECH: Is slightly DIFFERENT in that—
(i) you are part of a team and will have to advance certain arguments allotted to you, whether or not you believe in them;
(ii) there is great emphasis on arguing the points;
(iii) you think on your feet. You may have prepared some of your speech, but you are expected to deal with points brought up by your opponents. Repartee or the ability to make a witty retort is valued and rewarded.

I HAVE A DREAM (EXCERPT)
Martin Luther King

This is an excerpt from the famous speech by Martin Luther King at the march on Washington on 28 August 1963.

I say to you today, my friends, that in spite of the difficulties and frustrations of the moment I still have a dream. It is a dream deeply rooted in the American dream.

I have a dream that one day this nation will rise up and live out the true meaning of its creed: 'We hold these truths to be self-evident: that all men are created equal.'

I have a dream that one day on the red hills of Georgia the sons of former slaves and the sons of former slaveowners will be able to sit down together at the table of brotherhood. I have a dream that one day even the state of Mississippi, a desert state sweltering with the heat of injustice and oppression, will be transformed into an oasis of freedom and justice.

I have a dream that my four little children will one day live in a nation where they will not be judged by the color of their skin but by the content of their character.

I have a dream today. I have a dream that one day the state of Alabama, whose governor's lips are presently dripping with the words of interposition and nullification, will be transformed into a situation where little black boys and black girls will be able to join hands with little white boys and white girls and walk away together as sisters and brothers.

I have a dream today. I have a dream that one day every valley shall be exalted, every hill and mountain shall be made low, the rough places will be made plains, and the crooked places will be made straight, and the glory of the Lord shall be revealed, and all flesh shall see it together.

This is our hope. This is the faith with which I return to the South. With this faith we will be able to transform the jangling discords of our nation into a beautiful symphony of brotherhood. With this faith we will be able to work together, to pray together, to struggle together, to go to jail together, to stand up for freedom together, knowing that we will be free one day.

This will be the day when all of God's children will be able to sing with new meaning, 'My country 'tis of thee, sweet land of liberty, of thee I sing. Land where my fathers died, land of the pilgrim's pride, from every mountainside, let freedom ring.'

And if America is to be a great nation this must become true. So let freedom ring from the prodigious hill-tops of New Hampshire. Let freedom ring from the mighty mountains of New York. Let freedom ring from the heightening Alleghenies of Pennsylvania!

Let freedom ring from the snowcapped Rockies of Colorado!
Let freedom ring from the curvaceous peaks of California!
But not only that; let freedom ring from Stone Mountain of Georgia!
Let freedom ring from every hill and molehill of Mississippi. From every mountainside, let freedom ring.

When we let freedom ring, when we let it ring from every village and every hamlet, from every state and every city, we will be able to speed up that day when all of God's children, black men and white men, Jews and Gentiles, Protestants and Catholics, will be able to join hands and sing in the words of that old Negro spiritual, 'Free at last! Free at last! Thank God Almighty, we are free at last!'

Reading

1. What is the main idea running through the first half of this speech (down to 'sisters and brothers')?
2. Mention two images the speaker uses to communicate the main idea, and comment on their effectiveness.
3. What is the speaker's attitude to his country in general? Refer to the text to support your answer.
4. What does the speech reveal about the character of the speaker?

Writing style

Notice 1: *Points clearly expressed*? There is really only one point repeated over and over in different ways: that racial inequality must end if America is to be a great nation. Repetition hammers home the point. So the content is simple and clear.

Notice 2: *Logically presented*? The ideas are linked by a repeated phrase, such as 'I have a dream.'

Exercise

What other repeated phrases do you notice, and are they effective?

Notice 3: *Colour*? He uses graphic imagery, which helps the listener to visualise the point, for example 'the red hills of Georgia!' or 'Mississippi, a desert sweltering with the heat of injustice.' He uses metaphors very effectively: 'sit down together at the table of brotherhood.' There is a suggestion of a family meal, togetherness.

Exercise

What other images do you find effective? Explain.

Notice 4: *Symmetry of sentences*? Many sentences are constructed in two contrasting halves, for example '... children will one day live in a nation where they will be judged not by the color of their skin but by the content of their character.' *Not by ... but by*. This gives an opportunity to raise and lower the voice and a poetic rhythm of speech.

Exercise

Can you find two other examples of this? Comment on their effectiveness.

Notice 5: *Building to a climax*? Examine how he builds to that emotional appealing finish.

Exercise

Do you find this speech moving and convincing. Why?

PRESIDENT ROBINSON'S ACCEPTANCE SPEECH
9 November 1990

1. Exactly one year ago today the Berlin Wall came down. Five months later, at the invitation of the Labour Party, I applied to the people of Ireland for the job as President. They said: 'Don't ring us, we'll ring you.' In other words, show us you are serious. The task ahead seemed daunting but straightforward enough in the quiet of my study. The tradition of easy-going elections—or indeed no elections—for the Presidency seemed to promise a fairly sedate seven months. In theory I would put a comprehensive and constructive case for a working Presidency before the people in a rational and responsible fashion, and on the basis of the policies put forward the Irish people would decide. The political soothsayers predicted the Irish people would give me a vote commensurate with that of the parties supporting me, in other words, third place. I began my campaign in many places like Limerick, Allihies in West Cork, the Inishowen peninsula and the islands of the West coast, in a journey of joy and discovery, of myself, of my country, of the people of Ireland. Now seven months later I find that these places did not forget me. The people of Ireland did ring me, and you gave me the job, and I don't know whether to dance or to sing—and I have done both.
2. That seven months seems like seven years. There is nothing rational or reasonable about the campaign which developed into a barnstorming, no holds barred battle between an ad hoc assembly of political activists, amateurs, idealists and romantic realists against the might, money and merciless onslaught of the greatest political party on this island. And we beat them.
3. Today is the day of victory and valediction. Even as I salute my supporters as Mary Robinson I must also bid them farewell as President-elect. They are not just partisans, but patriots too. They know that as President of Ireland, I must be a President of all the

people. But more than that I want to be a president for all the people. Because I was elected by men and women of all parties and none, by many with great moral courage who stepped out from the faded flag of the civil war and voted for a new Ireland, and above all by the women of Ireland, mná na hÉireann, who instead of rocking the cradle rocked the system, and who came out massively to make their mark on the ballot paper and on a new Ireland.

4. Some say a politician's promises are worthless. We shall see. I mean to prove the cynics wrong. What I promised as candidate I mean to deliver as President. Áras an Uachtaráin will, to the best of my ability, become a home as well as a house; a home for all those aspirations of equality and excellence which have no other home in public life. The first step in that process is to preserve and protect the building itself; and one of my first acts as President will be to consult with An Taoiseach, whose regard and respect for our arts and heritage I admire and acknowledge, and whom I know will give this aspect of affairs his best attention. But the material fabric is only the envelope of the enterprise, of that quest for equality and excellence of which I mean the Presidency to be the symbol.

5. I have a mandate for a changed approach within our Constitution. I spoke openly of change and I was elected on a platform of change. I was elected not by parties of Ireland but by the people of Ireland, people of all parties. I will be a President for all the people, a symbol of reconciliation as well as renewal, not least in my commitment to pluralism and peace on this island. But I am not just a President of those here today but of those who cannot be here; and there will always be a light on in Áras an Uachtaráin for our exiles and our emigrants, those of whom the poet Paul Durcan so movingly wrote:

> Yet I have no choice but to leave, to leave,
> And yet there is nowhere I more yearn to live
> Than in my own wild countryside,
> Backside to the wind.

6. But as well as our emigrants abroad we have exiles at home; all those who are at home but homeless; the poor, the sick, the old, the unemployed, and above all, the women of Ireland who are still struggling on the long march to equality and equity. To all those who have no voice or whose voice is weak I say: take heart. There is hope. Look what you did in this election. You made history. As President I hope we will make history together.
7. Dóchas linn, Naomh Pádraig—agus treise libh, mná na hÉireann, a bhuail buille, ní amháin ar bhur son féin ach ar son ceart an duine!

Reading

1. According to paragraphs 1 and 2 of the text, did it seem likely at the beginning and during the election campaign that Mary Robinson would win?
2. In paragraph 2, what does the speaker mean by 'Even as I salute my supporters as Mary Robinson I must also bid them farewell as President-elect'?
3. On the evidence of paragraphs 3, 4, 5, and 6, how does the speaker see the role or function of the President of Ireland (i.e. what should the President be)?

Writing style

Is it a good speech? Examine it under the headings (*a*) points clearly expressed, (*b*) colourful expressions, (*c*) repeated key phrases, (*d*) the build-up of excitement or tension in each paragraph.

Exercises

1. Write a speech to be delivered to an assembly of parents and teachers, advocating that there be two pupil representatives on the boards of management of all schools.
2. The motion for your next debate is 'That it would be better for the world if the differences between peoples in language and customs were to disappear'. [Junior Certificate examination, 1992]
3. Write out a speech you would make for or against the motion 'That school uniforms should be banned.'

The essay

1. The essay is a vehicle that allows you to express your views and opinions on a subject.
2. Points are made and arguments are constructed, so it is a piece of analytical writing
3. Usually the arguments are set out in a logical sequence, and good use is made of examples and references in order to convince the reader.

A COOL AND LOGICAL ANALYSIS OF THE BICYCLE MENACE
And an examination of the actions necessary to license, regulate, or abolish entirely this dreadful peril on our roads
P. J. O'Rourke

Our nation is afflicted with a plague of bicycles. Everywhere the public right-of-way is glutted with whirring, unbalanced contraptions of rubber, wire, and cheap steel pipe. Riders of these flimsy appliances pay no heed to stop signs or red lights. They dart from between parked cars, dash along double yellow lines, and whiz through crosswalks right over the toes of law-abiding citizens like me.

In the cities, every lamppost, tree, and street sign is disfigured by a bicycle slathered in chains and locks. And elevators must be shared with the cycling faddist so attached to his 'moron's bathchair' that he has to take it with him everywhere he goes.

In the country, one cannot drive around a curve or over the crest of a hill without encountering a gaggle of huffing bicyclers spread across the road in suicidal phalanx. Even the wilderness is not safe from infestation, as there is now such a thing as an off-road bicycle and a horrible sport called 'bicycle-cross.'

The ungainly geometry and primitive mechanicals of the bicycle are an offence to the eye. The grimy and perspiring riders of the bicycle are an offence to the nose. And the very existence of the bicycle is an offence to reason and wisdom.

Principal Arguments Which May Be Marshalled Against Bicycles
1. Bicycles are childish.
Bicycles have their proper place, and that place is under small boys delivering evening papers. Insofar as children are too short to keep motorcycles upright at intersections, bicycles are suitable vehicles for them. But what are we to make of an adult in a suit and tie pedalling his way to work? Are we to assume he still delivers newspapers for a living? If not, do we want a doctor, lawyer, or business executive who plays with toys? St. Paul, in his First Epistle to the Corinthians, 13:11, said, 'When I became a man, I put away childish things.' He did not say, 'When I became a man, I put away childish things and got more elaborate and expensive childish things from France and Japan.'

Considering the image projected, bicycling commuters might as well propel themselves to the office with one knee in a red Radio Flyer wagon.

2. Bicycles are undignified.
A certain childishness is, no doubt, excusable. But going about in public with one's head between one's knees and one's rump protruding in the air is nobody's idea of acceptable behaviour.

It is impossible for an adult to sit on a bicycle without looking the fool. There is a type of woman, in particular, who should never assume the bicycling posture. This is the woman of ample proportions. Standing on her own feet she is a figure to admire—classical in her beauty and a symbol, throughout history, of sensuality, maternal virtue, and plenty. Mounted on a bicycle, she is a laughingstock.

In a world where loss of human dignity is such a grave and all-pervading issue, what can we say about people who voluntarily relinquish all of theirs and go around looking at best like Quixote on Rosinante and more often like something in the Macy's Thanks-giving Day parade? Can such people be trusted? Is a person with so little self-respect likely to have any respect for you?

3. Bicycles are unsafe.
Bicycles are topheavy, have poor brakes, and provide no protection to their riders. Bicycles are also made up of many hard and sharp components which, in collision, can do grave damage to people and the paint finish on automobiles. Bicycles are dangerous things.

Of course, there's nothing wrong, *per se*, with dangerous things. Speedboats, racecars, fine shotguns, whiskey, and love are all very dangerous. Bicycles, however, are dangerous without being any fun. You can't shoot pheasants with a bicycle or water-ski behind it or go 150 miles an hour or even mix it with soda and ice. And the idea of getting romantic on top of a bicycle is alarming. All you can do with one of these ten-speed sink traps is grow tired and sore and fall off it.

Being dangerous without being fun puts bicycles in a category with open-heart surgery, the war in Vietnam, the South Bronx, and divorce. Sensible people do all that they can to avoid such things as these.

4. Bicycles are un-American.
We are a nation that worships speed and power. And for good reason. Without power we would still be part of England and everybody would be out of work. And if it weren't for speed, it would take us all months to fly to L.A., get involved in the movie business, and become rich and famous.

Bicycles are too slow and impuissant for a country like ours. They belong in Czechoslovakia.

5. I don't like the kind of people who ride bicycles.
At least I think I don't. I don't actually know anyone who rides a bicycle. But the people I see on bicycles look like organic-gardening zealots who advocate federal regulation of bed-time and want American foreign policy to be dictated by UNICEF. These people should be confined.

I apologise if I have the wrong impression. It may be that bicycle riders are all members of the New York Stock Exchange, Methodist bishops, retired Marine Corps drill instructors, and other solid citizens. However, the fact that they cycle around in broad daylight making themselves look like idiots indicates that they're crazy anyway and should be confined just the same.

6. Bicycles are unfair.
Bicycles use the same roads as cars and trucks yet they pay no gasoline tax, carry no license plates, are not required to have insurance, and are not subject to DOT, CAFE, or NHSTA regulations. Furthermore, bicyclists do not have to take drivers' examinations, have eye tests when they're over sixty-five, carry registration papers with them, or submit to breathalyser tests under the threat of law. And they never get caught in radar traps.

The fact (see No. 5, above) that bicycles are ridden by the very people who most favour government interference in life makes the bicycle's special status not only unfair but an outright incitement to riot.

Equality before the law is the cornerstone of democracy. Bicycles should be made to carry twenty-gallon tanks of gasoline. They should be equipped with twelve-volt batteries and a full complement of taillights, headlamps, and turn signals. They should have seat belts, air bags, and safety-glass windows too. And every bicycle rider should be inspected once a year for hazardous defects and be made to wear a number plate hanging around his neck and another on the seat of his pants.

7. Bicycles are good exercise.
And so is swinging through trees on your tail. Mankind has invested more than four million years of evolution in the attempt to avoid physical exertion. Now a group of backward-thinking atavists mounted on foot-powered pairs of Hula-Hoops would have us pump%%ing our legs, gritting our teeth, and searing our lungs as though we were being chased across the Pleistocene savannah by sabre-toothed tigers. Think of the hopes, the dreams, the effort, the brilliance, the pure force of will that, over the aeons, has gone into the creation of the Cadillac Coupe de Ville. Bicycle riders would have us throw all this on the ash heap of history.

What must be done about the bicycle threat?
Fortunately, nothing. Frustrated truck drivers and irate cabbies make a point of running bicycles off the road. Terrified old ladies jam umbrella ferrules into wheel spokes as bicycles rush by them on sidewalks. And all of us have occasion to back over bicycles that are haplessly parked.

Bicycles are quiet and slight, difficult for normal motorised humans to see and hear. People pull out in front of bicycles, open car doors in their path, and drive through intersections filled with the things. The insubstantial bicycle and its unshielded rider are defenceless against these actions. It's a simple matter of natural selection. The bicycle will be extinct within the decade. And what a relief that will be.

Reading

1. Summarise, in your own words, the principal objections that the author expresses against bicycles in the introductory five paragraphs (from 'Our nation is afflicted' to 'an offence to reason and wisdom').
2. Why does the writer consider bicycles as suitable only for children?
3. 'Bicycles are unsafe.' The author puts forward some unusual notions

under this heading. Do you agree?
4. Why does the author consider the bicycle to be unsafe, and what is his solution?
5. What does this essay reveal about the author's attitude to exercise?
6. How would you describe the tone of his solution to the bicycle problem?

Writing style
<u>Notice</u>
1. The introduction has a striking opening sentence, which is simple, yet the good 'catchy' metaphor of the plague indicates the author's attitude to bicycles and sets the tone for the essay—a sneering yet humorous one.
2. The impression of uncontrolled movement is carried by the verbs—'dart', 'dash', 'whiz'.
3. Paragraphs 2, 3 and 4 of the introduction proceed in a logical order: 'in the city'; 'in the country'; 'even in the wilderness'.
4. Repetition of the word 'offence' pounds home the argument.
5. Imagery and pictures are used to good effect, for example 'a gaggle of huffing bicyclers.' 'Gaggle' is normally associated with geese so suggests here creatures of a lower intelligence. 'Huffing bicyclers' is not the usual advertisement for fitness and health.

Exercise
Bearing some of these stylistic features in mind, write the introduction for an essay on one of the following: lorry drivers; skateboarders; the 'ghetto-blaster'; queuing for the telephone.

Other features of style
6. P. J. O'Rourke writes thematic headings for the different arguments he puts forward. This is unusual in an essay. Normally you would allow the reader to comprehend the key ideas for himself or herself. What are your views on this device?
7. Humour is achieved through many devices:
   (*a*) Exaggerated images such as 'going about in public with one's head between one's knees and one's rump protruding in the air is nobody's idea of acceptable behaviour.'
Write about one other effective exaggeration you notice.
   (*b*) Bathos, or a sharp fall-off in the style and tone of a particular sentence or paragraph. For example, when he is admiring the woman of ample pro-

portions: 'classical in her beauty and a symbol, throughout history, of sensuality, maternal virtue, and plenty. Mounted on a bicycle, she is a laughingstock.'

(*c*) Unexpected contrasts, which act like repartee or the quick retort in conversation; for example: 'Bicycles are good exercise. And so is swinging through trees on your tail.' Or: 'What must be done about the bicycle threat? Fortunately, nothing.'

Exercise

Do you notice any other features of style that create the humour?

8. Use of rhetorical questions. This provides good variety and breaks up any boring patterns of sentences.

9. Use of examples to back up arguments. 'Of course there is nothing wrong *per se* with dangerous things. Speedboats, racecars, fine shotguns, whiskey, and love are all very dangerous.'

Exercise

Mention one other good use of examples, and say why it is effective.

10. Tone. The tone reflects the attitude of the author to his subject. Think of the tone of voice the author would use when reading the piece aloud. The tone could be serious, worried, enthusiastic, angry, humorous, cynical, sarcastic, nostalgic, regretful—in fact any tone capable of being created by the human voice.

Exercise

What do you think is the author's intended tone in this piece? Explain your choice by analysing at least two passages from the essay.

Writing

1. Make a list of any words, phrases or images that you thought particularly effective and that you might use in your own writing.
2. Compose a cool and logical analysis of 'The Teacher Menace' or 'The young brother/sister menace' or 'The Parent Menace'.

On your way
Orla Bourke *offers advice for prospective hill-walkers*

Summer is gone and autumn is here—a prime time for walking outdoors. As far as the Irish walker is concerned, the coolness of autumn and even winter frosts are infinitely preferable to clammy summer days.

You needn't be a masochist to venture out on the Irish hills, especially if you stick to one of Cospóir's way-marked routes. These 'ways' can provide breaks that are scenic and cheap and are an ideal way of surveying the nation's pubs. Further, they can be the start of a great love affair with the rolling hills, heather-clad slopes and brown stretches of bog that are so quintessentially Irish.

Walking a way can be daunting at first. It's just you, your rucksack and your trusty feet taking you across a vast strip of land. It can even be a freedom that scares, but within minutes of your journey's start, those doubts seep away to be replaced by great excitement.

Walking companions should be chosen with care. You should not bring a dog. Nor should you bring your car. Both are a major tie, the dog dragging you after anything white and woolly that runs and the car demanding complex backtracking just so you can pick it up again at night. Most importantly as regards walking companions, if you do take a friend, it must be one who sympathises with your blisters and sores and can withstand the outpourings of gobbledygook that walking through long stretches of coniferous plantations seems to induce. It also helps if your friend likes the same habitats as you, especially the ones frequented by *Homo sapiens* and on which thoughts are exclusively focused for the remaining half of each walk—the pub of course, and the soothing pint that awaits you there.

People who abhor inclines of any type will be pleased to hear that the ways are reasonably flat, though there's the odd up and down to be tackled here and there like the side of Mount Brandon on the Dingle Way and equally daunting Mullacor on the Wicklow Way.

A cash reserve is always handy when starting off on a way—you won't find Pass machines in spots as remote as the Maharees and they're unheard of in windswept Slea Head. Accommodation is mostly at B and Bs where you'll also get evening meals. There are twelve ways in total, ranging from short skip to long trek. The Burren and Cavan Ways will take only two days to complete (15 miles approximately) whereas the Kerry and Dingle Ways take up to two weeks (100 miles each).

Packing for a walking trip is a great lesson in thrift. The lighter your load, the more enjoyable the walk. It's really a toss-up between toothbrush and comb; and the most you can afford to bring, whether walking for one day or ten, is just one change of clothes. It still means that you get to taste one of life's great sensuous experiences at each day's end: putting on a dry pair of socks.

Opinions vary as to how you should be shod whilst walking a way, since terrain can be wet and squelchy at times and at other times bone dry. Essentially footwear should be one of two types: runners with a good grip for forest tracks and boreens and for the wetter spots like bogs, strong worn-in leather walking boots. The other piece of essential paraphernalia for anyone contemplating a walking trip is a rainjacket. All information and maps on the ways can be got from Cospóir and Bord Fáilte.

To avoid reaching exhaustion where the balls of your feet are about to fall off and the ravens circling overhead seem to be watching you with a hungry eye, the average fit person should cover no more than 10 miles daily. On average, two miles are walked in an hour.

Walking a way is addictive. As soon as you've returned to the civilisation of your own home, the bustling streets and the wardrobe full of clean clothes, you find your hand reaching for the brochure again, wondering what the other routes must be like. With twelve of them to keep you busy, it's an addiction you'll keep fed for years.

Reading

1. According to the author, what is the best time of year for walking outdoors?
2. What arguments does the author put forward to encourage us to venture out on the hills?
3. What advice is given about walking companions?
4. 'The writer offers us invaluable advice on preparation for walking trips.' Would you agree with this statement?
5. Is the tone of this piece very excited, neutral, quietly enthusiastic, or what? Write a paragraph justifying your opinion.
6. 'The style of this piece is greatly enhanced by the sparing use of simple but effective imagery.' Comment on this statement.

Writing

Write on one of the following:
—The advantages and disadvantages of a camping holiday
—Why I would recommend canoeing trips (or rock climbing or any outdoor pursuit)
—'To travel hopefully is a better thing than to arrive, and the true success is to labour' (Robert Louis Stevenson)

On donkeys
John D. Sheridan

I am very fond of donkeys. I like their grey muzzles, their pathetically skinny legs, and their noble, loganberry-shaped heads. But what I like most of all about them is their air of relaxation, for the donkey is never tense, and you can ease the strain of life merely by looking at him. He is never anxious to do anything, except to eat, nor to go anywhere, except as far as the next tuft of grass: and even when he is moving he preaches the glory of standing still.

Stupid people think that donkeys never learn, but the truth is that donkeys have no need to learn. Their business is to teach. If you want to see wisdom at its best, look at the next donkey-cart you meet. Or look at the drivers of donkey-carts. Look at the eyes of a boy bringing a pig to market, or at the lined face of a countrywoman going to town for a stone of meal. People who do business with donkeys have a proper outlook on life—they must have, otherwise they would not be fit to do business with donkeys. The donkey knows his own, and he gives them a limited and conditional obedience.

You must let him stand and think now and again, and you must not press any argument too far. If he likes you he will take you into partnership: you can choose the direction, but he sets the pace. If he doesn't like you he will break your heart slowly, and blunt your temper against the rock of his dignified and passive resistance.

I am glad to see that donkey-racing has almost died out; not because it sometimes involves a little physical cruelty to donkeys but because it always involves a great deal of mental cruelty to donkeys. Competition is for men, and wolves, and horses: not for donkeys. The donkey has a proper sense of his own importance, and he is as much out of place on a race-field as a professor under a hod of bricks. The whip may bother him a little, but what really hurts him is the outrage to his nature, for he knows that he was made for higher things.

The donkey is a born contemplative, and his place is outside the hurly-burly. He doesn't wrinkle his forehead, as we do: he wrinkles his whole body, and he does it so quickly that you might easily mistake the movement for a shiver of cold, or think that he had just swallowed a morsel of electrified nettle. And the twitch is always followed by a period of complete calm, for though the donkey thinks great thoughts he never thinks them for very long, and anything that he can't solve easily he dismisses almost at once.

When you compare him with other animals you see his real stature. Seals can be trained to balance coloured balls on their noses, horses to keep time to music (though what really happens in this instance is that the music keeps time with the horses), and goldfish to see a connection between the ringing of a bell and a meal of ants' eggs. Even the humble flea, I understand, can be trained to drag a little carriage after him—in return for grazing rights on the person of his impresario. But the intelligence of the donkey has never been exploited by showmen, and he is the only animal that baffles Barnum.

A lot of nonsense is written about the intelligence of animals. Some people, for instance, regard the ape as an unlucky first cousin who might have done very well for himself if his ancestors had had the wit to turn right instead of left at some stage of the slow, hypothetical movement upwards from the primeval slime. But the only evidence in favour of the ape is that his bony scaffolding is something like our own, that he can skin bananas with his finger-nails, and can be trained to ride a bicycle. For my own part I have never felt this way about apes. I am not impressed by Darwin and the boys, and I think that they have allowed an obvious similarity to blind them to a still more obvious dissimilarity.

I look down on monkeys. I look down also on snakes, elephants, musical horses, and educated fleas. But I am not so sure about donkeys. I feel sometimes that the donkey is laughing at me from behind his sober mask, and that he is vastly amused by this great, unending circus in which we ourselves are the star performers.

In really progressive environments, of course, there is no room for the donkey: a fact which, in itself, is sufficient condemnation of really progressive environments. He has plenty of room on the little roads of Connacht, but Wall Street is too narrow for him. He refuses to adapt himself to noise and hurry, and he is the pioneer of passive resistance.

I like him because he is a sturdy rebel, a quiet philosopher, a penniless aristocrat who refuses to rehabilitate his fortunes by marrying money or moving with the times. But I often wonder what thoughts he is turning over in that quaint, loganberry-shaped head of his, and I cannot get rid of the notion that he refuses to keep pace with civilisation because he knows that civilisation is going the wrong way.

Reading

1. What does the author like about donkeys?
2. Why, according to the author, have donkeys no need to learn?
3. (*a*) The author explains that donkeys have a particular attitude to life. Describe this, in your own words. (*b*) The author uses particular metaphors and similes to convey this attitude. Examine any two of them and say how effective you think they are.
4. (*a*) Why, according to the author, is the donkey superior to many other animals? (*b*) Does he argue this convincingly?
5. Does the author feel that the donkey has any worthwhile function in the modern world? Explain.
6. Write a paragraph on the tone adopted by the author in this essay.
7. What do you admire or dislike about the author's style of writing in this piece? Comment on any two features of the style.

Writing style
How a paragraph can be structured

Notice 1
OPENING PARAGRAPH:
—has memorable description
—has a variety of sentence types
—builds to a strong finish

There is a simple opening sentence, followed by a good graphic description of the animal, followed by the unusual idea of exploring the donkey's philosophy of life!

Notice how this pick-up in pace is reflected in the variety of sentence structure:

No. 1. Simple sentence

No. 2. More complex (loose) sentence, listing the qualities.

No. 3. A balanced compound sentence, showing the effect a donkey can have on humans.

No. 4. A compound symmetrical sentence in three parts. The first two parts have a similar structure: (*a*) 'never anxious to do anything, except to eat,' (*b*) 'nor to go anywhere, except as far as … ' and so it builds up to the final amusing paradoxical (or contradictory) phrase: (*c*) 'and even when he is moving he preaches the glory of standing still.'

Paragraph 6 also builds up to a point. The author begins by listing what other animals can be trained to do. Examine how he structures his ideas in phrases and *links them with different conjunctions*—a growing list of animals: 'seals can be trained ... horses to keep time ... *and* goldfish ... *Even* the humble flea ... *But* ... the donkey ...' and it ends in that alliterative and memorable phrase, 'the only animal that baffles Barnum.'

Exercise
Examine and explain the structure of any other paragraph.

Notice 2
SENTENCE STRUCTURES. Paragraph 2 opens with a fine balanced sentence, i.e. the second half reflects back on the first. 'Stupid people think that donkeys never learn, but the truth is that donkeys have no need to learn.'

Exercise
Where else does the author use this device, and what is the effect? Examine at least two other examples of this structure of sentence.

Notice 3
The author uses sparse but memorable IMAGERY, usually to reinforce a point he is making; for example, 'the rock of his dignified and passive resistance.' This metaphor suggests the immovable and almost elemental nature of the donkey's stubbornness. It is also quaintly humorous in that it attributes sophisticated rebel reasoning to the animal—i.e. passive resistance.

Exercise
Examine any two images, metaphors or similes you find, and comment on the effectiveness of each and their appropriateness.

Writing
1. Make a list of any words, phrases or images you think particularly effective and that you might use in your own writing.
2. Compose a piece on cats, elephants, worms, or any other creature that interests you,
or
Plan the ideas for the above, and concentrate your energies on writing a really interesting opening paragraph!

The personal experience essay

Sometimes the essay writer draws on his or her own personal experience of an event to demonstrate something about society or human beings, etc. So the points that the writer makes come across in an indirect way through the narrative and the reflections of the author.

This type of essay often reveals a great deal about the personality of the writer.

These next pieces are also good examples of humorous writing.

THE DOG THAT BIT PEOPLE
James Thurber

Probably no one man should have as many dogs in his life as I have had, but there was more pleasure than distress in them for me except in the case of an Airedale named Muggs. He gave me more trouble than all the other fifty-four or -five put together, although my moment of keenest embarrassment was the time a Scotch terrier named Jeannie, who had just had six puppies in the clothes closet of a fourth floor apartment in New York, had the unexpected seventh and last at the corner of Eleventh Street and Fifth Avenue during a walk she had insisted on taking. Then, too, there was the prize-winning French poodle, a great big black poodle—none of your little, untroublesome white miniatures—who got sick riding in the rumbleseat of a car with me on her way to the Greenwich Dog Show. She had a red rubber bib tucked around her throat and, since a rain storm came up when we were half way though the Bronx, I had to hold over her a small green umbrella, really more of a parasol. The rain beat down fearfully and suddenly the driver of the car drove into a big garage, filled with mechanics. It happened so quickly that I forgot to put the umbrella down and I will always remember, with sickening distress, the look of incredulity mixed with hatred that came over the face of the particular hardened garage man that came over to see what we wanted, when he took a look at me and the poodle. All garage men, and people of that intolerant stripe, hate poodles with their haircut, especially the pom-poms that you got to leave on their hips if you expect the dogs to win a prize.

But the Airedale, as I have said, was the worst of all my dogs. He really wasn't my dog, as a matter of fact: I came home from a vacation one summer to find that my brother Roy had bought him while I was away. A big, burly, choleric dog, he always acted as if he thought I wasn't one of the family. There was a slight advantage in being one of the family, for he didn't bite the family as often as he bit strangers. Still, in the years that we had him he bit everybody but mother, and he made a pass at her once but missed. That was during the month when we suddenly had mice, and Muggs refused to do anything about them. Nobody ever had mice exactly like the mice we had last month. They acted like pet mice, almost like mice somebody had trained. They were so friendly that one night when mother entertained at dinner the Friraliras, a club she and my father had belonged to for twenty years, she put down a lot of little dishes with food on them on the pantry floor so that the mice would be satisfied with that and wouldn't come into the dining-room. Muggs stayed out in the pantry with the mice, lying on the floor, growling to himself—not at the mice, but about all the people in the next room that he would have liked to get at. Mother slipped out into the pantry once to see how everything was going. Everything was going fine. It made her so mad to see Muggs lying there, oblivious of the mice—they came running up to her—that she slapped him and he slashed at her, but didn't make it. He was sorry immediately, mother said. He was always sorry, she said, after he bit someone, but we could not understand how she figured this out. He didn't act sorry.

Mother used to send a box of candy every Christmas to the people the Airedale bit. The list finally contained forty or more names. Nobody could understand why we didn't get rid of the dog. I didn't understand it very well myself, but we didn't get rid of him. I think that one or two people tried to poison Muggs—he acted poisoned once in a while—and old Major Moberly fired at him once with his service revolver near the Seneca Hotel in East Broad Street—but Muggs lived to be almost eleven years old and even when he could hardly get around he bit a Congressman who had called to see my father on business. My mother had never liked the Congressman—she said the signs of his horoscope showed he couldn't be trusted (he was Saturn with the moon in Virgo)—but she sent him a box of candy at Christmas. He sent it right back, probably because he suspected it was trick candy. Mother persuaded herself it was all for the best that the dog had bitten him, even though father lost an important business association because of it. 'I wouldn't be associated with such a man,' mother said, 'Muggs could read him like a book.'

We used to take turns feeding Muggs to be on his good side but that didn't always work. He was never in a very good humour, even after a meal. Nobody knew exactly what was the matter with him but whatever it was it made him irascible, especially in the mornings. Roy never felt very well in the morning, either, especially before breakfast, and once when he came downstairs and found that Muggs had moodily chewed up the morning paper he hit him in the face with a grapefruit and then jumped up on the dining-room table, scattering dishes and silverware and spilling the coffee. Muggs' first free leap carried him all the way across the table and into a brass fire screen in front of the gas grate but he was back on his feet in a moment and in the end he got Roy and gave him a pretty vicious bite in the leg. Then he was all over it; he never bit anyone more than once at a time. Mother always mentioned that as an argument in his favour; she said he had a quick temper but that he didn't hold a grudge. She was forever defending him. I think she liked him because he wasn't well. 'He's not strong,' she would say, pitying, but that was inaccurate; he may not have been well but he was terribly strong.

One time my mother went to the Chittenden Hotel to call on a woman mental healer who was lecturing in Columbus on the subject of 'Harmonious Vibrations'. She wanted to find out if it was possible to get harmonious vibrations into a dog. 'He's a large tan-coloured Airedale,' mother explained. The woman said that she had never treated a dog but she advised my mother to hold the thought that he did not bite and would not bite. Mother was holding the thought the very next morning when Muggs got the iceman but she blamed that slip-up on the iceman. 'If you didn't think he would bite you, he wouldn't,' mother told him. He stomped out of the house in a terrible jangle of vibrations.

One morning when Muggs bit me slightly, more or less in passing, I reached down and grabbed his short stumpy tail and hoisted him into the air. It was a foolhardy thing to do and the last time I saw my mother, about six months ago, she said she didn't know what possessed me, but he twisted and jerked so, snarling all the time, that I realized I couldn't hold him that way very long. I carried him to the kitchen and flung him on to the floor and shut the door on him just as he crashed against it. But I forgot about the backstairs. Muggs went up the backstairs and down the frontstairs and had me cornered in the living-room. I managed to get up on the mantelpiece above the fireplace, but it gave way and came down with a tremendous crash throwing a large marble clock, several vases, and myself heavily to the floor. Muggs was so alarmed by the racket that when I picked myself up he had disappeared. We couldn't find him anywhere, although we whistled and shouted, until old Mrs Detweiler called after dinner that night. Muggs had bitten her once, in the leg, and she came to the living-room only after we assured her that Muggs had run away. She had just seated herself when, with a great growling and scratching of claws, Muggs emerged from under a davenport where he had been quietly hiding all the time, and bit her again. Mother examined the bite and put arnica on it and told Mrs Detweiler that it was only a bruise. 'He just bumped you,' she said. But Mrs Detweiler left the house in a nasty state of mind.

Lots of people reported our Airedale to the police but my father held a municipal office at the time and was on friendly terms with the police. Even so, the cops had been out a couple of times—once when Muggs bit Mrs Rufus Sturtevant and again when he bit Lieutenant-Governor Malloy—but mother told them that it hadn't been Muggs' fault but the fault of the people who were bitten. 'When he starts for them, they scream,' she explained, 'and that excites him.' The cops suggested that it might be a good idea to tie the dog up, but mother said that it mortified him to be tied up and that he wouldn't eat when he was tied up.

Muggs at his meals was an unusual sight. Because of the fact that if you reached toward the floor he would bite you, we usually put his food plate on the top of an old kitchen table with a bench alongside the table. Muggs would stand on the bench and eat. I remember that my mother's Uncle Horatio, who boasted that he was the third man up Missionary Ridge, was splutteringly indignant when he found out that we fed the dog on a table because we were afraid to put his plate on the floor. He said he wasn't afraid of any dog that ever lived and that he would put the dog's plate on the floor if we would give it to him. Roy said that if Uncle Horatio had fed Muggs on the ground just before the battle he would have been the first man up Missionary Ridge. Uncle Horatio was furious. 'Bring him in! Bring him in now!' he shouted. 'I'll feed the — on the floor!' Roy was all for giving him a chance, but my father wouldn't hear of it. He said that Muggs had already been fed. 'I'll feed him again!' bawled Uncle Horatio. We had quite a time quieting him.

In his last year Muggs used to spend practically all of his time outdoors. He didn't like to stay in the house for some reason or other—perhaps it held too many unpleasant memories for him. Anyway, it was hard to get him to come in and as a result the garbage man, the iceman, and the laundryman wouldn't come near the house. We had to haul the garbage down to the corner, take the laundry out and bring it back, and meet the iceman a block from home. After this had gone on for some time we hit on an ingenious arrangement for getting the dog in the house, so that we could lock him up while the gas meter was read, and so on. Muggs was afraid of only one thing, an electrical storm. Thunder and lightning frightened him out of his senses. (I think he thought a storm had broken the day the mantelpiece fell.) He would rush into the house and hide under a bed or in a clothes closet. So we fixed up a thunder machine out of a long narrow piece of sheet iron with a wooden handle on one end. Mother would shake this vigorously when she wanted to get Muggs into the house. It made an excellent imitation of thunder, but I suppose it was the most roundabout system for running a household that was ever devised. It took a lot out of mother.

A few months before Muggs died, he got to 'seeing things'. He would rise slowly from the floor, growling low, and stalk stiff-legged and menacing towards nothing at all. Sometimes the Thing would be just a little to the right or left of a visitor. Once a Fuller Brush salesman got hysterics. Muggs came wandering into the room like Hamlet following his father's ghost. His eyes were fixed on a spot just to the left of the Fuller Brush man, who stood it until Muggs was about three slow, creeping paces from him. Then he shouted. Muggs wavered on past him into the hallway grumbling to himself but the Fuller man went on shouting. I think mother had to throw a pan of cold water on him before he stopped. That was the way she used to stop us boys when we got into fights.

Muggs died quite suddenly one night. Mother wanted to bury him in the family lot under a marble stone with some such inscription as 'Flights of angels sing thee to thy rest' but we persuaded her it was against the law. In the end we just put up a smooth board above his grave along a lonely road. On the board I wrote with an indelible pencil 'Cave Canem'. Mother was quite pleased with the simple classic dignity of the old Latin epitaph.

Reading

1. From your reading of the first paragraph, how would you describe the writer's attitude to dogs?
2. List the main characteristics exhibited by the dog Muggs. Support your accusations with references.
3. From the evidence of this piece, what kind of person is the writer's mother?
4. What do we learn of the personality of the writer from a reading of this essay?
5. How does the author create the humour in this essay? Examine any two techniques or two episodes.
6. Do you think Thurber is an effective writer? Explain your views in two paragraphs.

Writing

Write an essay or prose composition under one of the following headings:
—Everyday horrors
—Mothers: everybody should have one
—The trouble with neighbours

THE TELEPHONE
(from An Irishman's Diary)
Kevin Myers

There was a time, and a great and glorious time it was too, when you could hear your telephone ring. In those days of course the telephone was connected to the outside world by heavy, coiled fabric-covered flex which was ideal, as a secondary use, for murder. If it had not been such an excellent conductor of telephonic messages one might have concluded that it was purpose-built for strangulation.

The telephone itself was big, black and Bakelite. Admittedly it was not exactly portable, normally requiring two hands just to lift it, which made dialling while holding it just a trifle difficult unless, of course, one had a particularly agile tongue. But in those days one didn't move telephones about any more than one moved the dining room table around. The telephone sat in the hall, a great black brooding eminence pregnant with consequence.

But the most outstanding feature of the telephone in its earlier incarnation was its bell. This bell did not ring—it bawled. A battleship clearing decks for action did not emit a noise to compare with that generated by this telephone when it wanted to attract your attention. The house would reverberate as if elephants were dancing a military two-step on the roof. Windows would rattle or even crack. Plaster would be loosened from the ceiling. Even the cry of a baby, normally considered the most ear-shattering din known to humankind, was dwarfed by the sheer tangible volume emitted by the old-fashioned Bakelite telephone.

And then along came new technology and somebody somewhere decided that this great big, comfortable Bakelite piece of furniture, handsome to look at and full of gravitas and enormous dignity, was old-fashioned and out of date. A comparable attitude was responsible for the installation of Formica surfaces over Victorian mahogany and for the replacement of old wooden window frames with aluminium ones.

And so the great old Bakelite telephones were pensioned off to retirement homes by the sea and modern trimline telephones came into our lives. They were slim and light and you could lift the entire unit with one hand and doubtless they seemed the mustard to the people at Bord Telecom who make the decisions regarding our telephonic future.

Except that the new electronic telephone does not have a bell. It emits a curious fluting noise, an electronic lisp that achieves the decibel level of dustfall. When I received the first of these creatures in my home—and it is a small home—I was unable to hear the telephone's simpering noise unless I virtually installed it in my ear.

Two rooms away the telephone was as audible as a moth's wingbeat in an iron foundry. So unless one was actually poised over the telephone waiting for it to ring one would miss those very few callers who bothered to ring one. And time without number, while one was sitting in the back garden, one would become mildly aware, above the din of a passing snail clearing its throat, of a mild bleating sound. The telephone.

Then one would realise that in fact that very noise had been ever so gently caressing one's inner ear for the last minute or so. With a bound one would be out of one's garden chair, would trip over the dog, crush the cat, knock over the garden table, sprint into the kitchen, upset the vegetable rack, break two cups, one saucer and a small ceramic device whose purpose one had never divined, and would get to the phone—only to find that it was a wrong number.

I have not pointed out that these phones are wallphones and they are made in Ballinasloe and are called Harmony; and if I were in Ballinasloe I would change my name, adopt a beard and go into hiding, with such a phone factory about the place.

Here's how it works, or doesn't. You put the receiver back into the recess designed to house it, and it gives the firm impression that it has been safely installed. So you walk away from it and it promptly leaps out of its mooring place and shatters on the floor, which, thanks to a flex of perfect length, it is just long enough to reach.

But the most irritating thing about the Harmony phone—may its bones rot alone on some distant beach—is that it has nothing to hold its receiver if you want to go and look for a pen or something. If you just let it go it shatters against the floor again—and of course being a wallphone there is no horizontal surface you can put the receiver on.

All that is required would be a small hanging device, such as I have in mind for Harmony's designer, which would take the responsibility of preventing the Harmony receiver from dashing itself to pieces on the stone floor of the kitchen.

This problem I have not solved; I have solved the problem of not being able to hear the telephone by enlisting the services of a choir of telephones which break into a housewide antiphonal chant whenever somebody rings and which can even be heard above the clatter of a butterfly fly-past.

But how I yearn for the days when I would read the latest, hottest news from *Dance Digest* over the big black telephone to my friend Margot Fonteyn: with a ballet paper in one hand and a Bakelite in the other.

Reading

1. List the writer's main objections to the new telephone.

2. What do you think were the purposes the writer had in mind when composing this piece—to inform, uplift, criticise, entertain, or what? Refer to the text to support your views.

3. Tone. Comment on the tone of the piece. Do you think this is an effective way of treating the issue the author wished to address? Explain your reasoning with reference to the text.

4. Examine the effectiveness of any two devices used by the author to create the humour. You might consider hyperbole or exaggeration; graphic imagery; unusual choices of words; structure of sentence or paragraph; or any other.

5. Make a list of any words, phrases or images you thought effective.

Satirical writing

A satire describes any work that attacks faults in people or society by mockery and cutting humour.

Jonathan Swift, Dean of St Patrick's Cathedral, Dublin, in the eighteenth century, was very critical of British policy in Ireland, which had resulted in mass starvation among the Irish. He composed an essay entitled 'A modest proposal for preventing the children of Ireland from being a burden to their parents or country', in order to deride the English government and show how despicable was its policy towards Ireland. This is an extract from that essay.

A MODEST PROPOSAL (EXTRACT)
Jonathan Swift

I shall now therefore humbly propose my own Thoughts; which I hope will not be liable to the least Objection.

I have been assured by a very knowing American of my Acquaintance in London; that a young healthy Child, well nursed, is, at a Year old, a most delicious, nourishing, and wholesome Food; whether Stewed, Roasted, Baked, or Boiled; and, I make no doubt, that it will equally serve in a Fricasie, or Ragoust.

I do therefore humbly offer it to publick Consideration, that of the Hundred and Twenty thousand Children, already computed, Twenty thousand may be reserved for Breed; whereof only one Fourth Part to be Males; which is more than we allow to Sheep, black Cattle, or Swine; and my Reason is, that these Children are seldom the Fruits of Marriage, a Circumstance not much regarded by our Savages; therefore, one Male will be sufficient to serve four Females. That the remaining Hundred thousand, may, at a Year old, be offered in Sale to the Persons of Quality and Fortune, through the Kingdom; always advising the Mother to let them suck plentifully in the last Month, so as to render them plump, and fat for a good Table. A Child will make two Dishes at an Entertainment for Friends; and when the Family dines alone, the fore or hind Quarter will make a reasonable Dish; and seasoned with a little Pepper or Salt, will be very good Boiled on the fourth Day, especially in Winter.

I have reckoned upon a Medium, that a Child just born will weigh Twelve Pounds; and in a solar Year, if tolerably nursed, encreaseth to twenty eight Pounds.

I Grant this Food will be somewhat dear, and therefore very proper for Landlords; who, as they have already devoured most of the Parents, seem to have the best Title to the Children.

Infants Flesh will be in Season throughout the Year; but more plentiful in March, and a little before and after: For we are told by a grave Author, an eminent French Physician, that Fish being a prolifick Dyet, there are more Children born in Roman Catholick Countries about Nine Months after Lent, than at any other Season: Therefore reckoning a Year after Lent, the Markets will be more glutted than usual; because the Number of Popish Infants, is, at least, three to one in this Kingdom; and therefore it will have one other Collateral Advantage, by lessening the Number of papists among us.

I have already computed the Charge of nursing a Beggar's Child (in which List I reckon all Cottagers, Labourers, and Four fifths of the Farmers) to be about two Shillings per Annum, Rags included; and I believe, no Gentleman would repine to give Ten Shillings for the Carcase of a good fat Child; which, as I have said, will make four Dishes of excellent nutritive Meat, when he hath only some particular Friend, or his own Family, to dine with him. Thus the Squire will learn to be a good Landlord, and grow popular among his Tenants; the Mother will have Eight Shillings net Profit, and be fit for Work until she produceth another Child.

Those who are more thrifty (as I must confess the Times require) may flay the Carcase; the Skin of which, artificially dressed, will make admirable Gloves for Ladies, and Summer Boots for fine Gentlemen.

As to our City of Dublin; Shambles may be appointed for this Purpose, in the most convenient Parts of it; and Butchers we may be assured will not be wanting; although I rather recommend buying the Children alive, and dressing them hot from the Knife, as we do roasting Pigs.

Reading

1. Do you think the author's opening statement is sincerely meant or is a conscious irony? How do you understand the tone of this opening?
2. Are there any other examples of irony in this essay? If so, explain the purpose and effect.
3. Swift goes into great detail on the method and advantages of his plan. Do you think it is his intention to shock the reader? Do you consider this approach effective? Comment on these points, supporting your views with reference to the text.
4. 'There is a wide divergence between the tone of the writing and the content of the proposals Swift is making.' Comment on this statement.
5. Do you think this is an effective satire? Explain your reasoning.

Writing

Compose your own 'modest proposal' for:
Reforming the education system
or
Solving traffic congestion in our cities
or
The better government of the country.

Writing Essays

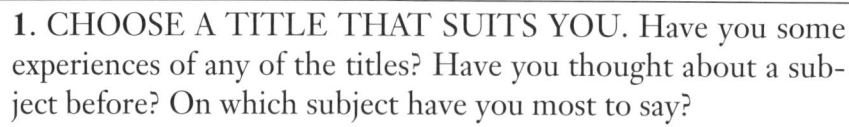

1. CHOOSE A TITLE THAT SUITS YOU. Have you some experiences of any of the titles? Have you thought about a subject before? On which subject have you most to say?

2. PLAN IN TWO STAGES:

(*a*) Write the title in the centre of the page and jot down all relevant ideas; for example on 'National characteristics' from the 1992 Exam.

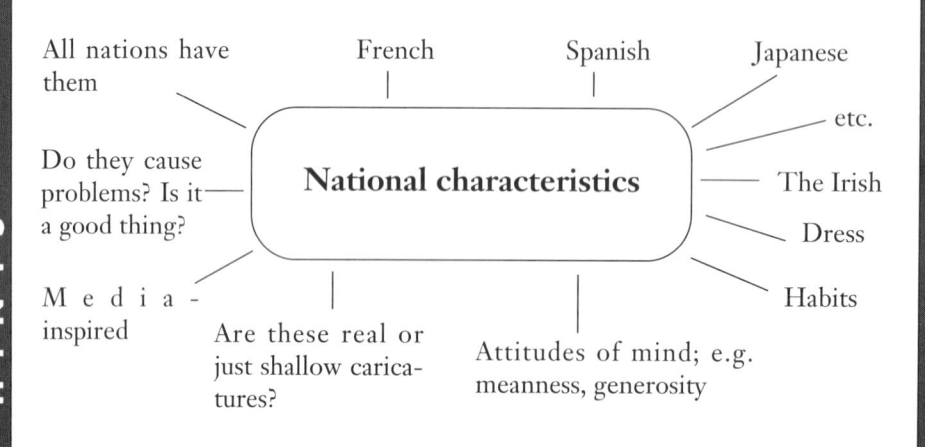

```
All nations have          French        Spanish        Japanese
them                        |              |
                                                        — etc.
Do they cause         ┌─────────────────────────┐
problems? Is it ──────│  National characteristics│────── The Irish
a good thing?         └─────────────────────────┘
                                                        ── Dress
M e d i a -                   |              |          
inspired        Are these real or     Attitudes of mind; e.g.   Habits
                just shallow carica-   meanness, generosity
                tures?
```

(*b*) Select the ORDER of your paragraphs:

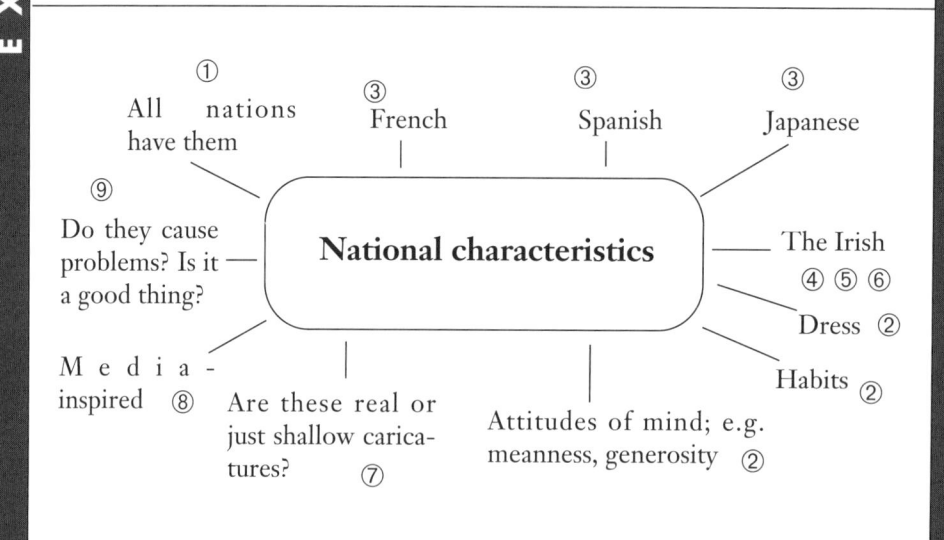

```
       ①
   All    nations       ③              ③               ③
   have them          French         Spanish          Japanese
  ⑨                     |              |
Do they cause         ┌─────────────────────────┐
problems? Is it ──────│  National characteristics│────── The Irish
a good thing?         └─────────────────────────┘       ④ ⑤ ⑥
                                                        Dress ②
M e d i a -                   |              |          
inspired  ⑧     Are these real or     Attitudes of mind; e.g.   Habits ②
                just shallow carica-   meanness, generosity ②
                tures?  ⑦
```

3. A GOOD OPENING PARAGRAPH could (*a*) be a general statement: dramatic, clever, funny, or just very true, (*b*) ask a question, (*c*) be a piece of dramatic dialogue, (*d*) be an interesting quotation.

   IT MUST CATCH ATTENTION

4. A STRONG CONCLUSION
—not necessarily a summary of what you said. Keep a fresh point for the conclusion and express it well.

5. SAY IT IN COLOUR. Make pictures; use
- adjectives
- adverbs
- similes, etc.

6. AVOID
- long introductions
- irrelevant points.

7. SUMMARY.

What you say:	How you say it:
—good ideas	—variety
—deep ideas	—colour.
—relevant ideas, etc.	

Be imaginative!

The personal writing question
What form of writing do I choose?

1. *What form of writing did you find easiest during the year*: descriptive writing; an autobiographical piece; a short story; diary writing; speech writing; the essay?

2. *What form of writing is suggested by or best suits the title?*
For example, take the title 'The suppression of emotion' (1992). Could you do a descriptive piece on it; on characters who must suppress real feelings, at least in public? It could be serious or funny.

Perhaps it is open to an autobiographical approach, using some incident or incidents from your own experience?

Or would you prefer to build a short story around an incident involving the suppression of emotion? Perhaps the diary of a disappointed mother or father, or a harassed teacher, or a student who is being bullied, or a heartbroken teenager? The diary of a failure might give the writing real fire.

A speech; on leaving home, school, or country?

A letter home (from abroad), not wishing to alarm parents? Saying goodbye to someone who is very ill?

Perhaps an essay dealing with such points as: 'boys don't cry'; emotion in relationships; saying what I feel, at home; what emotions are usually suppressed: jealousy, anger, fear? Deal with defeat; crowds; sports; some nationalities are more emotional than others; etc. Would this form give you a wider scope for your ideas?

LET LOOSE; BE IMAGINATIVE.

Examination Questions
(Junior Certificate Examination, 1992) [70 marks]

Write a composition on any one of the following topics. Except in the case of the debate topic, you are free to write in any form you wish, e.g. narrative, descriptive, dramatic, short story, etc.

1. National characteristics.
2. How my attitude has changed as a result of a particular experience.
3. Prejudices.
4. The suppression of emotion.
5. An interesting character.

6. Body language.
7. A difference of opinion.
8. Travel or biographical literature I have read—a personal viewpoint.
9. The motion for your next debate is 'That it would be better for the world if the differences between peoples in language and customs were to disappear.' Write out the speech you would make either for or against this motion.

Exercise

(i) In the case of each of four of these titles, decide the form of writing you would choose and draw up a brief outline plan for each.
(ii) Compose introductory paragraphs for any two of them.
(iii) Write a full composition for any one of the titles you have thought about.
(Time: forty-five minutes; this allows ten to fifteen minutes for the plan and introduction already composed—one hour if beginning from scratch.)

Section 3 — Functional writing

Report writing

> **EXAM HINTS**
>
> A REPORT INFORMS THE READER OF THE FACTS OF A SITUATION.
> So it must be:
> —FULL. Leave out nothing. A report is of little use if the writer has included only selected information or has examined only one side of the case.
> —FACTUAL. A report deals in accurate facts. If the report writer gives his or her opinions, then these should be marked clearly as such so that the reader can distinguish between fact and opinion.
> —PRECISELY STATED. You will notice that the language used is often technical, in an effort to express precisely what the situation is. But if the language becomes too technical, it can be understood only by an expert in that field. So in your reports try for a style of language that is precise without being too technical. But it is certainly not a time for being poetic or emotional.
> —LAID OUT CLEARLY AND LOGICALLY. You could try titled sections something like this:
>   Outline of problem
>   Description of effects
>   Exploration of reasons for problem
>   Possible solutions
>   Conclusion and recommendations
> or any structure you think suits the report.

MIGRAINE
Kathryn Holmquist

The term migraine is the French version of a Greek word meaning 'half a head', for migraine is usually felt on one side of the head, often behind the eye. At least one in ten people—and perhaps as many as one in three—get migraine headaches, which affect women three times more commonly than men. Migraine runs in families; children as young as three can have a first occurrence.

So-called 'classic' migraine, the rarer type, is preceded by an 'aura' or warning signal, which often includes flashing lights, zig-zag lines or a blind spot, which may precede the headache by five to thirty minutes. Rarely, tingling, numbness or weakness of part or all of one side of the body or difficulty with speech may develop. 'Common' migraine develops slowly, building to pain of varying intensities, and is often accompanied by nausea and vomiting, hence the term 'sick headache'.

While migraine is still poorly understood, the most popular theory is that migraine headaches begin with spasm of the arteries near the surface of the brain. The arteries then dilate excessively, resulting in throbbing pain so severe that the sufferer may seek a dark, quiet place in which to lie down.

Many migraine sufferers can pinpoint the triggers which set their headaches off. Stress, bright lights and glare and, for women, hormone pills may be involved. Foods rich in tyramine and phenylethylamine have been found to cause migraine in scientific studies.

Tyramine is found in aged cheeses, fermented sausages, sour cream, avocados, peanuts, pickled herring and red wines. Phenylethylamine is found famously in chocolate, but also in red wine and certain cheeses. Alcohol, nitrites (the food preservatives in bacon, ham, etc.) and aspartame (a sweetener) have also been known to trigger migraines.

Exercise

Evaluate this report under the headings:
- Factual nature;
- Precise language;
- Logical layout.

THE OZONE LAYER

The depletion of the ozone layer is one of the three most desperate environmental problems facing humankind. The other two are the destruction of the tropical rain-forests and the greenhouse effect. All three are interrelated.

Since ozone loss is much more easily stopped than the others, it is a test case. How we handle it will give some indication of whether life, as we know it, on this planet will continue.

What is ozone?
Ozone (O_3) is an altered form of the oxygen molecule (O_2). This form of oxygen is present in the atmosphere some 10 to 30 km above the Earth. Though only present in very small amounts, the ozone layer has been protecting us from damaging ultraviolet (UV) radiation for millions of years.

The effects of ozone loss
Ozone loss is far more serious than has been admitted until recently. Globally the Earth's ozone layer is getting thinner—by some 6 per cent during winter over most of Ireland. A 1 per cent drop in ozone cover allows a 2 per cent increase in the level of UV radiation to get through from the Sun. This in turn is estimated to cause an 8 per cent increase in the incidence of skin cancers—which have actually doubled here since 1974. Increased UV

also causes eye cataracts and reduces our resistance to disease. It breaks down molecules in plant cells, slowing photosynthesis and thus reducing crop yields.

At a high enough level, UV is capable of killing all terrestrial plant and animal life. But it is the marine food chain which is under the most immediate threat. UV radiation has already increased by about 10 per cent over the southern oceans. This is close to the level at which the plant plankton living in them will be killed. Scientists say that the plankton is already under very severe stress, and if it dies, the creatures which depend on it, from krill to penguins to whales, will die too. The loss of plankton would accelerate the greenhouse effect, as plankton absorbs the main 'greenhouse gas', carbon dioxide, in order to grow.

Carbon dioxide is also absorbed by trees, and with the ongoing destruction of the tropical rain-forests it's certain that our Earth is facing a very serious problem.

What is destroying the ozone layer?
Two groups of gases are mainly responsible: chlorofluorocarbons (CFCs) and, to a lesser degree, halons. Both these gases are very safe and stable at ground level, but when they float up into the stratosphere, UV radiation from the Sun breaks them down to release chlorine atoms from the CFCs and bromine atoms from the halons. These free atoms go blundering through space, breaking up the ozone, until they bump into one of their own kind and form a stable molecule which falls back to Earth. It is estimated that one chlorine atom will destroy 100,000 ozone molecules before finding a mate and settling down. Bromine atoms are even more destructive.

This process has been known for some time. However, what has alarmed scientists and caused the recent flurry of international conferences is that the reaction is accelerated many times by the presence of ice particles, which is why it is over the poles that the ozone holes have appeared, when the Sun returns at the end of the polar winters.

Do CFCs do other damage?
Yes. They are also a greenhouse gas and have 10,000 times the heating effect of CO_2. Fiona Weir, Friends of the Earth's specialist in this area, reckons that this damage is at least as bad as their effects on the ozone layer.

What are CFCs used for?
CFCs are widely used—
• as cleansing agents in the electronics and dry-cleaning industries;
• as blowing agents in the production of polyurethane and polystyrene foams for furniture, building insulation and packaging;
• as a refrigerant in the coil in your fridge.
   Halons are used mainly as a smothering gas in fire extinguishers.

Can they be replaced?
Phasing out CFCs in aerosols—about a third of total consumption—is no problem. Neither is their elimination from cleansers and flexible foams. In other areas there is no 'drop-in' alternative, so manufacturing processes will have to be extensively modified or stopped altogether.

For example, rigid foam—the type used as insulation in fridges—might have to be abandoned, but, since other insulating materials are not as effective at keeping heat out, fridges will need more of them. This will probably mean a return to bigger fridges.

Some of the alternatives are CFCs themselves but ones with much less destructive effects because they have less chlorine or none at all. However, some of them may be flammable, poisonous or carcinogenic, and testing is still going on. Replacement refrigerants have been developed but will be more expensive when they get into volume production in 1991. There are no substitutes yet for halons except traditional fire extinguishers like water and CO_2.

Who caused the problem?
The developed countries. The OECD countries produce 80 per cent of the world's CFCs, and their consumption—about 900 grams per head a year—is about ten times that of people in the poorer parts of the world. The EC makes about 33 per cent of the 1 million tonnes world output, the United States slightly less.

What is being done to correct the situation?
The key agreement is the Montreal Protocol, which came into effect only in January 1989. It commits its developed-country signatories to halve their consumption (not their production—they can make and export) of CFCs by 1999. Developing countries that signed were given a ten-year deferment, so the result would be a 35 per cent reduction in world use.

Forty-five countries have signed (but not necessarily ratified) the protocol, and another twenty-two said they would do so at a meeting on the crisis in London in March 1989. However, it is agreed by everyone except the USSR, which wants more research, that the protocol is much too weak and that 85 per cent reduction is the least that would do any good. Many experts want a 100 per cent ban. And, since the CFCs which have already been released will continue to do their damage for as long as a century, the cuts should be made as soon as possible.

Negotiations to stiffen the protocol began in May 1989. The EC has already committed itself to a complete ban by 1999 and the United States has said it will follow suit. There is a catch, however. Most developing countries feel they should not have to make sacrifices to help cure a crisis brought on by the greed of the west. The Chinese could soon become the world's biggest producers of CFCs as a result of their programme to put a fridge into every household. They have already announced plans for a tenfold increase in CFC production. The key issue for the west is how to buy off this by providing them with ICI and Dupont's technology for making the replacement chemicals and by giving them cash to help meet the higher costs involved. The UN Environment Programme, co-sponsor of the London meeting, has suggested a World Atmosphere Fund to pay for this.

Have we gone too far?
Enough CFCs to sterilise the seas might already be on their way up to the ozone layer. Scientists are already suggesting restoring it by injecting 5,000 tonnes of ozone a day into the stratosphere for the next century. They think this could be done by attaching ozone generators to aircraft on ordinary commercial flights or shooting frozen ozone into the sky with special guns.

What is the situation in Ireland?
Ireland has agreed to phase out CFCs by the year 2000 in line with the rest of the EC. However, some other countries in the EC have taken much stronger individual stances,

with the elimination targets set for the mid-1990s and short-term measures in full swing. These include recycling CFCs from fridges and labelling aerosol cans. The Irish Government is now considering implementing such schemes.

Reading

1. What, according to this report, are the principal damaging effects of ozone loss?
2. What, according to the report, could be done to alleviate the problem?
3. In your own words, describe what is being done to correct the situation.
4. Comment on the layout and language of this report.
5. Is this report couched in solely factual terms or are there opinions hidden in it? Do you think the writer has a point of view on this issue? Write your opinions on this, referring to specific examples to support your answer.

Writing

1. Compile a report on the problem of noise in a street or road in your area.
2. Compile a report on the problem of late arrival in school, which may be affecting your class.
3. You want to run a disco in the school hall. Prepare a report for the school principal, outlining your plans, what you propose to do about potential problems, costings, etc. Indeed you should give detailed arrangements for all aspects of the night.
4. You have been asked to draw up a set of basic rules for the smooth running of a youth club where you are a member. This club caters for boys and girls from the ages of twelve to sixteen.
5. Draft the report that a teacher might send to a parent after a pupil has been seriously injured on the sports field.
6. Write a report for your school magazine describing an excursion or field trip undertaken by your class. Since the report will be read by parents as well as pupils, the editor wants you to strike a note of some formality and to cover aspects such as

　—what was the aim of the trip;
　—what happened on the day;
　—what benefits were gained by the students.
　[Junior Certificate examination, 1992]

Writing instructions

HOW TO PLANT A TREE

While awaiting planting, tree roots must be protected from drying winds and frost by covering them with soil or sacking. The planting pit should be at least 18 inches square and 18 inches deep, and the topsoil, which is the darker upper layer, should be retained and the lighter-coloured subsoil removed and replaced with additional topsoil or peat moss.

Place the tree in the pit and position a stake so that it doesn't interfere with the roots. Remove the tree and drive the stake into the ground leaving about 2 feet above ground level.

Cut all dead or broken roots and place the tree in the pit to the same depth at which it was growing in the nursery. This is the part near the roots where the stem colour gets darker.

Roots should be first spread out before covering them with soil. Then shake the stem slightly to remove air pockets from around the roots. Cover with more soil, shake again and finally firm the soil to prevent the tree from moving in the wind. After planting, the soil should be slightly raised above ground level to allow for settlement. Secure the stake with a tree-tie approximately 1 inch below the top of the stake. Then water the ground around the tree with approximately one bucketful of water.

After-care of the tree should include the following:
- Check the tree tie and adjust if necessary to allow for increased growth in stem thickness.
- Ensure that the stake is firm.
- Remove weeds from the base of the tree.
- Lightly fork in 3 oz of general organic fertiliser in April or May.
- Water if necessary during the summer.
- Cut back broken branches and remove growth which arises from the base of the tree.

Exercises

1. How many steps are outlined in this process? List them in order. Is this logical and clear?
2. Comment on the language used under the headings of vocabulary and sentence structure.
3. Write the instructions for one of the following: mending a puncture; cooking your favourite meal; painting a room; washing the dog; doing homework.

122 ACCURATE DESCRIPTION OF A SCENE

■ Accurate description of a scene

EXAM HINTS

1. The same report WRITING guidelines apply when you are writing an accurate description of a scene or photograph:
   —FULL
   —FACTUAL
   —PRECISE LANGUAGE
   —LOGICAL LAYOUT.

2. It may be helpful to DIVIDE THE PICTURE, in your mind, into sections and deal with each of these in turn: background; foreground; left; right; centre.

Exercise

Write an accurate description of one of the following scenes.

Accurate Description of a Scene 123

124 Accurate Description of a Scene

Agenda and minutes of a meeting

The agenda is the running order of business for the meeting and is usually circulated to the members at least a week in advance. It normally looks like this:
1. Minutes of last meeting.
2. Matters arising from the minutes (i.e. discussion of any points that arose out of the last meeting).
3. Officers' reports (i.e. report from secretary, treasurer, etc.).
4. ⎫
5. ⎬ Points of business
6. ⎭
7. Any other business (AOB): i.e. matters that arose since the agenda was set up and so couldn't be included.

The minutes of a meeting are a concise record of the progress of the meeting, such as a very brief summary of each speaker's contribution and a record of the decisions taken.

Exercise

Record the minutes of this residents' association meeting, called to discuss the proposed building of a council estate on the grounds of the local disused orphanage. The residents are all seated around a large dining-room table. They are drinking tea and chatting.

Chairman: Ladies and gentlemen, if I can call the meeting to order ... [The meeting shuffles and coughs, then settles down.] Thank you. Now I think you all know why this meeting has been called, so we'll get straight down to business. I imagine you will all have pretty strong opinions concerning the redevelopment of the orphanage site. [Comments of 'Hear, hear,' 'Disgraceful,' etc.] The buildings themselves are of some local architectural interest. They were designed by Sir Alexander Plumme.
Resident 1: If they build all over the place I won't have anywhere to walk my dog.
Chairman: That's hardly the point at issue. The thing is—
Resident 2: I've never heard of Sir Whatsisname, but I know how I'd feel with an enormous tower block overlooking my garden. If they do anything with the place they should turn it into a nice park. With proper gardens. And benches.

Resident 3: And 'Keep off the grass' signs. We don't want hooligans running about the way they do now. The council should keep them out of there. It's not a playground.
Resident 1: Something nice and respectable, that's what we need. And quiet.
Resident 2: Have you thought what a big council estate would do to property prices? It would bring down the value of our houses considerably.
Resident 3: And we'd be paying for it out of our rates. It would come from our own pockets in the end.
Resident 2: Four hundred and fifty houses. All with children. There's enough children around here already. And they'd be bound to have their fair share of troublemakers. Council estates always do. [General sounds of agreement from the others: 'Hear, hear,' etc.]
Resident 2: It's not what we want, not what we want at all.
Chairman: I think we're all more or less agreed then. The area would make an ideal public garden, properly organised and maintained. With shrubberies and ornamental flower gardens.
Resident 3: I wouldn't object to a couple of tennis courts.
Resident 1: I suppose we could agree to a small children's play area. You know, swings and things. If it were unobtrusive and properly fenced in.
Chairman: Quite. But nothing that would lead to any rowdiness.

Letters

We are going to look at two different types of letter: the personal letter and the business letter. With each we will concentrate on two features:
—Layout
—Language style

The personal letter

Layout: There are no set rules for layout other than the general principle that the page should look neat and orderly. So it doesn't matter if the address is laid out vertically or slanted, provided the signing off is of a similar style.
   Here is a suggested format:

Letters

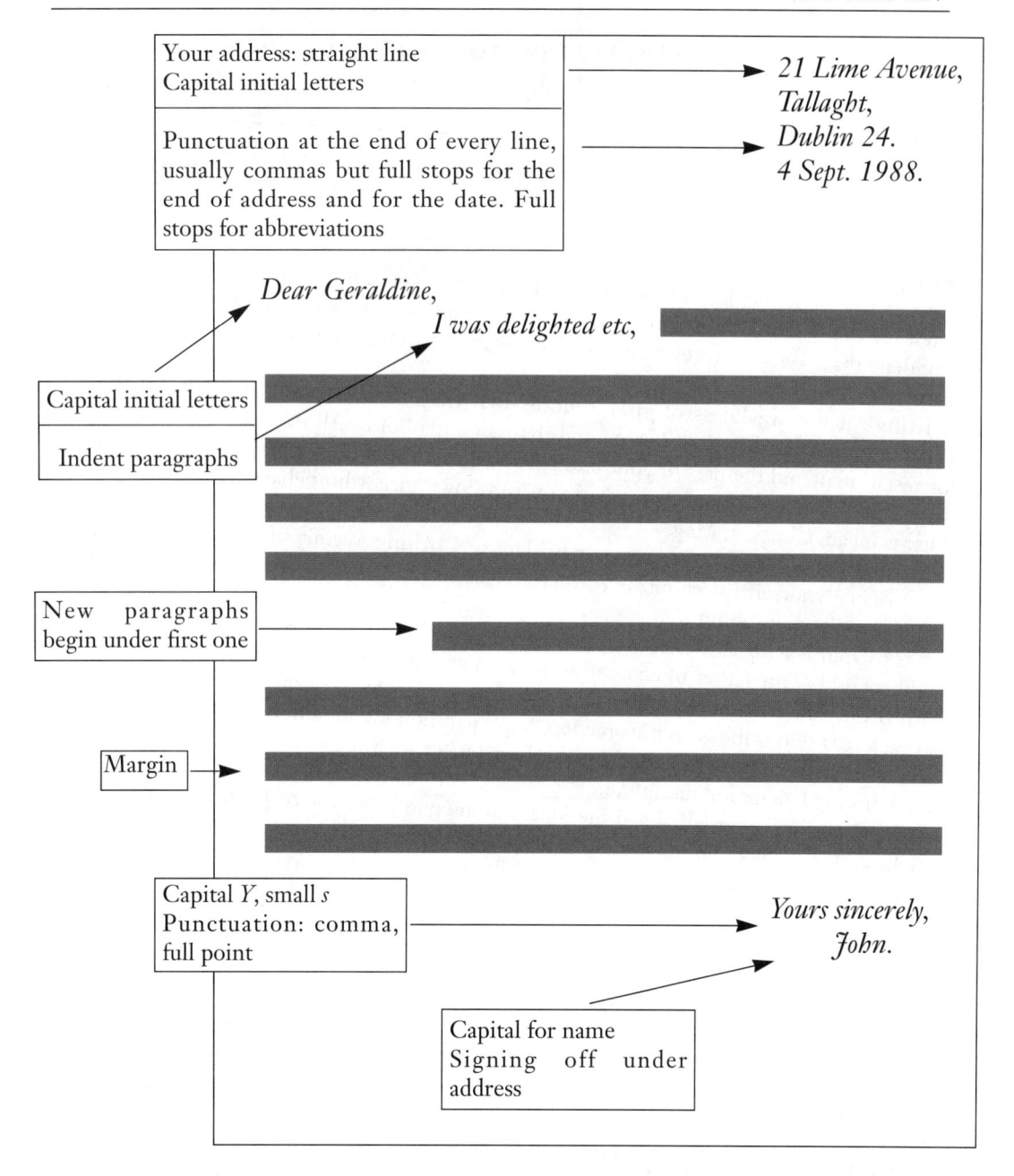

Your address: straight line
Capital initial letters → *21 Lime Avenue, Tallaght, Dublin 24.*

Punctuation at the end of every line, usually commas but full stops for the end of address and for the date. Full stops for abbreviations → *4 Sept. 1988.*

Dear Geraldine,
    I was delighted etc,

Capital initial letters
Indent paragraphs

New paragraphs begin under first one

Margin

Capital Y, small s
Punctuation: comma, full point → *Yours sincerely, John.*

Capital for name
Signing off under address

Language style

The style of a personal letter is always informal, personal, even intimate. You can express yourself freely. Indeed a letter is very revealing of the writer's own feelings, attitudes, mood, and general character.

Two Letters to a Daughter
Evelyn Waugh

Combe Florey House
3 June [1957]

Darling Meg

A sad and saddening letter from you. I am sorry you are in hot water. You do not have to tell me that you have not done anything really wicked. I know my pig. I am absolutely confident that you will never never be dishonourable, impure or cruel. That is all that matters.

I think it is a weakness of girls' schools that they have no adequate punishments. When a boy is naughty he is beaten and that is the end of it. All this admonition makes for resentment and the part of your letter that I don't like at all is when you say the nuns 'hate' you. That is rubbish. And when you run down girls who behave better than you. That is mean. Chuck it, Meg.

It is only three weeks since Mother Bridget was writing warmly of your 'great efforts' to reconcile yourself to school. If you have lapsed in the meantime it is only a naughty mood. Don't whine about it.

As to your leaving early—we can discuss that next holidays. I was miserable at Lancing and kept asking my father to take me away. I am very glad now that he did not. The same with Bron. The whole of our life is a test & preparation for heaven—most of it irksome. So each part of our life is an irksome test & preparation for something better. I think you would greatly enjoy Oxford and get the best out of it. But you can't get there without much boring labour and discipline.

Don't get into your silly head the idea that anyone hates you or is unfair to you. You are loved far beyond your deserts, especially by your
Papa

Combe Florey House
7 June [1957]

Darling Meg

I send you all my love for your birthday. I hope it is a very happy day despite the savage persecution of Mother Bridget.

You have certainly made a resourceful & implacable enemy in that holy lady. She has written to both Colonel Batchelor and Mrs Critchley-Salmonson strong denunciations of your moral character and behaviour. I have sent these documents to my solicitors and hope you will soon appear in the courts suing her for libel. Damages will be so heavy that no doubt the school will have to close down.

She has done more than that. She has written to the committee of the St James's Club warning them not to admit you to luncheon on 23rd. I have had a letter from the

Chairman asking whether it is true that you steal the silver when asked to luncheon. She also told them that you are invariably drunk & disorderly. I call that a bit thick.

But her most cruel move has been to circularise all the London fishmongers warning them under pain of mortal sin not to have any white-bait during your visit to London. The poor men are so frightened of her that they have forbidden the fishermen to catch any for the next fortnight.

Her powers are infinite. She has agents everywhere. I fear you have got yourself into an appalling predicament.

I have just received a letter from Lady Diana who writes: 'Since learning from Mother Bridget of Margaret's terrible wickedness I wish you to destroy the photograph of her and me which was taken last year. I do not want there to be any evidence of my ever having met the odious girl.'

All this malevolent campaign must, I am afraid, rather over-cloud your birthday. Nevertheless I hope you have some pleasure in eating the cakes which, I know, the other girls will refuse to share with you.

Sweet Meg, don't be a donkey. Everyone loves you—particularly I—me? which I wonder is grammatical.

Your loving
Papa

Exercises

1. Describe the attitude of the writer towards his daughter. Refer to the letters to support your views.
2. What kind of person do these letters reveal the writer to be?
3. Describe the tone of each letter. Which tone do you consider to be most effective? Give reasons.
4. Compose the two letters that Margaret Waugh might have written and that gave rise to these replies.

Love letters often make amusing and embarrassing reading! See James Joyce's letter of 1904 to Nora Barnacle.

James Joyce to Nora Barnacle

James Joyce, 1882–1941, novelist; Nora Barnacle, later his wife. Written about 1 September 1904 on Joyce's return to Dublin at the time of his mother's death.

7 S. Peter's Terrace, Cabra, Dublin

Sweetheart I am in such high good humour this morning that I insist on writing to you whether you like it or not. I have no further news for you except that I told my sister about you last night. It was very amusing. I am going out in half an hour to see Palmieri who wants me to study music and I shall be passing your windows. I wonder will you be there. I also wonder if you are there will I be able to see you. Probably not.

What a lovely morning!

That skull, I am glad to say, didn't come to torment me last night. How I hate God and death! How I like Nora! Of course you are shocked at these words, pious creature that you are.

I got up early this morning to finish a story I was writing. When I had written a page I decided I would write a letter to you instead. Besides, I thought you disliked Monday and a letter from me might put you in better spirits. When I am happy I have an insane wish to tell it to everyone I meet but I would be much happier if you gave me one of those chirruping kisses you are fond of giving me. They remind me of canaries singing.

I hope you haven't that horrible pain this morning. Go out and see old Sigerson and get him to prescribe for you. You will be sorry to hear that my grand-aunt is dying of stupidity. Please remember that I have thirteen letters of yours at present.

Be sure you give that dragoon's stays to Miss Murphy—and I think you might also make her a present of the dragoon's entire uniform. Why do you wear these cursed things? Did you ever see the men that go round with Guinness's cars, dressed in enormous frieze overcoats? Are you trying to make yourself like one of them?

But you are so obstinate, it is useless for me to talk. I must tell you about my nice brother, Stannie. He is sitting at the table half-dressed reading a book and talking softly to himself 'Curse this fellow'—the writer of the book—'Who in the devil's name said this book was good' 'The stupid fuzzy-headed fool!' 'I wonder are the English the stupidest race on God's earth' 'Curse this English fool' etc etc

Adieu, my dear simple-minded excitable, deep-voiced, sleepy, impatient Nora. A hundred thousand kisses.

Jim

Exercises

1. Describe the mood of the writer as indicated by this letter.
2. What is his attitude to Nora Barnacle? Refer to the text to substantiate your views.
3. Comment on any two features of the style of this letter.

Letters of sympathy

Letters of sympathy are notoriously difficult to compose. It is often difficult to express meaningful sentiment without being too lugubrious. The letters of Captain Scott and George Bernard Shaw adopt very different approaches to the same theme.

Captain Scott to Mrs Bowers

Robert Falcon Scott (1868–1912), Antarctic explorer; Mrs Bowers, mother of 'Birdie' Bowers. This is another of the letters found with Scott's body. Bowers was one of the two companions who perished with him.

> My dear Mrs. Bowers, [March 1912]
>
> I am afraid this will reach you after one of the heaviest blows of your life.
>
> I write when we are very near the end of our journey, and I am finishing it in company with two gallant, noble gentlemen. One of these is your son. He had come to be one of my closest and soundest friends, and I appreciate his wonderful upright nature, his ability and energy. As the troubles have thickened his dauntless spirit ever shone brighter and he has remained cheerful, hopeful, and indomitable to the end.
>
> The ways of Providence are inscrutable, but there must be some reason why such a young, vigorous and promising life is taken.
>
> My whole heart goes out in pity for you.
>
> Yours,
> R. Scott.
>
> To the end he has talked of you and his sisters. One sees what a happy home he must have had and perhaps it is well to look back on nothing but happiness.
>
> He remains unselfish, self-reliant and splendidly hopeful to the end, believing in God's mercy to you.

Bernard Shaw to the Hon. Mrs Alfred Lyttelton

George Bernard Shaw, 1856–1950, playwright; Edith Lyttelton, née Balfour, one of the 'Souls'. Alfred Lyttelton MP, to whom Edith had been married for twenty-one years, had died that day following surgery necessitated, apparently, by his exertions ten days previously in a charity cricket match.

> 10 Adelphi Terrace WC
> 5th July 1913
>
> My dear DD
>
> So Alfred has the start of us by a few years. He might have waited for you; but I suppose he couldn't help himself. We get our marching orders; and off we must go, leaving our wives and all our luggage behind. He will be at a loss without you for a while, and will fret like a lost child; but he will be so popular that he will have to marry some pushing angel or another out of sheer goodnature, and annoy her from time to time by telling her, with a sigh, how nice DD could be without wings.
>
> Don't order any black things. Rejoice in his memory; and be radiant: leave grief to the children. Wear violet and purple. Dying is a troublesome business: there is pain to be suffered, and it wrings one's heart; but death is a splendid thing—a warfare accomplished, a beginning all over again, a triumph. You can always see that in their faces.
>
> Be patient with the poor people who will snivel: they don't know; and they think they will live for ever, which makes death a division instead of a bond. And let the children cry a little if they want to; it is natural.
>
> And come and close my eyes too, when I die; and see me with my mask off as I really was. I almost envy him.
>
> Yours, dear DD, still marching on
> G.B.S.

Exercises

1. How does Scott attempt to comfort the mother?
2. Do you think Scott's is an effective letter of condolence? Explain your reasoning.
3. Contrast both letters under the headings of
—appropriate tone
—formality of language.

The formal or business letter

Layout: The layout is similar to any other letter except that the name, job title and address of the person to whom you are sending the letter are inserted at the top left side of the page, two or three lines down (see page 000).

Language style
1. The style of language is formal and precise.
2. Address the person formally with Mr, Ms, Mrs, Sir, Madam, as appropriate.
3. Sign off 'Yours faithfully'.

The type of business letter you are most likely to use at this stage of your life is one for a job application. JOB APPLICATION letters generally fall into three categories:

1. A simple request for an application form.
2. Requests for information about a job you think might suit you and for which you may apply.
3. A full letter of application for a particular job. This letter will include your personal details, either in the body of the letter or on a separate page called a curriculum vitae (CV).

Here is a check-list of points for a job letter. Select the points you think necessary to include in your particular letter.

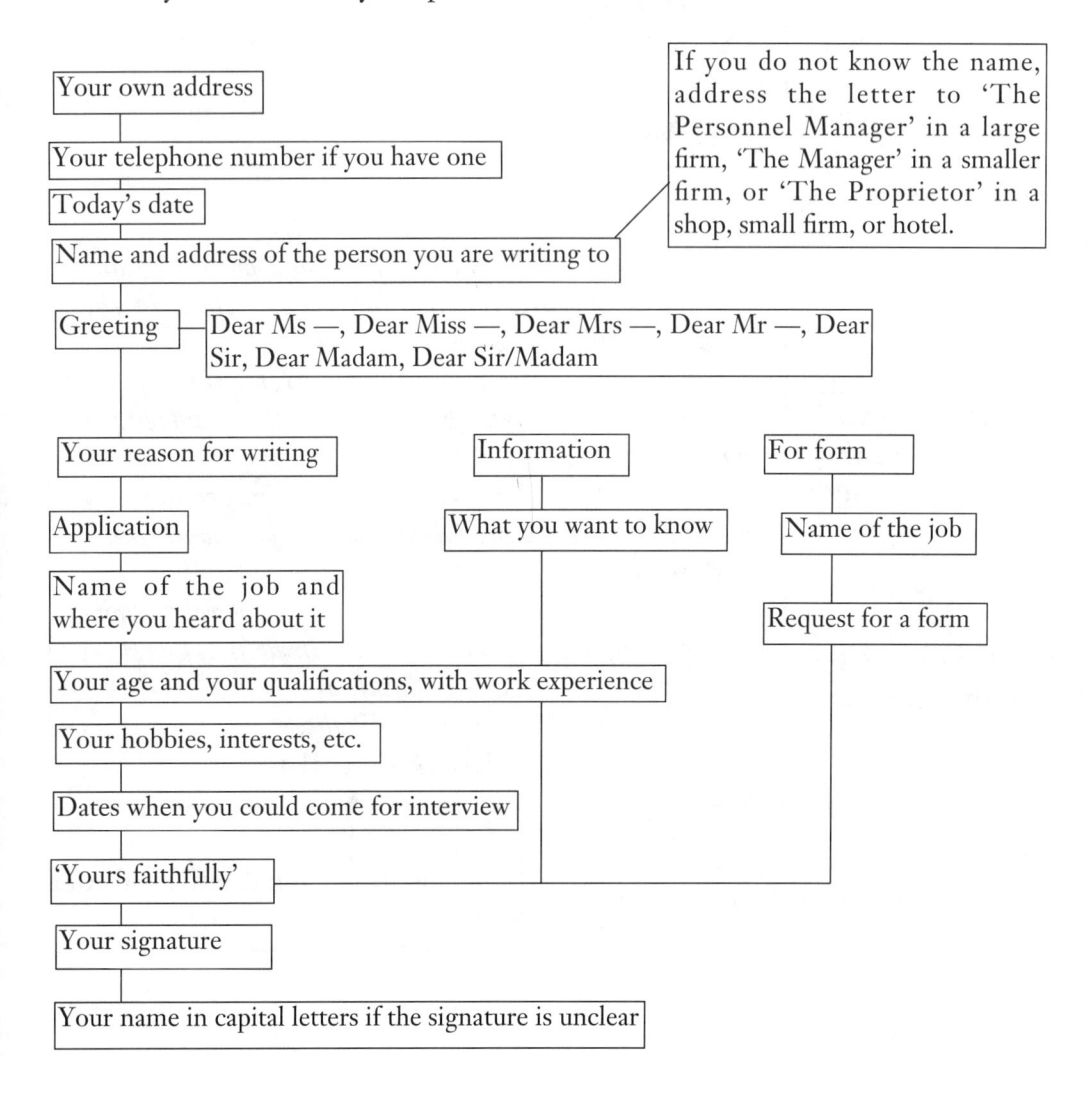

- Your own address
- Your telephone number if you have one
- Today's date
- Name and address of the person you are writing to

  If you do not know the name, address the letter to 'The Personnel Manager' in a large firm, 'The Manager' in a smaller firm, or 'The Proprietor' in a shop, small firm, or hotel.

- Greeting — Dear Ms —, Dear Miss —, Dear Mrs —, Dear Mr —, Dear Sir, Dear Madam, Dear Sir/Madam

- Your reason for writing
  - Application
    - Name of the job and where you heard about it
  - Information
    - What you want to know
  - For form
    - Name of the job
    - Request for a form

- Your age and your qualifications, with work experience
- Your hobbies, interests, etc.
- Dates when you could come for interview
- 'Yours faithfully'
- Your signature
- Your name in capital letters if the signature is unclear

Layout of a business letter

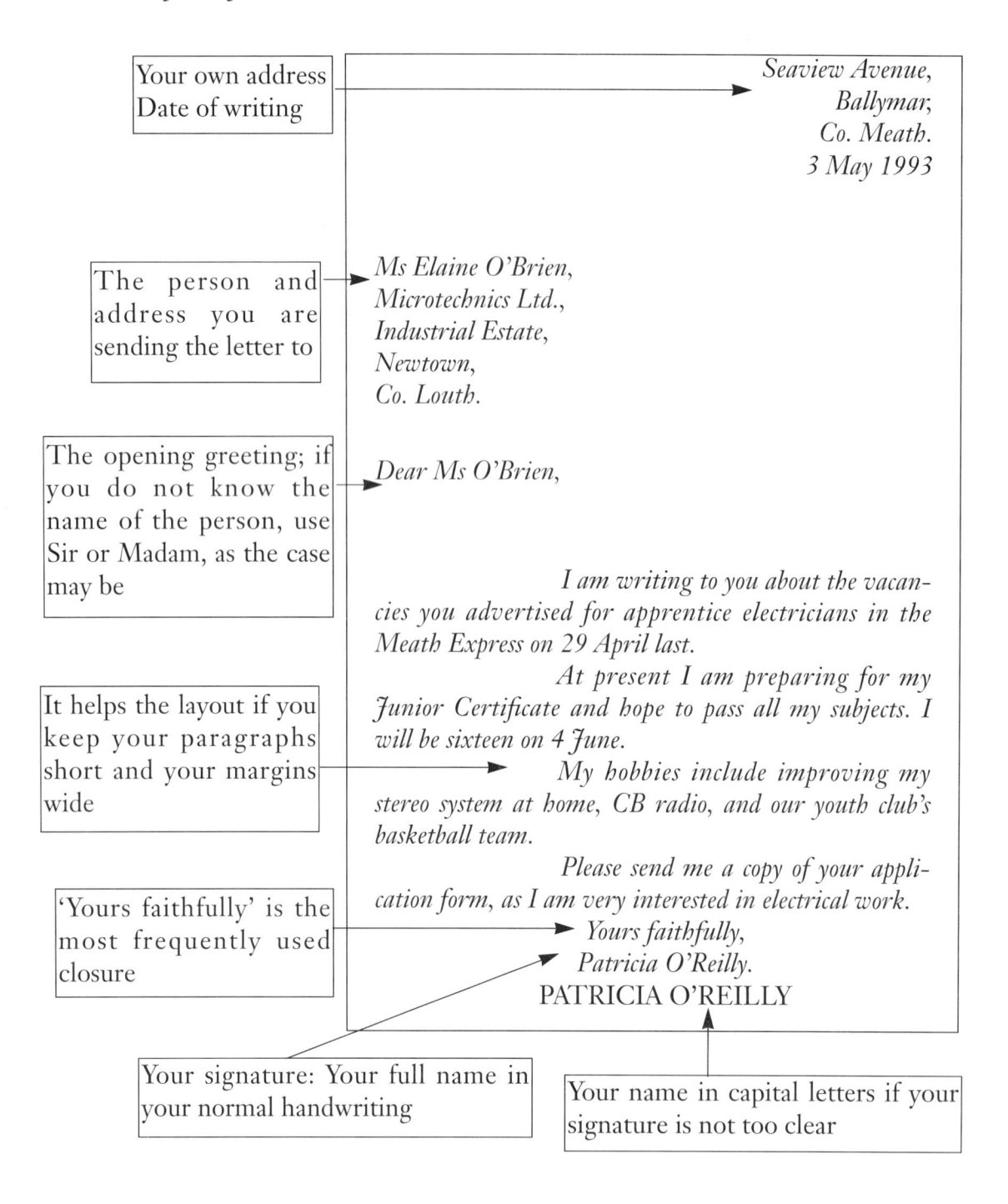

Your own address / Date of writing →

Seaview Avenue,
Ballymar,
Co. Meath.
3 May 1993

The person and address you are sending the letter to →

Ms Elaine O'Brien,
Microtechnics Ltd.,
Industrial Estate,
Newtown,
Co. Louth.

The opening greeting; if you do not know the name of the person, use Sir or Madam, as the case may be →

Dear Ms O'Brien,

I am writing to you about the vacancies you advertised for apprentice electricians in the Meath Express on 29 April last.

At present I am preparing for my Junior Certificate and hope to pass all my subjects. I will be sixteen on 4 June.

It helps the layout if you keep your paragraphs short and your margins wide →

My hobbies include improving my stereo system at home, CB radio, and our youth club's basketball team.

Please send me a copy of your application form, as I am very interested in electrical work.

'Yours faithfully' is the most frequently used closure →

Yours faithfully,
Patricia O'Reilly.
PATRICIA O'REILLY

Your signature: Your full name in your normal handwriting

Your name in capital letters if your signature is not too clear

Exercises

1. Write a letter to the Careers Information Section of the Department of Labour Affairs asking for an information leaflet about a career of interest to you.

2. Write a letter to a firm (imaginary or real) asking if they have any vacancies. Let them know what sort of work you are suited for.

3. Write to request an application form for the following position:

County Dublin Mental Health Service

Location: Cluain Phádraig, Sandyford, Co. Dublin. The centre provides a comprehensive community-based adult psychiatric service in south County Dublin.

Post: Driver.

Ideal candidate: The service wishes to recruit suitably qualified personnel for placement on a panel to provide cover, as required, during the absence of its full-time drivers. Successful candidates must possess a class D driving licence. Good interpersonal skills and previous experience essential.

Application forms are available by sending a SAE to: Administrative Manager, Cluain Phádraig, Sandyford, Co. Dublin, to whom completed applications must be returned by **Wednesday 2 June 1993**.

---

4. Compose a letter requesting information about any one of the following positions:

Wanted
Volunteer secretary with experience.
Five hours per fortnight. Might suit retired person. Apply ISLD, 32 Wicklow Street, Dublin 2.

Bush Hotel, Carrick-on-Shannon, requires experienced cooks, chefs, housekeeping, bar and waiting staff. Apply in writing to Manager.

Mechanic required
by leading Dublin garage. Must be fully qualified. Apply Box C1774.

5. Compose a full application for one of the following positions:

> Young American family with working mother needs housekeeper with some child care, near Chicago. Flexible hours, immediate position. Apply with photo and phone no. to Margaret Levin, 115 Mountain Rd, Arlington, Illinois 60024; tel. 001 708 5119091.

> **Accountants**
> Small Dublin city centre practice requires experienced semi-senior clerk or technician to prepare work to draft accounts stage. Some form of transport preferred. Send CV and state salary to Box C1284.

6. Write a letter of complaint to a restaurant where you found the prices high, the food inedible, and the staff rude.

7. Write a letter of apology to a former friend whose books you dumped in the canal because of a misunderstanding.

8. Write a letter of thanks to your school principal, who has attempted to provide an education for you. The tone of the letter may be embarrassingly grovelling, boringly sincere, or laced with sophisticated irony.

9. Write a letter to RTE either (*a*) praising or protesting about a programme or programmes you have recently seen on television or heard on radio or (*b*) commenting on some social problem that was covered in a news or current affairs programme.
[Junior Certificate examination, 1993]

Filling application forms

EXAM HINTS
1. First do a rough version of the answers.
2. Use capital letters unless told otherwise.

APPLICATION FOR EMPLOYMENT
(Complete this form in capital letters.)

Surname: Mr/Mrs/Ms	First name:	Nationality:	Date of birth:

Home address:

Telephone number:

Correspondence address (if different):

Application for position of:

Details of any disability or serious illness:

Education:	
Name and address of primary school:	Dates attended:
Postprimary school or college:	Dates attended:

Please state any examinations taken or to be taken. Indicate subjects, levels, dates, and results, where applicable.

Positions of responsibility held at school:

Special training (if any):

Details of previous employment:

Dates:	Name and address of employer:	Position:

Details of any other relevant experience:

Interests, hobbies:

Why do you think you are suited for this position?

Names, addresses and telephone numbers of two referees:

Curriculum vitae

You may decide to present the personal information on separate pages, called a curriculum vitae (CV).

Your CV should be professionally typed, signed, and dated, and should include the following information.

1. PERSONAL DETAILS:	Name, Address, Tel. No. Date of Birth.
2. EDUCATIONAL DETAILS:	Names and addresses of schools and/or colleges, with dates when attended; subjects studied with details of levels and results of any exams taken.
3. PRESENT POSITION:	Brief details, address etc
4. WORK EXPERIENCE:	Consider all work done, outside of home and school, whether paid or voluntary.
5. POSITION OF RESPONSIBILITY:	In work, school or leisure activities.
6. INTERESTS:	List all main hobbies, leisure activities and skills.
7. ANY OTHER RELEVANT INFORMATION:	Anything that might make an employer think about you.
8. REFEREES:	Names, addresses, telephone numbers; usually of TWO referees. Ask their permission first!

Section 4 — The media

Newspaper writing
News   Editorial   Features   Letters   Reviews

Writing the news
1. Structuring the report.

Notice
HEADLINES BY-LINE INVERTED PYRAMID STRUCTURE PHOTO AND CAPTION

—HEADLINES are used to grab the reader's attention. To do this they often employ puns, alliteration, violent verbs, etc.

—The BY-LINE identifies the journalist and his or her area of responsibility.

—INVERTED PYRAMID: The main facts (i.e. what, who, where, when, why) are given in the first and second paragraphs. Background and other peripheral questions are dealt with further down the report. The information becomes thinner and less important as the report progresses, hence the notion of inverted pyramid.

—A PHOTOGRAPH is immediately eye-catching. 'A picture is worth a thousand words.'

WRITING THE NEWS

Daily Mirror — Friday, May 28, 1993 — PRINTED IN IRELAND — 45p

Allan Hall's IRISH EYE — Dateline New York—see page 6

REVENGE: Lamont

Ghost of Lamont is set to haunt Major

By JOHN WILLIAMS

NORMAN Lamont was last night plotting revenge on John Major from his political grave.

The ex-Chancellor is furious that he was axed in the Premier's panic reshuffle which has split the Tory Party.

His friends said he feels "very angry and hurt" and badly let down by Mr Major.

Senior Tories fear Mr Lamont will now turn on his former friend. And one Cabinet Minister said: "We're dreading what he will do."

Mr Lamont stalked out of the Prime Minister's study in a rage after being

TARGET: Major

told in a face-to-face showdown that Kenneth Clarke was getting his job.

He threw the offer of a switch to Environment Secretary back in Mr Major's face – as an insult.

And last night in an extraordinary gesture of defiance which rocked the Cabinet, he refused to write the traditional letter of "resignation".

Instead – after enjoying a champagne lunch – Mr Lamont issued a menacing statement.

In it there were NO usual courtesies and NO normal promises of loyalty.

Those were seen by senior Tories as clear signs that he may be dead but he won't be lying down.

They are worried he will rise gunning for his old boss – just as Sir Geoffrey Howe turned fatally against Mrs Thatcher. For the

● Turn to Page 3

PLEASED TO MEET YOU.. AFTER 400 YEARS

PRESIDENT Mary Robinson had an historic meeting with Queen Elizabeth at Buckingham Palace yesterday – signalling a new era in Anglo-Irish relations.

The last Irish national figure to meet a British monarch was the great female warrior Granuaile exactly 400 YEARS ago.

And then it was Queen Elizabeth I who invited the legendary pirate queen to England to make peace – because she had caused the English so much trouble.

Yesterday's talks were strictly private. The two heads of state exchanged a wide range of views on a variety of issues.

President Robinson joked later: "Unlike Granuaile, we did not speak in Latin."

She added: "It was a friendly and cordial meeting.

"It indicates what warm relations exist between the two countries."

The President said the meeting was "significant because of the bond between the countries and because so many Irish people lived in Britain."

She said the Queen greeted her and her husband Nicholas in a very friendly manner.

"She made us feel very relaxed and very much at home.

"We had wide-ranging discussions and a frank exchange of views."

President Robinson arrived at Buckingham Palace at 3.00pm, 15 minutes early.

Irish people gathered outside the famous gates carrying tricolours and waved at her as her black Mercedes drove in.

A guard of honour greeted her in the courtyard.

Then she met the Queen in a reception room on the first floor overlooking the palace gardens.

Mrs Robinson was accompanied by the Irish Ambassador to London, Joseph Small.

Later she and her husband, Nicholas, met the Queen alone.

No officials were allowed into the room.

Both Dublin and London described the meeting as a "courtesy call."

We Can't Afford Not Invite You Back – Page 5

Queen's guest last time was a girl pirate

By JOHN KIERANS

HEAD START: President Mary and the Queen yesterday

2. Writing styles

Individual newspapers develop their own distinctive style of writing. By far the most obvious difference in style is that between 'broadsheet' (large-page) or quality newspapers and the 'tabloid' (small-page) newspapers.

Notice

Tabloids have:
SENSATIONAL HEADLINES
MORE PICTURES, LESS TEXT
SHORTER SENTENCES
EMOTIONAL LANGUAGE
EXAGGERATED OR SENSATIONAL SLANT
MORE HUMAN INTEREST OR PERSONAL ANGLE

Exercises

1. Contrast the approaches of the *Irish Independent* and the *Star* in covering this tragic story.

Family make life-saving plea

By CLODAGH SHEEHY

AN anguished family last night appealed for a life-saving heart for a 44-year-old Dublin man who has been given only days to live.

Noel Murphy of Grangemore Drive in Raheny had two major heart attacks this weekend, and surgeons say his only hope is a transplant operation.

The father of three had been on the transplant waiting list since last November, but his condition became critical on Friday, when he slumped over the wheel of his car as he was driving through town.

His sister May Walsh of Seapark, Malahide, told how Noel was now in the intensive care unit in the Mater Hospital coronary unit.

"He's so weak that, although he can speak, they've asked his wife, Marie, not to talk to him. She's the only one allowed in to see him at the moment."

Noel and Marie Murphy have two daughters, Marie (17) and Susan (20) and a son, Robert (21).

May said Noel was in great pain on Friday and was driving home to Raheny to get medication when he had the attack.

"He was in the car with his wife and one of his daughters and he got as far as Dame Street. Marie ran across the road to get a woman to ring an ambulance, and when she got back to the car Noel practically fell into her arms.

"The ambulance took him to the Meath and the family were told he had to be moved to the Mater within ten minutes. He was moved with a Garda escort. The staff in both hospitals were marvellous."

May explained that her brother had been born with heart defects, "but he didn't find out until he was 29. Both our parents had heart defects."

Irish Independent

ONLY DAYS TO LIVE

This man will die in the next few days unless his family's prayers are answered.

Father of three Noel Murphy needs a new heart.

And doctors say time is running out for the 44-year-old Dubliner.

Surgeons carried out a life-stretching operation after Noel suffered a near-fatal heart attack.

But he suffered another severe attack yesterday.

And last night doctors said his only hope of survival was an immediate transplant.

Anxiety

Noel, of Grangemore Drive, Raheny, was waiting for a miracle in the intensive care unit at the Mater Hospital in Dublin.

His wife Marie and their children Robert (21), Susan (20) and Marie (17) were at the hospital.

And as they prayed for Noel, his sister May Walsh told how years of fear and anxiety finally came to a head on Friday as the former auctioneer drove through Dublin.

She recounted how Noel came within 10 minutes of dying from a massive heart attack.

Only prompt action by his wife, emergency services and hospital staff saved him.

May, of Seapark, Malahide, said Noel slumped over the wheel of his car as he drove along with his wife and one of the girls.

"Marie ran across the road to get a lady to ring an ambulance and when she got back to the car, Noel practically fell into her arms," she said.

"The ambulance took him to the Meath Hospital and the family were told that he had to be moved to the Mater within 10 minutes.

"He was, with a police escort."

Noel was born with heart defects—although he did not know it.

His problem was finally diagnosed when he was 29.

Since then he has suffered declining health.

Last November doctors warned him that he would need a transplant.

"He is so weak that although he can speak, they have asked Marie not to talk to him," May said.

"She is the only one allowed to see him at the moment."

Dad will die if he can't get a new heart

By Fraser Macmillan

Star

---

2. Your school has been destroyed by fire. Compose two reports covering the event, (*a*) for the *Irish Times* and (*b*) for a tabloid newspaper.

3. Read the following news reports and, in the case of each, indicate whether you think it comes from a quality or a tabloid newspaper. Give the reasons for your choice in each case.

KIDS ARE GRABBED AT JAMIE SERVICE

A MANIAC attacked a child while his parents sat in church listening to a sermon on the Jamie Bulger case.

He dragged the boy out of mass along with two of his young friends and punched him repeatedly in the face. The parents did not see what was going on.

But a member of the congregation heard the screams and scuffles outside St Anne's Catholic church in Shankill, Co Dublin, and rescued the children aged seven, eight and 12 before they were seriously hurt.

Last night police confirmed they were hunting the mystery attacker. They said the crazed man wore a headband and "looked like something out of the Vietnam war."

It is believed he got annoyed because the three young friends were making noise.

Abuse

He also screamed abuse at a young woman with a baby in her pram as he fled from the church.

He was last seen taking a train out of the area.

By JOHN KEIRANS

A shocked churchgoer who witnessed the attack, Mr Joe Doyle, said: "One of the children was punched several times in the head outside the door of the church. They were lucky someone rushed out and saved them. Ironically the priest was talking about Jamie Bulger at the time."

Father Norman Fitzgerald said the assault came as a total shock.

"We heard noises from the back of the church but did not realise what was happening. Nobody knows who the attacker is but he is definitely not local."

Police said the father of the child most seriously beaten was annoyed some people in the church turned a blind eye to what was going on.

One officer said: "He felt it was just like the abduction of little Jamie when people saw him being taken but declined to do anything."

MUSIC MURDER

A POT-SMOKING heavy metal fan strangled a neighbour with his dressing gown cord after he pulled the plug on his blaring rock music ... at 5am.

Neighbour Alexander Cook, 54, switched off the power after rocker Mark Smith – who'd been smoking cannabis – refused to turn down his stereo.

Music fan Smith, 25, had been listening to heavy metal band Metallica in his bed-sit with two girls who'd taken "magic mushrooms," Plymouth Crown court heard.

By DAVID NEWMAN

But he had a row with the neighbour Mr Cook after he silenced his music by turning off the power at 5am.

Smith later attacked Mr Cook as he left the bathroom and throttled him.

Yesterday Smith of Barnstaple, Devon, admitted manslaughter due to diminished responsibility – but denied murder.

The trial continues.

Ghost of Lamont is set to haunt Major

By JOHN WILLIAMS

NORMAN Lamont was last night plotting revenge on John Major from his political grave.

The ex-Chancellor is furious that he was axed in the Premier's panic reshuffle which has split the Tory Party.

His friends said he feels "very angry and hurt" and badly let down by Mr Major.

Senior Tories fear Mr Lamont will now turn on his former friend. And one Cabinet Minister said: "We're dreading what he will do."

Mr Lamont stalked out of the Prime Minister's study in a rage after being told in a face-to-face show-down that Kenneth Clarke was getting his job.

He threw the offer of a switch to Environment Secretary back in Mr Major's face – as an insult.

And last night in an extraordinary gesture of defiance which rocked the Cabinet, he refused to write the traditional letter of "resignation".

Instead – after enjoying a champagne lunch – Mr Lamont issued a menacing statement.

In it there were NO usual courtesies and NO normal promises of loyalty.

Those were seen by senior Tories as clear signs that he may be dead but he won't be lying down.

They are worried he will rise gunning for his old boss – just as Sir Geoffrey Howe turned fatally against Mrs Thatcher. For the underlying message of an angry fax which Mr Lamont sent to Number 10 was: That he was the man who cleared up the economic mess left by Mr Major and history would vindicate him.

He declared: "I have always been willing to be judged on my record.

"I believe the success of the policies I have put in place will become increasingly clear with the passage of time."

The big fear is that Mr Lamont will tell the story of how Mr Major lost his nerve on Black Wednesday – often hinted at, but never told.

Last night the Tory Party was divided and disappointed with the reshuffle Mr Major has dithered over for months.

Clarke replaces sacked, angry Lamont

MR NORMAN LAMONT was sacked yesterday as Britain's Chancellor of the Exchequer after refusing the humiliating offer from the Prime Minister, Mr Major, of being demoted to Environment Secretary.

Mr Major has tried to restore the battered authority of his government by moving Mr Kenneth Clarke from Home Secretary to replace the angry and embittered Mr Lamont.

This was one of the six switches he made in his cabinet reshuffle, apart from the 18 alterations to those below cabinet rank.

Ending a power struggle that had threatened his government, Mr Major balanced the elevation of the centrist pro-European Mr Clarke with the appointment of the right wing Euro-sceptic, Mr Michael Howard, as Home Secretary.

The changes were soured by the acrimony surrounding Mr Lamont's departure. Mr John Redwood was the only new appointment to the cabinet, taking the post of Welsh Secretary.

In spite of the other changes, the former Chancellor and the manager in 1990 of Mr Major's leadership campaign was left in no doubt that the principal objective of the changes was his removal from the Treasury.

After refusing to accept the Environment post, Mr Lamont gave public vent to his anger by issuing a terse statement in which he failed conspicuously to pledge his continuing support for Mr Major.

Senior Ministers said that Mr Major's decisive action in dismissing Mr Lamont had restored his personal political authority.

Editorials

While news reports should contain only verifiable facts, the editorial is the proper place for opinion, personal views, the political bias of the newspaper, etc.

Exercises

1. Read the following editorials and, in the case of each one, (*a*) list what facts are contained there and, (*b*) in your own words, state what opinions are expressed.

THE CLARE CHAMPION

Shannon betrayal

The next time a Government minister or politician preaches the virtues of regional development—have a sad, cynical laugh. Because regional development and regional policy in Ireland has been buried this week by the Coalition Government of Fianna Fáil and the Labour Party.

Without doubt the mid-west has led the way over the past thirty-odd years in developing a climate of enterprise, in attracting new industry, in providing jobs for thousands of people. The airport, through the dynamism of its executives and the active support of regional bodies, has become one of the big success stories of the country. And the airport has been the key to much of the success of the region.

Now the party that have always claimed the kudos for the Shannon success are, with the Labour Party, in the process of destabilising and ultimately destroying their showpiece creation. They would by advised to consider the situation carefully.

Nobody questions the urgent need to bring Aer Lingus back from the brink, or indeed the need for fairly drastic measures to make the airline viable once again. In the process it makes no sense at all to place Shannon Airport's future in jeopardy. Shannon's status has now been dumped by Fianna Fáil and the Labour Party. The fact that the stop-over has had little or no bearing on Aer Lingus losses has been ignored. Also ignored has been the fact that 70 per cent of all people travelling from North America to Ireland have opted to disembark at Shannon.

Shannon's success has been a thorn in the side of the Dublin business lobby. Now they have got their way. Fianna Fáil deputies, who form the greater part of the Government, have given assurances on Shannon as late as six or seven months ago. Now they have reneged. The Labour Party leader, Dick Spring, has in the past pledged his support for Shannon's status. So has the Taoiseach, Deputy Reynolds, and the new Minister for Justice, Deputy Máire Geoghegan-Quinn. No doubt all of them will find reasons to wriggle out of commitments given.

Clare deputies Tony Killeen and Síle de Valera, honest and honourable people, have the courage of their convictions and have resigned from the Fianna Fáil parliamentary party. While Deputy Killeen is in the Dáil, Deputy de Valera is in the U.S.A. attending a women's conference. Deputy Bhamjee and Deputy Jim Kemmy voted with the Government.

Deputy Killeen and Deputy de Valera can rest assured that their political futures will be enhanced rather than endangered by their dignified approach. They have made the right decisions, and Clare voters will not forget it.

The problems facing Aer Lingus are due to a lack of initiative on the part of previous Ministers, particularly Séamus Brennan, and the inability of executive and board members to come to grips with them. The company was incurring losses and little was done to stop the rot.

Now the Government intends to inject £175 million in new capital over a period of years, but it requires 1,450 redundancies and the dropping of Shannon's status to allow direct flights from Dublin to North America. The airline's chain of hotels and its computer company are to be sold.

Employees of Aer Lingus and people in the mid-west are justified in their angry responses to the plan now adopted by the Government. They have been let down badly by their political masters, and in the mid-west there is growing concern for the future. It has been a bad week for Shannon and the people who work there.

[*Clare Champion*, 9 July 1993]

The Irish Times

A bad act of rebalancing

There is public outrage and a deep sense of sharp dealing over Telecom Éireann's increased telephone charges. And rightly so. No obvious consultation, some carefully placed rumours about the scale of the rise, plámás from the Minister. The whole thing reeks of the cheapest form of ad-man's engineering of plain English: 'rebalancing', when what is meant is a substantial transfer of costs to the domestic user, in effect a new tax to support industry; 'pro-consumer', when the public perception overwhelmingly is that the reverse is the case. All combined with a shameless attempt to hide behind Culliton, the thrust of whose proposal has been perverted.

Nor do the statistics produced by the company—nearly three-quarters of all peak-time local calls are of less than three minutes, and virtually all off-peak calls are less than a quarter of an hour—have much genuine relevance to subscribers. If true, the figures are made meaningless by being a composite picture of very different circumstances. An ideal customer of Telecom frequently rings Australia outside peak hours and will see a significant reduction in charges. But a more typical one—with teenagers, or running a small business in a suburb of Cork, or fighting off loneliness with long calls to relatives or friends—will be rebalanced upwards with a vengeance. And necessarily so, because if costs to business are to be reduced to an extent that benefits its profitability, the offsetting gain for Telecom must be commensurate.

If Mr Cowen believed that the methods of the PR manipulator are any substitute for sane judgement and the proper use of the Government's authority, he must by now know that he was wrong. The public has not been adequately informed, either about the effects of the increases or, indeed, about their extent. In its presentation of the new charges, Telecom erred by failing to note the percentage rise in the price of local calls (which make up by far the largest proportion of the bills of poor and vulnerable subscribers) while highlighting the size of the drop in the cost of trunk calls to Britain and the rest of the world. More seriously, it misled the public by publishing the charges without incorporating the imminent new VAT rates, and this, of course, means that the percentage reductions claimed are simply not correct. At best, this was disingenuous of Telecom.

Mr Cowen allowed himself to be complicit in this charade; and perhaps this was inevitable because the Government itself has sedulously followed an anti-consumer policy of telecommunications charges, and therefore must accept a large share of blame for the disincentive to industry. The VAT rate is the second-highest in Europe, after Denmark, and many of our competitors—for it is on the basis of competition that the new tariffs have been devised—have zero-rated phones. Far from being 'pro-consumer', the charges sanctioned by Mr Cowen mean that a 12-minute local call at the peak rate will be the second-dearest in the European Community after Britain, and a six-minute call third by a squeak after Italy. If there is anger over the charges as such, there is still more over the hamfisted attempt to deceive.

Telecom Éireann will not have missed the deeper note of dissatisfaction in the public's reaction. It is perceived, because of its policy towards customers who have difficulty in paying their bills, as arbitrary and unjust. It is ruthless towards those who question unexpectedly high bills, using its monopoly position to wield the ultimate threat of disconnection. It is not accidental that the most numerous complaints dealt with by the Ombudsman relate to its decisions.

In giving its consent to the radical restructuring of telephone charges (with some minor cosmetic changes), the Government has not dealt fairly with the public. There is also a serious shortfall in democratic openness. Should there not be a recognised process of consultation, including a consumer input, where monopoly price-setting is concerned? Is there not now a case to introduce some competition for Telecom? Certainly, there must be few who can believe that the necessary savings could not have been found by increasing its efficiency.

[*Irish Times*, 13 May 1993]

2. Write an editorial for an edition of your school magazine that contains, among other items, reports on: alcohol drinking habits among students; the high failure rate in last year's Junior Cert English exam; and the banning of a planned school disco.

Feature articles

Feature articles provide an opportunity for treating an issue in more depth.

> *Notice:*
> —Because it is longer, the style can be looser—no need for the inverted pyramid.
> —Often shaped like an essay: stylish opening paragraph, organised and structured ideas, and a striking conclusion.
> —Use made of examples, statistics and quotations from relevant experts.
> —Still a piece of reportage, so it is based on fact rather than fancy.

Here come the giants with sweets for your children

Nicola Davidson and Rajeev Syal on how food and drinks merchants are using video games to advertise.

We have come a long way since Space Invaders. You cannot innocently obliterate Martians on your home computer these days. You can, however, collect Penguin biscuits with your Robocod, munch on Quavers with Colin Curly, and find out that Coke is it with your very own computer Olympics. The food and drinks industries are cashing in on the game boys and girls in the computer market.

We are in an age when most homes have a computer or games system, with one in every two children aged between seven and fourteen regularly playing computer games, and this fact has not been lost on the manufacturers of the perfect accompaniment to screen-game shenanigans: junk food.

'Children and teenagers constitute the mainstream consumers of snacks, and their number 1 interest, as researched, is in computers and computer games,' says Sally Hollowell of Smiths Crisps. As the manufacturer of Quavers cheese snacks, it has brought its television ad character Colin Curly to a game called Pushover, for the Commodore Amiga system, where Colin, a dog, spends his time trying to retrieve his Quavers.

One of the first games to incorporate a product in a computer game was the bizarre 'James Pond 2: Robocod'. During the opening credits, large chocolate-dripping graphics tell you that the McVities goodies are 'the chocolatiest biscuits' around. As the game unfolds, Robocod, a fish-like character, collects Penguin biscuits, some of which are half the size of the entire screen, from the course.

Martin Sutherland, the brand group manager of McVities, says that the campaign has been 'hugely successful; awareness among young people increased dramatically and has considerably helped Penguin's contemporary image'—while helping to reap even larger profits for the company. 'The use of computer games as a medium coincided with record Penguin sales,' he says.

These games were originally written by software publishers, but had to be adjusted to incorporate the brand 'characters'. Others are based on the kind of events that in real life are sponsored by food and drinks companies, and those same sponsors have been quick to make an appearance. In an Olympic game for the Sega system, a Coca Cola balloon drifts by the score-board in between rounds. In a motor racing game, 7-Up—which is actually a sponsor of real Formula 1—is advertised on the trackside hoardings.

The company that is setting up the deals between the game manufacturers and the food giants is Microtime Media. Although its representatives were reluctant to disclose exactly how much McVities had spent on the campaign, which incorporates Penguin's branding into six new home computer and video games, it is believed to be in the region of £200,000.

Daniel Bobroff, Microtime's managing director, claims that the campaign has the potential to reach 30 per cent of all seven to fourteen-year-olds. For example, he believes the James Pond game will be played by more than a million children for an average of twenty-five hours each. By including Penguin bars as a reward in the Robocod game, he says, 'we can help build positive brand values as well as exposure.'

But should parents be worried by their children being bombarded by yet more images of brand names? Should they be worried by chocolate and the association with winning? Dr Tim Lobstein, the co-director of the Food Commission and author of the book *Children's Food: the Good, the Bad, and the Useless*, does not approve of the ad-man's images for children.

'The association of junk food with success and social success is a false image for children, because they will become overweight and spotty and will probably be the least successful,' he says. 'This is another example of commercial exploitation of our children.'

However, while the food giants believe they will increase the overall consumption of convenience foods by this tactic, Lobstein has not found any evidence to back this up. 'While adults' consumption of junk food has increased, children's eating habits have not changed by any significant amount for many years.'

Dr Mark Griffiths, an expert in computer games from the University of Plymouth, has studied many of the effects of computer games and believes that their addictive nature may well help the advertisers.

'Games have the potential to addict children. If they sit in front of a screen playing the game for hours at a time, they can become hooked. If children begin to associate the euphoria of doing well in the game with the chocolate bars and the drinks, then the advertisers could be on to something.'

But Margaret Shotton, a psychologist at Nottingham University, believes there are benefits to be reaped from computer games. They have been shown to 'improve concentration, especially among children who have concentration difficulties.' Shotton thinks the advertising will be effective, but gains consolation from the fact that such games as Robocod, which will have groups of children urging the player to 'pick up the Penguin,' will be less harmful than some computer games that can be both sexist and violent. But where is this ad trend leading us? As Griffiths points out, 'the advertising world will jump onto any opportunity to reach their target market, but children are subject to trends and will always move on to the latest fad.'

With the production of three-dimensional images through the technological advances of virtual reality, it will only be a matter of time before imaginary sweets, crisps and chocolate can be picked up, unwrapped and very nearly eaten at the touch of a button.

Sunday Times

Reading

1. State briefly and in your own words what is the central point or notion that this article examines.
2. (*a*) Explain the reasoning, according to the article, of the food and drinks industry, which has cashed in on the computer game market. (*b*) Outline their strategy.
3. Does this article reveal a bias for or against this new advertising trend? Explain your reasoning by referring to details in the text.
4. Do you consider this a good headline? Explain your views.
5. Do you think the photograph is effective? Why?

▬▬ Letters to a newspaper

Layout

> **Notice**
>
> The form of address is slightly different. As you are writing to an editor, the usual convention is to begin 'Sir,' not 'Dear Sir,' and you sign off simply 'Yours etc.'

Writing style

> **Notice**
>
> The subject matter. It is usually semi-formal; not as chatty as a personal letter, but not quite as stiff as a business letter.

Here are some published examples.

Closing Sellafield

Sir,—For many years now Sellafield has been polluting our land, our sea and our air. Now they plan a second plant. The thermal oxide reprocessing plant will begin its thirty-year life early next year. This plant will import nuclear waste from Japan, continental Europe and other UK nuclear power stations. These other countries have considered the waste too dangerous to reprocess at home. Why, then, is it safe enough to reprocess on our doorstep?

When Germany tried to build a plant of this type it was stopped because of public protest. Now the Irish public is protesting. It remains to be seen whether or not we are listened to. It is no longer enough for politicians to voice disapproval. This environmental disaster and potential time-bomb must be stopped.—Yours, etc.,

Sinéad Mulready (aged 14),
50 Calderwood Road,
Dublin 9.

Driving and Roads

Sir,—The weekend before last seven people lost their lives in accidents on Irish roads. My family and I have returned from a holiday in the west of Ireland all in one piece. Our car, unfortunately, is a write-off. It ended upside down in a bog after trying to avoid a car pelting in the opposite direction but on the wrong side of the road. The road—a main one—was narrow and badly surfaced and had an unmarked two-foot gulley running along the edge.

I would respectfully suggest that before the Minister for the Environment raised the speed limits on roads and motorways—to comply, as he puts it, with European speed limits—he might have ensured that all our roads were built to exacting European safety standards.—Yours, etc.,

Maureen Keenan,
Newcourt Road,
Bray, Co.Wicklow.

Women in the Home

Sir,—What a pity that the Mothers Working at Home association were interviewed by your correspondent before they had had an opportunity to study and digest the report of the Second Commission on the Status of Women, instead of relying on press reports and individual opinions. As a member of the commission, I had a particular interest in women who, like myself, were full time in the home. Indeed, as most members had either had or were having this experience, I found this to be a special interest of the commission at all times, and also part of our brief from the Government.

Members broke into eleven working groups on the relevant subjects, which in turn reported their findings to the whole commission for discussion and, with rare exceptions, consensus. This was not always easy, but we felt it worth while to achieve our goal. The women and child care group, which I chaired, took particular note of submissions from mothers who chose to be at home but often felt lonely and worthless in the eyes of a society that seemed to equate money-earning with status.

We looked for ways, such as drop-in centres, that might give them support and renewed confidence by providing a place where they could talk to their peers for an hour or two while their children played together, as well as giving them information on their legal, social and health entitlements as new legislation is introduced.

I think that if the MWAH members read the full report (which is available from Government Publications, Molesworth Street, Dublin 2, price £12.50) they would lose their feeling of Them and Us between 'feminists' and women at home. They would realise that there is no conflict where all of us are working towards the same goal, the true status that women should have in Irish society today—in all its different aspects.—Yours, etc.,

Joy McCormick,
Greencastle,
Co Donegal.

Sir,—In the recent MRBI poll on the role of women in society (16 February) 74 per cent of the women polled saw motherhood and caring for their family as their most important role. I would also see motherhood as my most important role, and I am anxious because the commission's Report on the Status of Women does not reflect this statistic.

Women who choose to stay at home to rear their families no longer want to be caught in a dependence trap; neither do they want to be forced into the workforce by economic necessity. The answer to this is basic income. The Green Party has long proposed that basic income would be a way of rectifying these two problems.

If society continues to ignore this problem, society in the end will suffer, as children do need to be cared for. I would urge women who feel as I do to put pressure on politicians or to become politically active themselves and to let their voices be heard.—Yours, etc.,

Felicity Coll,
Ballyroan,
Dublin 14.

WOMEN'S DAY AND AFTER

Sir,—The 'International Women's Day' page of the *Irish Times* (8 March) was an incredible collection of platitudes and fashionable absurdities. Women have become deluded into thinking that the world would be a much happier and fairer place if half or more of the people in 'top management and government' were female; that when women control 'the power points where decisions are made', somehow a new millennium of peace and joy will emerge from the shambles of the late twentieth century. Anyone who challenges this trendy consensus is written off as a misogynist or a 'sniper' in the infantry of some vague anti-feminist 'backlash'.

The assumption behind such notions is that women are intrinsically more caring and co-operative than men and will therefore make a huge difference to the way humanity organises its affairs, once women are 'empowered'. I question such an assumption, because my experience tells me that women are as capable of exalted and depraved emotions and thoughts as men are—and just as capable of acting on them, for good or ill.

Feminists complain about under-representation of women in politics, yet 51 per cent of the electorate are women. If, for whatever reason, their appeal to the voters of their own sex falls on deaf ears, they can hardly blame men, although that's precisely what they do, calling it 'submissive role conditioning'. How can one argue with such sophistry?

The way to achieve a free and equitable society is to discard the very idea of 'top management' and hierarchical power-politics; for the state is the enemy of the Irish people, even though it has a woman at its head. Neither the land nor the capital of the nation is ours to call our own. Without practical economic democracy, our polling cards are useless bits of paper, props in the mummery called 'election day'. And while this farce continues once every four years, feminism will remain the Great Red Herring, distracting us from the true source of political and social evils: greed, an emotion that stirs equally in the hearts of men and women, and which has impoverished the world.

Yours, etc.,
Robert Francis,
Dublin 6.

PRESIDENT'S VISIT TO BELFAST

A Chara,—Had the Queen of England met the leaders of the UVF, or had An Taoiseach met the leader of the IRA/Sinn Féin, there would be a (justifiable) public outcry and indignant calls for their resignation. When Dr James McDaid shook hands with a constituent of his who had been found innocent of IRA membership, the behaviour of Fine Gael and the PDs at the time ensured the complete devastation of his political career.

However, the President of Ireland—representing the Irish Government and state—has now met, and briefly conversed with, a man who publicly and unashamedly supports violence of the most sickening kind. While this may not necessarily be a resigning matter, it was an utterly inexcusable diplomatic *faux-pas*, to say the least, and one that the Government must ensure will never be repeated.

I wonder if Mr McDowell and his colleagues would be as silent and content as they are now if the President were a Fianna Fáil nominee?—Is mise le meas,

David Carroll,
Boyle,
Co Roscommon.

Sir,—Since de Valera went to the German embassy to offer sympathy on the death of Hitler, there has surely been no greater *faux-pas* than the meeting of President Mary Robinson and Gerry Adams.

Did the utter misery of the parents of Warrington not touch her at all?—Yours, etc.,

Dr Patrick Golding,
Truro,
Cornwall.

Sir,—It would appear to me that Mary Robinson's act of shaking hands with Gerry Adams was perfectly logical when one bears in mind the nature of her office. The President, as we know, is politically neutral. This means that when, as Mrs Robinson recounted subsequently in her statement, Mr Adams was introduced to her, she would have had no valid grounds for distinguishing him on the basis of his political outlook. Mrs Robinson was thus acting clearly within the spirit of her office by acknowledging and responding to Mr Adams as she presumably would do to any other person, even to the extent of shaking hands with him.—Yours, etc.,

Conor Verdon,
Dublin 11.

HARE COURSING AND RURAL ETHOS

Sir,—The bias displayed in your editorial of 22 June on hare coursing is unworthy of an Irish newspaper of your stature. I suggest that you are out of touch with the ethos of the rural people of Ireland. Fortunately, our politicians are not, and Tony Gregory's private member's bill to ban hare coursing will be rejected in the Dáil by the three main political parties.

Tony Gregory represents an unfortunate electorate in Dublin's inner city. They, through no fault of their own, have no knowledge or appreciation of the countryside and of field and country-sport activities. They and you, sir, fall into the anthropomorphic trap, which, as Alan Dukes explained to the Dáil, means 'viewing the world of animals through the eyes of humans.' They see them as little furry friends with human instincts.

However, for the rural dweller whose lives and daily living is spent in close proximity to animals, there is a healthy respect for all animals, both domestic and wild. In the farming community, where animals are part of one's livelihood, they live, die, come and go, but no tear is shed for their passing. When a farm animal is lost through illness or accident, it is quickly carted away to be disposed of by the hounds at the nearest hunt kennel.

Likewise, when the rural community turns to field and country sport, animals play a major part in this recreation. The prowess of man to use rod or gun is tested on fish, game birds, and animals. The coursing of a hare is a contest between two greyhounds, and the killing of the hare is not the objective. Hunting fox and hare with hound and beagle is a test of breeding, hound prowess, and horsemanship. That wild animals get killed in these recreational pursuits is part of man's heritage from time immemorial.

Man does not go out deliberately to kill animals; indeed it is a poor sportsman who does not have a healthy respect for the preservation of the game he pursues. It is the field and country-sport activists who are our greatest conservationists. They restock the countryside with game birds and hares, and our rivers with salmon and trout. It is the field and country-sports activists who conserve our countryside and who are the first to protest at the destruction of habitat.

Legislation that seeks to restrict the recreational activities based on the natural rural ethos of this country is both sinister and dangerous. Far better that Tony Gregory would seek to provide his Dublin city centre constituents with the opportunity of enjoying a day's hunting, shooting or fishing in the country. It would also be better for you, sir, instead of listening to a vociferous minority that you would listen to the majority of the plain people living in rural Ireland, whose roots are in nature and in field and country-sport activity.—Yours, etc.,

David J. Daly,
Carrigaline,
Co Cork.

Sir,—In view of the current Dáil bill to amend the Wildlife Act and make hare coursing illegal, I would like to urge the TDs to have a free vote and to support the amendment. It seems that most people want them to put an end to the scandal given at home and abroad by the barbarous Irish 'sport' of tearing hares apart and frightening them to death through heart failure. I, for one, intend to take note of the voting, and to be influenced by it in future elections.—Yours, etc.,

(Father) Ignatius Fennessy OFM,
Killiney,
Co Dublin.

A stimulating letter often elicits a reply, sometimes a chain of replies, such as these to the *Times*.

Unfair daffodils

From Dr M. D. Croft
Sir,

The daffodils in our front garden are all pointing towards the street and away from our house. I bought them so that I could look at them out of the window, but they seem to reserve their beauty not for me but for passers-by, who did not fork out last autumn for the bulbs, as I did.

My wife tells me they are looking towards the sun, but that does not explain the behaviour of the daffodils in the back garden, which are also facing the other way. Is there something fundamentally wrong about the way we planted them, or are we doing something of which they disapprove?

Short of wringing their necks, or cutting off the flowers and placing them in a vase on the dining-room table, or changing our highly provocative life-style, can anything be done? We need an answer fast, as their attitude is already beginning to infect the primroses.

Yours faithfully,
Michael Croft

From Mr R. Norton Ellen
Sir,

Re the letter of 23 April, there are no such complaints from the Lake District.

Perhaps Dr Croft should try gazing at his daffodils from afar, or 'at a glance', instead of so critically staring at them from the window of his house, back and front. Or, perhaps, join them in sprightly dance, or, at any rate, do something to show them that he is 'gay in such a jocund company.'

This should meet with their approval, and may cause Dr Croft to think what wealth the show to him had brought.

Yours faithfully,
R. Norton Ellen

From Mrs Olga Lockley
Sir,

Mr Croft's daffodils are obviously reluctant to turn their faces to the walls of his house. Perhaps if he lined the said walls with some reflective material his flowers might reconsider. After all, they are narcissi!

Yours faithfully,
Olge E. Lockley

From Mr Geoffrey Yorke
Sir,

The uncooperative daffodils in Dr Croft's garden are simply turning towards the best source of light. Planted near the house, they will turn away from it to where the sky is more visible. If Dr Croft has a front garden wall or hedge, daffodils planted near it will look towards the house.

I have north-facing daffodils against a fence on my southern boundary, and south-facing ones on the opposite side of the garden.

It's only natural, if you come to think of it. You would not sit on your patio staring at the house, would you?

Yours faithfully,
Geoffrey Yorke

From Mrs E. Murray
Sir,

With regard to Dr Croft's daffodils, I am surprised that he does not know the old Celtic legend in which the defenders of the marches, being attacked from the rear while facing the enemy, stood back to back and fought to the last man; their bereaved womenfolk planted daffodils on the site, and ever since, daffodils planted in rows have grown back to back.

There is a reference to this in the

Green Book of Llantrisant (Cenhinen Rhyfelwr). The only thing to do is to confuse the daffodils by planting them in odd-shaped flower beds or at random all over the lawn.

Yours faithfully,
Elaine Murray

From Ms Patricia A. Tyrrell

Sir,

I am delighted to learn from Dr Croft that I am not the only person being ostracised by daffodils.

Mine insist on facing the street when they bloom and are consequently at right angles to the house. I agree that sun direction has nothing to do with it and have come to the conclusion that they disapprove of my life-style but wish to keep track of me with an occasional sideways glance.

Yours faithfully,
Patricia A. Tyrell

From Mrs Barbara Milne

Sir,

Dr Croft should really not complain about a flower with such highly placed poetic connections, and his wife, as he observes, is quite wrong to tell him that they are looking at the sun. What they are looking at, being aesthetic by nature, is the view.

We have many daffodils in our woodland, which faces north-east, but they too turn their backs on the sun to admire the magnificent view over Porlock Vale and the sea towards Wales, their homeland!

Dr Croft should realise that flowers with such sensitivity cannot be dragooned; rather, he must learn from them and seek solace and peace in these things of beauty, thereby acquiring 'joy for ever'!

Yours faithfully,
Barbara Milne

From Mr T. Larsson

Sir,

In the spring of 1946, being in need of a complete change, I decided to spend three months in Sweden's Lappland, just north of the Arctic Circle.

I took with me from Stockholm some two dozen daffodil bulbs in pots which had started to sprout, and planted them out early in May.

At that time of the year the sun does not set but only dips towards the horizon at midnight and then goes around in a circle, rising comparatively high at midday.

The daffodils grew rapidly and within three weeks were in full bloom. Then tragedy. They insisted on following the sun for its full circle, and within one week had strangled themselves. All of them.

Yours faithfully,
Theo Larsson

Exercise

Compose a letter as if to a newspaper on any contentious topic, such as unemployment; pollution; the cost of school books; or any other scandalous or amusing topic.

All the letters are then pinned to the notice board. For the second round of letters each student replies to any letter of choice, and so on until a few controversial chains develop.

Entertainment

Reviews of
> BOOKS
> FILMS
> MUSIC
> THEATRE
> ETC.

There is no set formula for a review, but it is useful to have a number of headings in your mind, some of which you might use in an exam. For example, a book review might contain some of the following:

—THEMES or ISSUES dealt with.

—General SETTING or LOCATION and something of the PLOT (without giving the full story away)

—Main character or CHARACTERS—complicated, deep—or thin characterisation—credible, interesting?

—STYLE OF WRITING—light and fast-moving, heavily descriptive, or what?

—Anything else you liked or disliked about the book?

—Why should one read this book?

Exercises

1. Write a review of a novel you studied or any novel you read carefully.
2. What important points should be covered in a film review or a review of a play or musical event?
3. Read the following reviews. (*a*) What information does the review give us about the book, play, or musical event? (*b*) Would you describe the reaction of the reviewer as positive, negative, or mixed? Explain. (*c*) Could the review be improved on? Make suggestions.

A cocktail of murder in murky back streets

The Journeyman Tailor
by Gerald Seymour.
Harvill, £14.99.

I'm sure many Irish readers have problems about books on Northern Ireland, especially 'thrillers'—a rather suave, deceptive word to describe that terrible cocktail of murder in wet back streets, white-faced fear, broken limbs and brutality that is the truth behind this 'thriller'. It's a crucible filled with hell rather than heroes.

But behind the paddywhackery and stereotypes of Gerald Seymour's latest opus lies a taut, tense story, told in that accomplished, effortless style of his, as if words were bullets and sentences rapiers. Seymour can write—and how, as the Yanks say!

Allowing for the fact that it's not easy for the veteran thriller reader, used to an exotic diet of luscious landscapes from Bali to Bangalore, populated with spies, nuclear weapons, and deadly secrets, to wrap his or her mind about names like Patsy Riordan or Jacko from Pomeroy, the story still belts along.

Bren, a young, keen agent, is despatched to County Tyrone to aid in an undercover operation masterminded by Parker, top man in his business. The latter's job is to foster and protect an informer in IRA ranks. Among those misty hillsides, Bren discovers a secret society, who see, hear and know nothing. Collaboration is a death sentence.

Meanwhile, in London, innocent people are being bombed to death. The IRA desperately want to close in on their 'tout'; in London, the police chase their murderer. The concentric circles of pursuit touch, intertwine compulsively propelling traumatic decisions with life and death at their centre.

The Journeyman Tailor is about fear, about taking sides, about human anguish, about betrayal. Seymour's previous books on Northern Ireland, *Harry's Game* and *Field of Blood*, were good; this one is better—a compulsive, unstoppable read. Even if, personally, I still have problems with fictional heroes with names like Jon Jo Donnelly ...

The research is impressive, the pace unflagging, even if we have to remind ourselves occasionally that the ugliness of the conflict in Northern Ireland has little to do in reality with the breathless, fictional world of Seymour's undercover war and an awful lot more to do with shabbiness and brutality.

Gerald Seymour is a craftsman. He turns out books with no evidence of pain—which I am sure isn't the case, but it does show the sign of a master.

If you like his themes, you'll love his stories, told in that sparse, clinical style of his, without frills, putting words on pages as if hammering small, steel nails onto metal.

Michael Keating

Satisfying revival of epic quality

The Man from Clare
at the Gaiety

There is a sturdy narrative drive to John B. Keane's *The Man from Clare* that seizes and holds the interest from start to finish. Wedded to the dramatic story are characters of flesh and blood, equipped with lyrical, idiomatic dialogue that has become the author's trade mark.

The revival that opened at the Gaiety Theatre last night has a cast hand-picked for their colourful roles, and they give an epic quality to a thoroughly satisfying production.

The scene and mood is set with the Clare football team waiting at a pier to cross the Shannon to engage again their rivals of north Kerry. For their captain, now thirty-five years old and losing his athleticism, the uninhibited camaraderie is like sunshine before a storm. They lose, and he spends the night in a local house, drinking and brooding. By morning he will have been physically beaten by a young heir to his throne, and forced to think about his life and future.

Brendan Gleeson is magnificent as the fading hero, and matched by Ruth McCabe as the girl whose position and pride parallel his. The two rejects turn defeat into victory in a simple, moving love story. Around them swirl sub-plots and people with their own humanity and humour.

Johnny Murphy is a joy as the widower who courts the postman's sister with parcels of pollack and a rumoured legacy from an aunt in Seattle. Mick Lally persuades as the slightly obsessed team trainer, and Conor McDermottroe is fine as the young bull on the way up.

The play evokes much laughter, much of it hilarious and all of it sympathetic. The author's insights into human nature and folly have a warmth of understanding that gives depth to his work, and raise it high above what might easily have been a comedy of rural personalities and manners.

Pat Laffan directs the large cast with an easy naturalism that does not neglect the wider reverberations. Brian Fahey's set and Rupert Murray's lighting provide creative support in this fine version of an enduring play.

Gerry Colgan

A young man with a lot to prove

Andrew Strong
at the Stadium

'It's great to be back in Dublin,' the seventeen-year-old star of *The Commitments* told the capacity crowd at Dublin's National Stadium last Friday night, tricking us for a moment into believing he was a seasoned and road-weary veteran.

Andrew Strong might be a new star but he worked the crowd for all he was worth, anxious to prove he had the stagecraft to match his voice. He tried a little too hard, though, running around among the audience and coaxing them to sing 'Yeah!' in between every song. It wasn't a very convincing effort, but it did get the fans into the spirit of things.

There's no faulting this young man's superb singing, either live or on celluloid, and it was when Strong pushed his voice to its limits that the audience really showed its appreciation. It will be a while, though, before the public accepts Andrew Strong as a bona fide rock star.

First, he will have to kick away the considerable prop given to him by Alan Parker's hit movie. With *The Commitments* still on general release, it's a safe bet that much of Friday night's crowd came to hear the classic songs from the sound track, and Strong delivered songs like 'Mr Pitiful', 'Take Me to the River' and 'Try a Little Tenderness', along with other soul classics of his choice. His backing band were more than ready to bring these hits to life, and the crowd were more than happy to sing along.

As soul revival shows go, this was one of the best, but Strong will have to transcend this 'Blues Brothers' style of revue before he can be taken seriously as a contender for mega-stardom. His own compositions are fairly lukewarm sub-soul tunes, written in the same way as the classics he admires, but they're hardly going to knock Michael Bolton off the number 1 slot in the U.S.A.

A few years' experience in the music business might shape Andrew Strong into a rock star of power and charisma, but for the moment he's just a voice—and a damn good one at that.

Kevin Courtney

Reading an advertisement

Check-list

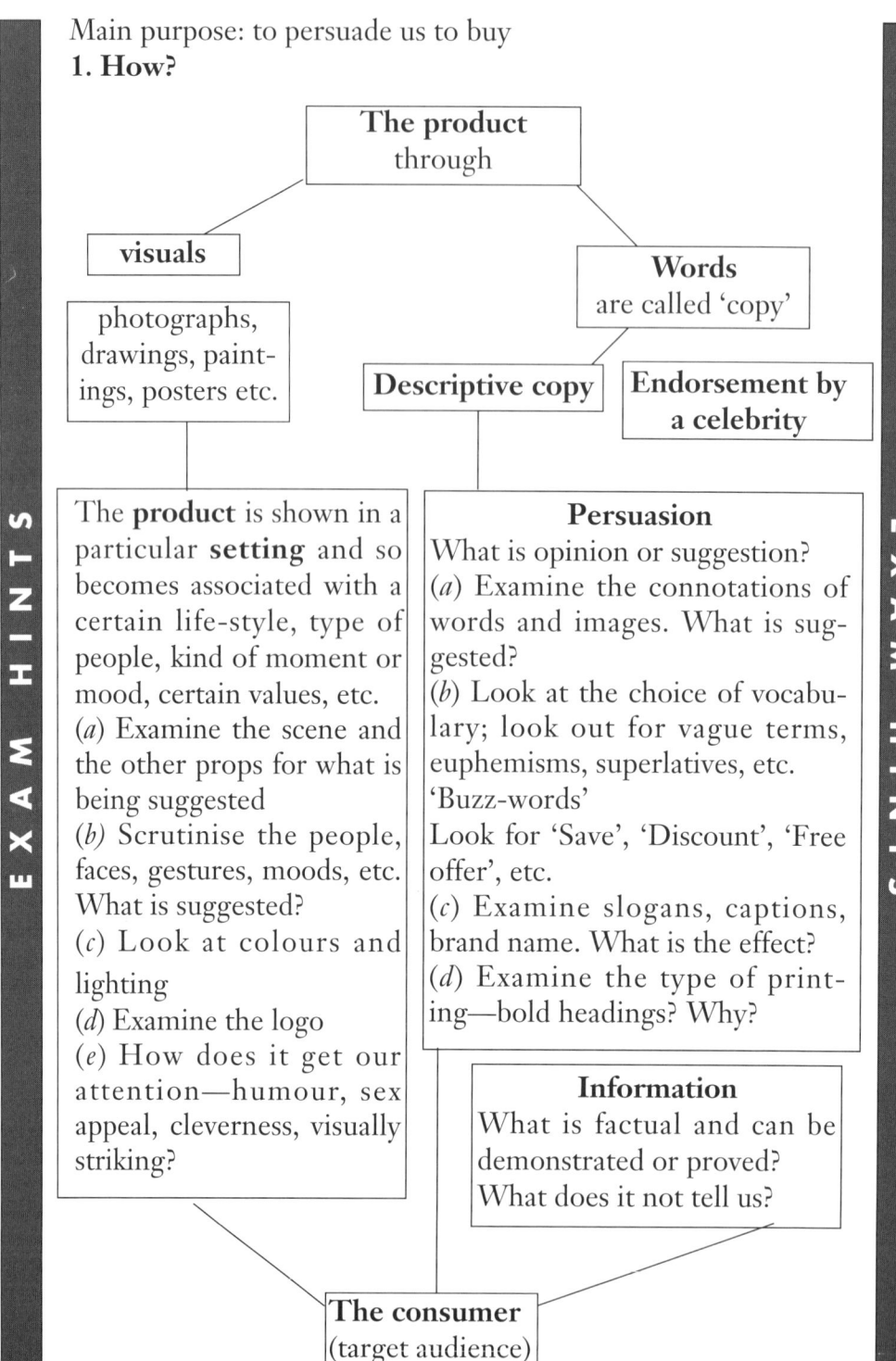

Main purpose: to persuade us to buy
1. How?

```
                    The product
                      through
                   /           \
            visuals             Words
                                are called 'copy'
     photographs,
     drawings, paint-
     ings, posters etc.    Descriptive copy    Endorsement by
                                                a celebrity
```

The product is shown in a particular **setting** and so becomes associated with a certain life-style, type of people, kind of moment or mood, certain values, etc.
(*a*) Examine the scene and the other props for what is being suggested
(*b*) Scrutinise the people, faces, gestures, moods, etc. What is suggested?
(*c*) Look at colours and lighting
(*d*) Examine the logo
(*e*) How does it get our attention—humour, sex appeal, cleverness, visually striking?

Persuasion
What is opinion or suggestion?
(*a*) Examine the connotations of words and images. What is suggested?
(*b*) Look at the choice of vocabulary; look out for vague terms, euphemisms, superlatives, etc. 'Buzz-words'
Look for 'Save', 'Discount', 'Free offer', etc.
(*c*) Examine slogans, captions, brand name. What is the effect?
(*d*) Examine the type of printing—bold headings? Why?

Information
What is factual and can be demonstrated or proved?
What does it not tell us?

The consumer
(target audience)

EXAM HINTS

2. What is the target audience? Who is this advertisement aimed at—what sort of person—what age, sex, occupation (and therefore spending power), etc.?

3. Does it use stereotyping? Stereotyping means reducing the complex traits of people into simple ones. For example, portraying women as only wives and mothers, or as glamorous consumers of cosmetics, or as appealing decoration for cars and other products targeted at men, is stereotyping—in other words, portraying women in a certain limited role.
Male stereotyping can also happen. Are men in advertisements often portrayed as tough, fit, powerful figures? Are children portrayed as dependent and in need of protection?

Exercises

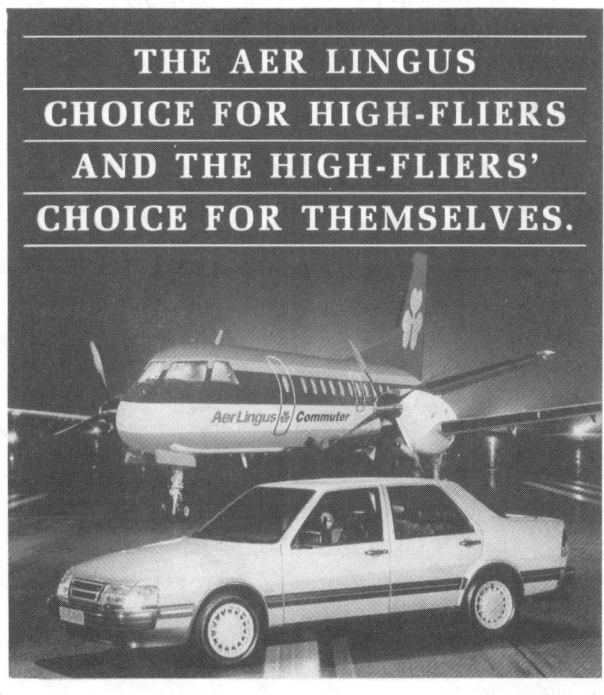

> **THE AER LINGUS CHOICE FOR HIGH-FLIERS AND THE HIGH-FLIERS' CHOICE FOR THEMSELVES.**
>
> To update their commuter services, Aer Lingus have turned to one of the world's most respected names in high-performance technology. Saab.
>
> Today, the first of four new Saab 340B turboprops goes into service, bringing the comforts of speed, space, wider seats and a pressurised cabin to commuter flying in Ireland.
>
> The Saab 340B was chosen by the airline "after careful analysis of its performance, economy and passenger appeal".
>
> The discerning motorist can give precisely the same reasons for choosing Saab.
>
> From the most demanding heritage of aeronautical technology, Saab design and build cars with the same commitment to safety, performance and comfort. They achieve the optimum balance between performance and practicality – building cars that are a pleasure to look at... a pleasure to drive. Prized by enthusiasts as much for their technological innovation as for their unconventional style, Saab offer an enviable blend of prestige and power.
>
> When you know you've arrived, but enjoy getting there, simply drive a Saab. And fly in the face of convention.
>
> **SAAB**
>
> CAR IMPORTERS: SCANVECO LTD., P.O. BOX 1419, LONG MILE ROAD, DUBLIN 12. TELEPHONE: (01) 504243. A MEMBER OF THE OHM GROUP.
> SAAB AIRCRAFT INTERNATIONAL LTD., LEWORTH HOUSE, 14–16 SHEET STREET, WINDSOR, BERKS. SL4 1BG. TELEPHONE: 03 0753 859991. FAX: 03 0753 856884.

(a) What product is being advertised here?
(b) What, in your opinion, is the purpose of the photograph in this advertisement?
(c) Comment on the effectiveness of the slogan.
(d) Examine the copy under the headings, (*i*) ideas and (*ii*) persuasive language.
(e) What type of consumer is this advertisement aimed at?

164 Reading an Advertisement

(a) The product is shown in a particular setting and so becomes associated with a certain life-style, type of people, kind of moment or mood, certain values etc. What association does this photograph attempt to create for the product?
(b) Do you find this advertisement effective? Explain your views.

(a) What is being promoted in this advertisement?
(b) What does the picture suggest about the product?
(c) Do you find the copy (words) effective? Explain.

Reading an Advertisement

When orange fizzes it's Fanta.

'Fanta' is a trade mark which identifies a product of The Coca Cola Company.

(a) What association does this advertisement want to create for the product?
(b) Do you think there is stereotyping here? Explain your views.
(c) Comment on anything else you noticed about the composition of this advertisement.

166 Reading an Advertisement

(a) What product is being advertised here? Is there anything unusual about the display of this product?

(b) Comment on the mood of the scene in this photograph and say how you think it persuades us to buy the product.

In 1950 Peter loved making things.

Now as a Consultant Engineer, he's built quite a reputation as well.

In the same year that Diners Club was founded, Peter built an aeroplane, two ships and a model of the Eiffel Tower.

He even built a model of a digger that swallowed things up – which is precisely what Peter wished the ground would do to him every time his father introduced him as 'the model son'.

It was his sense of attention to detail and the confidence to break new ground that helped Peter rise to where he is today. And why he carries a Diners Club Card.

The first-ever chargecard, it's consistently at the forefront with new services for its members – like £75,000 medical insurance abroad and up to £400 credit for necessities when baggage is delayed over 4 hours.

Whether it's travelling abroad, entertaining clients, or shopping for himself or his family, Peter reckons Diners Club measures-up perfectly.

Diners Club.   First – and still ahead.

For an application form, call Dublin (01) 6779444.

(a) What type of consumer is this advertisement aimed at? Explain your views.
(b) What does the photograph suggest about the product and the consumer?
(c) How does the text attempt to persuade us to use the product?

Junior Certificate examination, 1993

Look carefully at the TWO advertisements, labelled A and B, which accompanied this examination paper, and discuss them under the following headings:

(*a*) The kind of publication in which each advertisement is likely to appear, and the kind of consumer targeted by each. Give reasons for your answer.

(*b*) The techniques of advertising used in each.

A

"Giles. The curtains!"

Between now and dinner, poor Giles will have drawn over one hundred David Whitehead curtains. In the process Giles will destroy this pleasing view from the lawn, but enhance the view from inside beyond measure. After all who wants to stand on the lawn all night?

make
your
home a
mansion
with

DAVID WHITEHEAD FABRICS

Only the look is expensive

B

CURTAIN DEPT.

Massive reductions on all in stock curtain material

MEDICI	BALI
54" wide Curtain Material, 4 colours to clear.	54" wide Curtain Material, 3 colours to clear.
Reduced by 25%.	Reduced by 25%.
NOW ONLY **£5.75** yd	NOW ONLY **£5.95** yd
PANDORA	**AMETEX**
48" wide Curtain Material, 2 colours to clear.	54" wide Curtain Material, 2 colours to clear.
Reduced by 25%.	Reduced by 25%.
NOW ONLY **£6.95** yd	NOW ONLY **£5.95** yd
JENNY WREN	**CURTAIN LINING**
54" wide Curtain Material (self lined)	Top Quality Contract Curtain Lining
Reduced by 33%.	Reduced by 20%.
NOW ONLY **£5.95** yd	NOW ONLY **£2.50** yd

FREE Interior Design Service available to all our Customers

* *Best Value*
* *Largest selection of Fabrics*

Persuasive writing

1.
Study the text of this advertisement.
(*a*) What image of the product does this advertisement want to create? What words and phrases carry this image?
(*b*) Is there anything unusual or different about the style of this text? Do you think it is effective?
(*c*) What factual information does this advertisement carry?
(*d*) What type of consumer does it target?

A LITTLE PIECE OF HISTORY

Although it was a long time ago, I remember it like it was yesterday. We were all getting togged-out for an important championship match when word came around that O'Buachalla, the County selector, had been spotted at the gate.

The whole atmosphere changed, the lads went quiet, it was as if everyone was working out their own game plan, looking for a way to shine.

Well he was out there all right, sitting away from the crowd on a small wooden bench, his collar turned up and his cap pulled firmly down. I expected him to have a clipboard or something, at least a pen and paper. He just sat there, I'll always remember this, with a bar of Cadbury's Chocolate, breaking off squares and popping them into his mouth.

It was a great game, both teams played their hearts out and as you can imagine there were a few spirited individual performances as well.

Anyway, it was a close match, there were only two points in it at the end, unfortunately they didn't belong to us. As the final whistle blew, all eyes turned to the bench where he was sitting, but he was gone, he hadn't even waited for the final score.

Three days later O'Buachalla sent word that he wanted me to try out for the County team and the rest, as they say, is history.

The funny thing is, every time I see a bar of Cadbury's Chocolate I think of O'Buachalla and the day I got my first big break.

2.

(*a*) This copy uses people's fears and insecurity in order to make an impact. What phrases are most likely to cause the reader to stop and think? Explain.

(*b*) This text is structured as a conversation. Do you think this is an effective technique? Explain your reasoning.

(*c*) Is the plan made to sound appealing? How?

(*d*) Do you think the picture is effective in the context of the whole advertisement? Explain.

(*e*) Comment on the target audience or intended consumer of this product.

(*f*) What do you think is the intended effect of the two logos 'Hi Hibernian Life' and 'Healthwise Critical Illness Plan'? Are they cleverly constructed?

Will she have to carry you some day?

"Of course not".

That's likely to be your first reaction. Right now, it's inconceivable that one day you may be dependent on the very people that, today, depend on you.

Yet, one out of every five people will suffer a major illness before the age of 65. If it happens to you, you'll most likely end up enjoying a satisfying life for a long time afterwards. But who's going to cope with the mortgage? Who's going to provide assistance in running the home, looking after the children, nursing care?

Wouldn't it be nice if you could still do all that?

With the "Healthwise" Critical Illness Plan you can.

It's a simple and straightforward plan, that'll provide a substantial lump sum, when critical illness reduces your ability to look after yourself and those you care for.

HEALTH*wise*
CRITICAL ILLNESS PLAN

When it happens, it's too late to take action. Better think about it while you can and contact your broker or Hibernian Life.

HIBERNIAN
LIFE

3. Traditionally, the language of property advertising often engages in flights of poetic fancy.

Examine these advertisements. Do you find the style of language persuasive or offputting? Explain your reactions to any one of them.

**Biscayne, Park Avenue, Castleknock
Auction: Tuesday 18 May (unless previously sold).**

An air of rural tranquillity pervades this delightfully bright detached residence (c. 1860) surrounded by almost an acre of wonderfully planted gardens. Elegance, charm, graciousness—what else can one say about a house that has both the room and the atmosphere that make it ideal for entertaining yet still retains a warmth that makes everyday living in it easy? Biscayne also enjoys a favoured location, being discreetly tucked away on this quiet residential road. Add all this to an excellent orientation, a swimming pool that enhances rather than breaches the integrity of the house, and a wealth of other notable features, and you have a property that serious purchasers simply must view.
Acc.: Gracious entrance hall, drawing-room, dining-room, study, play room, 4 bedrooms (en suite bath & dressing-rooms), bathroom, shower room, sauna. Hardwood kitchen with terraced balcony off, utility room, boot room, OFCH. Outside: Extensive gardens, including former tennis court, heated swimming pool (40 by 20 ft). 2 garages. Various outbuildings.
Viewing: Strictly by appointment.
Solicitors: Doyle & Sons, 15 Upper Leeson Street, Dublin 2.

Tithe Cottage, College Road, Blackrock, Co. Dublin
Auction: Wednesday 5 May
(unless previously sold).

A haven of peacefulness! Simply irresistible cottage full of Old World charm and atmosphere, enjoying total seclusion yet ideally located close to Blackrock. Requiring modernisation but offering a wonderful opportunity to do your own thing and create the cosiest cottage in Blackrock.
Acc: 2 bedrooms, bathroom, separate w.c., living-room, dining-room, kitchen. Various outhouses. Wonderfully mature and secluded south-facing garden.
Viewing: Saturday 3–4:30 p.m. or by appointment.
Solicitors: Murphy & Co., 78 Rathfarnham Road, Dublin 14.

149 Foxrock Road, Dublin 18
Auction: Tuesday 4 May

Woodview: a fascinating odyssey, south by south-west.
Materials, vivid colours and the language of space are built into the structure and soul of Woodview. A hospitable openness to the unexpected compounds the pageantry of indoor reflections with those of the garden and startles the interior into extra life. Dual heating.
2 Large reception, kitchen/breakfast-room, 5 bedrooms, double garage. The wooded earth is remarkably pleasing with a sense of great age. An inviting, timeless, private refuge.
Solicitor: Dónall Greene & Co., 7 Morehampton Road, Dublin 4.

Exercise

Make out the *text* of an advertisement that you would devise to sell any one of the following products: (i) a particular record of your choice; (ii) an item of cosmetics; (iii) a motorcycle or car; (iv) a teenage clothing outfit, i.e. 'gear'.

[Junior Certificate examination, 1992]

Examination Hints: Paper II

1. TIME: 2½ hours. Three sections—about 45 minutes per section. Each section has two parts: unseen—25 minutes; studied text—20 minutes (25 maximum).

2. READ EACH QUESTION CAREFULLY. Notice:

(*a*) How many PARTS to the question? There may be some subsections that are not marked (*a*) or (*b*); for example, 'Do you think the picture captures the drama and sadness of this scene?' [1992 drama question]. Two subsections: (*a*) *drama* and (*b*) *sadness*.

(*b*) What exactly am I being asked? Study and underline the KEY TERMS in the questions. For example:

'*Describe*': this is straightforward.

'*Describe in your own words*': you must not just 'lift' whole sentences and phrases from the piece. Translate it into your own words.

'*Show*': demonstrate something by reference to the text. Prove the point.

'*Discuss*': you put points for and against the statement or idea.

'*Trace*': this suggests that you look at someone or something over a longer period, usually showing how it developed, how it leads on, etc. You may end up listing high points in the growth of something.

'*How well is it portrayed?*';

'*Why is it good?*';

'*Why do you think it appropriate?*': these ask you to EVALUATE, give your opinion on something. Your opinion should be based on whether or not it works in the context, not on some vague personal liking or dislike. You should have a REASON for your opinion. Ask yourself (i) what is it trying to communicate; (ii) does it succeed or not; (iii) why?

3. Make as many POINTS as you can in the time allowed. One point per paragraph.

4. QUOTE or refer to texts, even printed ones, in order to back up each point.

5. Use the TERMS of the question in your answer. This means that you keep the answer relevant.

Section 5 Drama

✓ Drama Check-list

☐ 1. **TITLE AND AUTHOR.** Have I got the correct title and can I spell it accurately?

2. **THE NARRATIVE**:

☐ (*a*) THEMES. Have I examined all the issues the play brings to light? What is the drama saying about life? What does it say about the behaviour of human beings in general? etc. Can I quote to support each theme or issue?

☐ (*b*) PLOT. Am I clear about the details of the story?

☐ (*c*) SCENES OR SECTIONS. Have I listed them in order, and am I clear in my mind about what happens in each? Have I made a detailed study of a few IMPORTANT SCENES; for example the opening scene; the concluding scene; a scene of great conflict or a particularly moving scene; a scene that is particularly effective on stage; a scene that is important for the main character or a key scene that best shows the essence of what the play is about? Can I quote from each scene?

Examining a scene: Framework for study or exam
What does a scene do?
(i) Advances the plot (tells more of the story).
(ii) Reveals more about the characters.
(iii) Shows a dramatic incident or confrontation.
(iv) Does all the above visually as well as orally. So consider how these contribute to the scene:
    —scenery, setting, props
    —lighting
    —costumes and make-up
    —expressions, gestures, movement

3. CHARACTERS
Writing about a character: Framework for study or exam

Examine:
(i) what he or she says —— dialogue
                             tone of the speeches

(ii) what he or she does —— actions
                             gestures, movements

(iii) Reactions of others

Using this three-point scheme, have I studied all the main characters well enough so that I could write a paragraph on each of the following headings concerning any one character?

(*a*) CHARACTER TRAITS. What kind of person; what motivates him or her? etc.

(*b*) VIEW OF LIFE. What is his or her view of life, attitude to people? etc.

(*c*) RELATIONSHIPS. Examine the relationships with other characters: antagonisms and friendships; who controls or influences most; opinions of others; etc.

(*d*) ROLE OR DRAMATIC FUNCTION. What is his or her role in the drama: hero, heroine, villain, victim, peacemaker, voice of the common person, or what?

(*e*) Examine A PARTICULAR SCENE that reveals something significant about the character. Quote to support each point.

4. CONFLICT
—How is the conflict brought about? → Characters' differing views on a particular topic or issue

↘ Clashing ambitions or needs

↙ Particular circumstances giving rise to conflict

↓ Different attitudes to life

- —Trace the development of the conflict throughout the play.

- —Study a scene of particular crisis. Where is the CLIMAX? Why is it dramatic? Is it resolved? How do the expressions, gestures and movement contribute to this?

- **5. LANGUAGE.** Is the language sophisticated or simple; poetical prose speech? Does the style of speaking suggest a rural or an urban setting? Are local expressions or slang used? It is witty, clever, etc.?

- —What do I notice about each character's particular style of speech?

- —Can I quote significant lines for each character and for important scenes?

EXAMINATION QUESTIONS

A. Drama: option 1

The following extract (in edited form) is taken from Shakespeare's play *The Life and Death of King John*.

Background information on the characters and story-line of the extract: Arthur is a young boy, nephew of King John of England. Arthur has a claim to the throne of England through his father, Geoffrey. Prior to this extract King John, who fears Arthur's claim, has taken him prisoner and has instructed a nobleman, Hubert, to murder him.

This extract shows Hubert's meeting with the boy Arthur in prison.

[*Enter Hubert and executioners.*]
HUBERT
Heat me these irons hot, and look thou stand
Within the arras.* When I strike my foot   *behind the curtain
Upon the bosom of the ground, rush forth
And bind the boy which you shall find with me
Fast to the chair. Be heedful. Hence, and watch.
[*Exeunt executioners.*]

HUBERT
Young lad, come forth; I have to say* with you.   *speak
[*Enter Arthur.*]

ARTHUR
Good morrow, Hubert.

Hubert
Good morrow, little prince.

ARTHUR
You are sad.

HUBERT
Indeed, I have been merrier.

ARTHUR
Mercy on me!
Methinks nobody should be sad but I.
By my Christendom,
So* I were out of prison and kept sheep,   * if
I should be merry as the day is long;
And so I would be here, but that I doubt
My uncle practises more harm to me.
He is afraid of me and I of him.
Is it my fault that I am Geoffrey's son?
No, indeed, is't not; and I would to Heaven
I were your son, so you would love me, Hubert.

HUBERT [aside]
If I talk to him, with his innocent prate*   *talk, chatter
He will awake my mercy, which lies dead:
Therefore I will be sudden and dispatch.

ARTHUR
Are you sick, Hubert? You look pale today.
In sooth,* I would you were a little sick,   *truth
That I might sit all night and watch with you:
I warrant* I love you more than you do me.   *guarantee

HUBERT [aside]
His words do take possession of my bosom.
Read here, young Arthur. [Shows him a paper.]
[Aside] I must be brief, lest resolution drop
Out of mine eyes in tender womanish tears.
[To Arthur] Can you not read it? Is it not fair writ?

ARTHUR
Too fairly, Hubert, for so foul effect.
Must you with hot irons burn out both mine eyes?

HUBERT
Young boy, I must.

ARTHUR
And will you?

HUBERT
And I will.

ARTHUR
Have you the heart? When your heart did but ache,
I knit my handkerchief about your brows,
And with my hand at midnight held your head,
And like the watchful minutes to the hour,
Still and anon cheered up the heavy time,
Saying, 'What good love may I perform for you?'
Will you put out mine eyes?
These eyes that never did nor never shall
So much as frown on you?

HUBERT
I have sworn to do it,
And with hot irons must I burn them out.

ARTHUR
Ah, none but in this iron age would do it!
And if an angel should come to me
And told me Hubert should put out mine eyes,
I would not have believed him—no tongue but Hubert's.

HUBERT [*stamps*]
Come forth.
[*Enter executioners with a cord, irons, etc.*]
Do as I bid you do.

ARTHUR
Oh, save me, Hubert, save me! My eyes are out
Even with the fierce looks of these bloody men.

HUBERT
Give me the iron, I say, and bind him there.

Answer question 1 and question 2.

1.

(*a*) Going ON THIS EXTRACT ALONE, give your impression of the kind of person young Arthur was. [10 marks]

(b) From what you have learnt of Hubert in this extract, do you think he will proceed with the murder of Arthur? Support your answer by reference to what you learn of Hubert IN THIS EXTRACT ALONE. [10 marks]

(c) This scene is likely to be very exciting and moving on the stage. Look at the picture of this scene that accompanies this examination paper. Do you think the picture captures the drama and sadness of this scene? Give reasons for your answer. [10 marks]

2. Basing your answer on any play studied by you, give an account of some scene or part of the play that you think would be most exciting or moving on stage. Give reasons for your answer. [30 marks]

You must give the playwright's name and the title of the play that you choose. (You must not use the drama extracts quoted on this paper as the basis for your answer.)

B. DRAMA: Option 2

The following extract is taken from Act Two of *The Power of Darkness*, a play by John McGahern. Read the extract carefully and then answer the questions which follow it.

Briefly, the story leading up to the scene is as follows:
The scene is set in the kitchen of aged and ill Peter King, a rich farmer. His young wife Eileen and her neighbour Baby are plotting against his life. Their aim is, first of all, to rob him, and then poison him. Eileen and Baby's son, Paul, are in love and it is the prospect of wealth for her son and herself that fuels Baby's murderous plans. Peter, as if he suspects something, has ordered his daughter Maggie (by an earlier marriage) to fetch his sister Martha, but Eileen blocks it. For the two plotters, the moment of decision has come.

> EILEEN
> Sometimes I feel so surrounded that I could do away with myself. I feel things beating around the place.
>
> BABY
> Don't worry about it, love. But we haven't much time. We have to find the money. Then we'll give him what's good for him. The poor thing will be off like a bird.
>
> EILEEN
> I'm afraid. Isn't it better that he be let go natural?
>
> BABY [*viciously*]
> What's natural? Is it natural that he's trying to put his sister in charge over his lawful wife?
>
> EILEEN
> I don't know what way to turn.
>
> BABY
> If you don't shift soon you'll find yourself out on the road and his sister will be cracking the whip.
>
> EILEEN
> I'd still have my rights as his wife.
>
> BABY
> If he gives her charge of the money you can whistle for your rights.
>
> EILEEN [*panicking*]
> I better go for Martha before he starts shouting. She'd be here already if Maggie had gone.

BABY
Are you out of your mind? Here. Do what I tell you. Put on the kettle again here. We'll give him a good stiff drink.

EILEEN
Suppose anything would happen?

BABY
There's no time for supposing. Just do what I tell you. Put on that kettle.

EILEEN [*in awe and fear*]
I'll put on the kettle.

BABY
That's more like it. [*Eileen stops in terror as Peter starts descending the stairs. Holding on to the wall, he gropes his way down. Baby retreats into the shadows of the room so that she can observe. Peter is too ill to notice her.*]

PETER
Did you not hear me calling? Is there no way to make you hear? I might as well be dead up there for all anybody cares.

EILEEN
Don't you know you're not fit to come down? Now we'll have to get you back up.

PETER
Did Maggie get back from Martha's yet?

EILEEN
She didn't go yet. I told her I'd go myself.

PETER
I warned her to go at once. Has nobody any heed any more?

EILEEN
I'm going for aunt Martha myself. Maggie is too giddy to go all that way on her own.

PETER
She's not half as giddy as what's left around here nowadays. I want my daughter to go. I want her to go this minute.

EILEEN
Of course I'm not trusted to go. I'm just the skivvy.

[*During the argument Baby stands in the shadows, a silent and sinister figure, unnoticed by Peter.*]

Answer **Question 1** and **Question 2** which follow.

Question 1.
(*a*) Which one of the three characters on the stage most dominates the above scene? Justify your choice by reference to or quotation from the scene. [10 marks]
(*b*) Briefly describe the nature of the relationship between husband and wife (i.e. Peter and Eileen) as it is revealed in the above scene. [10 marks]
(*c*) How is the presence of evil suggested and evoked in the scene?
 [10 marks]

Question 2.
Choose an important scene in a play you have studied and show—
(*a*) What it tells you about the principal character, and [15 marks]
(*b*) How that scene is related to the rest of the play. [15 marks]

You must give the playwright's name and the title of the play that you choose.
[You must NOT use the drama *extracts* quoted on this paper as the basis for your answer.]
 [*Junior Certificate examination, 1992*]

Sample answers (Option 1)
1.
(*a*) *This is a question on a* CHARACTER, *so remember the framework. Examine what he says (dialogue, tone); what he does (actions, gestures); and the reactions of others.*

He appears to be a boy of very simple desires, merely wishing to be out of prison: 'So I were out of prison and kept sheep, I should be merry as the day is long.'

Yet he is not totally naïve and innocent, because he is aware of the political situation. He fears his uncle, the king, and knows that his uncle fears him. 'My uncle practises more harm to me. He is afraid of me …'

Still he is innocent enough not to suspect Hubert of any ill intentions. Ironically, he seems to want him for a father. He is even unwilling to accept the reality when it is pointed out to him. 'If an angel should come to me … I would not have believed him.' The innocent tone of some of his comments adds to the sadness of the situation. 'I would you were a little sick / That I might sit all night and watch with you.' Indeed Hubert too vouches for Arthur's 'innocent prate' (reactions of others).

He is a kind, caring boy: 'When your heart did but ache, I knit my handkerchief about your brows.'

He talks a lot, like most children. He is also very persuasive, and pleads with Hubert emotionally and convincingly in that speech, 'Have you the heart? …'

(b) There are some suggestions that Hubert is reluctant to proceed with the murder of Arthur. For a start, he admits to being in bad form ('I have been merrier'). He also admits, in the aside, that he is in danger of softening—'His words do take possession of my bosom'—and that he is at least able to be touched. He also feels that he must do the deed quickly before he weakens: 'I must be brief, lest resolution drop / out at mine eyes in tender womanish tears.'

But there are also compelling indications that he will go through with it. He has hardened his heart: 'If I talk to him, with his innocent prate / He will awake my mercy, which lies dead.' Also he has sworn an oath. He adopts a very stern and resolute air of command, which would lead us to believe that he will go through with it. He stamps his foot authoritatively (gesture). He speaks curtly in a cold tone of command. 'I must. I will … Do as I bid you … Give me the iron, I say.' Overall I think he will go through with it.

(c) *Examine the key terms:* DRAMA, SADNESS. *How many* PARTS *are there in the question?*

It certainly is a dramatic scene, and it certainly captures the conflict between Hubert and Arthur, with the child kneeling, grasping Hubert's legs, pleading. This conflict is shown also through the symbolism of the costumes, the evil man in black dominating the small, innocent boy dressed in white.

The rough, violent-looking executioners also add to the dramatic effect, as indeed do the horrific props of the glowing-hot blinding irons. It seems as if the child can hardly survive this brute force.

The picture also hints at Hubert's internal drama—showing him with hand to head, a dramatic gesture betraying his uncertainty.

It is also a very sad scene—sad in that it shows human nature in a very bad light, displaying the horrific cruelty of which people are capable. We see the blinding irons, and cannot but notice the pleading look in the upturned eyes of the innocent child. The crucifix prop highlights a sad irony: that this horrific act is to take place under a symbol of religion. It is a scene of stomach-turning horror and sadness that well reflects the dialogue in the extract.

Section 6 — Poetry

Poetry Check-list

☐ 1. Have I studied a RANGE of poems dealing with a variety of themes? The themes listed so far, in the 1992 and 1993 examinations, were: childhood; memories; a happy or an unhappy experience; love; war; a personal experience of the poet; a picture of a rural or an urban scene.

Remember: each poem you study will probably deal with a number of themes, so it can be used to answer under a few of the categories. For example, Séamus Heaney's poem 'Mid-Term Break' could be used to answer under childhood, or memories, or an unhappy experience, or a personal experience of the poet.

☐ 2. Have I included at least TWO CONTRASTING POEMS dealing differently with the same theme? See the 1992 question: 'From the poetry you have studied select any two poems that you think deal with the same theme. Discuss the similarities and/or dissimilarities in the treatment of the theme in both poems.'

☐ 3. A short study of AN INDIVIDUAL POET is necessary. Two to four poems should be sufficient.

☐ 4. Have I some experience at reading and reacting to an UNSEEN POEM (without the help of prior discussion or study)?

Framework for examining a poem, unseen or studied text
THEMES—What is the poem about? What is the central theme? What other issues does the poem touch on? Quote to support. Has the poem a message?
IMAGERY—The poet uses pictures to communicate the themes. Examine the images; similes; metaphors; symbols; etc. What atmosphere do they create? What do they suggest about the theme, setting and mood of the poem? Do a number of them have anything in common—for instance, dealing with nature or city life or children or people or animals, etc.? Are the pictures striking, graphic, or subtle and subdued? Do you think they are effective in getting the ideas across to the reader?

CHOICE OF WORDS—The poet has chosen to use certain words. Examine some of them. Think about the connotations of a word—i.e. what it suggests to you, reminds you of, etc. Think of the nuances—different shades of meaning. Is the poet being clever, witty, subtle? Is the vocabulary mainly simple or is it sophisticated and difficult? What is the effect of these? Are the terms used vague or precise? Are there dialect words, or slang or jargon? Any puns, new or unusual words, or words made up by the author? Are there any words you think oddly placed? Why?

FEELINGS—What feelings or emotions does the poet wish to convey? What attitude does the poet communicate? This is usually referred to as the TONE. It can be happy, sad, angry, humorous, serious, sarcastic, ironic, regretful, etc. There are as many tones as the human voice can carry. What words, phrases or images convey this tone best?

SOUNDS OF WORDS—The musical qualities of the language. Think about rhyme, end rhyme, and internal rhyming sounds (assonance). Examine words where the sound carries the meaning (onomatopoeia). Examine other sound effects, such as long vowel sounds to suggest mourning or unhappiness, etc.

Other musical qualities can be found in the rhythm or beat; alliteration also sets up a sort of beat in words following each other. What do these sound qualities contribute to the poem?

APPEAL—How does the poem appeal to the reader: through the head (logical), or the heart (emotional), or the senses (sensuous)? If it appeals to the senses, which senses and where?

PERSONAL REACTION—Apart from the technical areas above, your own reactions to a poem are important and valid if based on some evidence in the text. What do you like or dislike about a poem, and why?

Note

Sometimes the terms of the questions are quite straightforward, when you are asked, for example, about pictures (images) or tone, or feelings, or choice of words or topic (themes), etc.

But some questions are made general and vague in nature. Then you must decide the terms of your answer, while keeping within the general direction or frame of the question; for example, 'discuss how the theme is treated' or 'discuss the way the poet conveys his message.' From the framework you can select some pointers that seem appropriate to the particular poem. Use these as pegs on which to hang your reactions to the poem.

| Themes

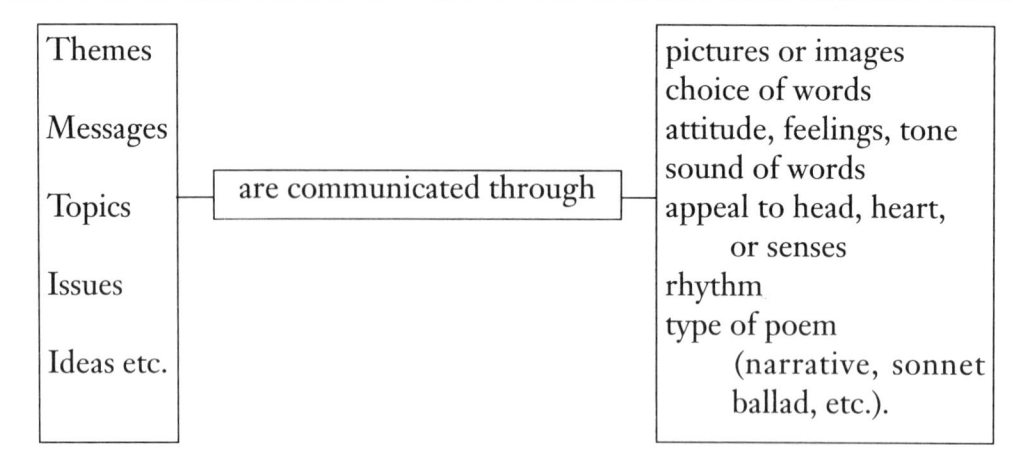

Messages

Topics

Issues

Ideas etc. | are communicated through | pictures or images
choice of words
attitude, feelings, tone
sound of words
appeal to head, heart, or senses
rhythm
type of poem (narrative, sonnet ballad, etc.). |

Examination Questions: unseen poetry

Read carefully the following poem and then answer the questions that follow it. [Junior Certificate examination, 1992]

Piano
D. H. Lawrence

> Softly, in the dusk, a woman is singing to me:
> Taking me back down the vista of years, till I see
> A child sitting under the piano, in the boom of the tingling strings
> And pressing the small, poised feet of a mother who smiles as she sings.
>
> In spite of myself, the insidious mastery of song
> Betrays me back, till the heart of me weeps to belong
> To the old Sunday evenings at home, with winter outside
> And hymns in the cosy parlour, the tinkling piano our guide.
>
> So now it is vain for the singer to burst into clamour
> With the great black piano appassionato. The glamour
> Of childish days is upon me, my manhood is cast
> Down in the flood of remembrance. I weep like a child for the past.

Answer question 1 and question 2.

1.

(*a*) Music is the link between the present and the past in this poem. In what way is this so? [7 marks]

(*b*) Are the pictures of domestic scenes remembered from the past happy ones? Support your answer by reference to the poem. [7 marks]

(c) Select two examples from the poem where you think the poet's choice of words is particularly good in describing a scene or conveying a feeling. In the case of each example say why you find it good. [8 marks]
(d) In the context of the poem as a whole, what do you think is meant by the following lines? [8 marks]

In spite of myself, the insidious mastery of song
Betrays me back.

2. Answer A or B in this question. [30 marks]
A. From the poetry you have studied, select a poem or poems dealing with any one of the themes below, and discuss how that theme is treated in the poem or poems chosen. You may not use the poem quoted above.
You must give the title(s) of the poem(s) chosen and the name(s) of the poet(s).
   (a) Childhood
   (b) Memories
   (c) A happy or unhappy experience
   (d) Love.

or

B. From the poetry you have studied, select any two poems that you think deal with the same theme. Discuss the similarities and/or dissimilarities in the treatment of the theme in both poems. You may not use the poem quoted above as one of the selected poems.
   You must give the titles of the poems chosen and the name(s) of the poet(s).

Sample answers (to question 1 above)

1.
(a) The speaker in the poem is listening to a woman playing the piano and singing to him. 'Softly, in the dusk, a woman is singing to me.' The music reminds him of his childhood, when he sat under the piano as his mother played. The music takes him 'back down the vista of the years,' and in that way it is a bridge between the present and the past.
(b) Yes, very happy indeed. He seems to have had an idyllic, trouble-free childhood, or at least that is what he remembers. The picture of the little boy under the piano pressing the feet of a mother 'who smiles as she sings' is an image suggesting a close, happy relationship between the boy and his mother, a mother who fills the house with music and joy.

The picture of Sunday evenings that he recalls suggests security and protection from the outside world, 'with winter outside / And hymns in the cosy parlour.' The adjective 'cosy' suggests comfort, warmth, contentment. So he felt he had a protected childhood. It was also a religious home, a hymn-singing Sunday evening suggesting goodness and freedom from any darkness or evil in his childhood.

And in the last verse he is openly sentimental and nostalgic for the past. 'A flood of remembrance' overcomes him and he weeps 'like a child for the past.' This image tells us how much he enjoyed his childhood, that he would willingly relive it.

(c) Remember—TERMS of the question: two examples of words describing a scene or words conveying a feeling.

(i) 'Pressing the small poised feet of a mother (who smiles as she sings).' The detail shows the physical contact between the little boy and his mother. It is an unusual little detail but very vivid and memorable. Her feet were small and delicate. 'Poised' makes you see the image very sharply: her feet were ready over the pedals, and he thought he was helping her to play. The choice of words, particularly the detailed observation, paints a memorable description but also suggests things about the relationship of mother and son—a close, loving relationship. So it also conveys a feeling.

(ii) 'The boom of the tingling strings.' 'Boom' conveys the great base sounds of the piano. It is an onomatopoeic word suggesting a huge sound. 'Tingling' describes well the more delicate sounds of the piano and also the actual physical sensation the boy might experience if he touched the strings. So the words describe very well the sounds and sensation of the piano.

(d) The poet seems to experience a conflict within himself about the past. On the one hand he has happy memories of the past, yet he seems reluctant to have these memories revived, perhaps because he knows that he will weep for past happy days. Perhaps that is why he says 'in spite of myself'. But the music is treacherous (insidious) and tricks him or forces him back. The music is that fatal link, and he finds himself remembering before he knows it.

Examination questions: studied poems
[Junior Certificate examination, 1993]

Answer A or B in this question. [30 marks]

A. From the poetry you have studied, select a poem dealing with any one of the following subjects and discuss the way the poet conveys his or her message, paying particular attention to the tone of the poem.
   (*a*) War.
   (*b*) A personal experience of the poet.
   (*c*) A picture of a rural or urban scene.
   You may not use the poem quoted above.
You must give the title of the poem chosen and the name of the poet.

or

B. Select the work of any one poet that you studied in depth and discuss the work of this poet, bearing in mind any *one* of the following points:
   (*a*) The poet's favourite theme(s) or topic(s).
   (*b*) The poet's special appeal for you.
   (*c*) How an event or events of the time in which the poet lived is reflected in his or her poetry.
   You must support the points you make by reference to at least two poems of the poet chosen. If the poet chosen is Sassoon, you may not use the poem quoted above.
You must give the name of the poet and the titles of the poems chosen.

Sample answer (to question B above)
Based on the following poems of Séamus Heaney: 'Mother of the Groom', 'Digging', 'St Francis and the Birds', 'Mid-Term Break', 'The Diviner', 'Death of a Naturalist'.
   (*a*) The poet's favourite themes or topics.

Humans and nature
In a number of the poems Séamus Heaney writes about the relationship between humans and nature. He explores two facets or aspects of this question. He writes about the close relationship, the empathy between humans and nature in 'The Diviner'. The ground yields up its secret store of water to the diviner: '*Spring water suddenly broadcasting / Through a green aerial its secret stations.*' This poem shows humanity dependent on the earth, but the

earth takes care of humanity with life-giving water, in the age-old way, despite modern technology. In another poem, 'Digging', the poet admires the father's and the grandfather's ability to cultivate the earth.

> 'He rooted out tall tops, buried the bright edge deep
> To scatter new potatoes that we picked
>   Loving their cool hardness in our hands.'

The earth even provides the inspiration for writing, in that poem:

> 'The cold smell of potato mould, the squelch and slap
> Of soggy peat, the curt cuts of an edge
> Through living roots awaken in my head.'

It is as if the earth, through its smells and sounds, awakens the idea in his head.

Humankind's love for the creatures of nature is dealt with in 'St Francis and the Birds'.

> 'When Francis preached love to the birds
> They listened, fluttered, throttled up
> Into the blue like a flock of words.'

Altogether, Heaney seems to dwell a lot on humanity's love of nature, our ability to be close to the soil and use nature. Nature, in turn, takes care of our needs.

But the poet also deals with the darker side of this relationship. A person can be frightened by nature: in 'Death of a Naturalist', '*I sickened, turned and ran.*' The boy is revolted by the frogs' reproduction; he refers to them as '*great slime kings*'. The boy has lost his innocent view of nature and needs time to come to terms with this new knowledge.

Family and family relationships
In 'Digging', the poet shows the importance of family tradition, a man being proud of his father's and grandfather's work on the soil. In 'Mother of the Groom' we see a mother feeling the loss of her son on his wedding day. She remembers him as a baby, and now, '*It's as if he kicked when lifted and*

slipped her soapy hold.' The poet deals with a young boy's reaction to the death of his brother in 'Mid-Term Break', and we experience the family grief '*as my mother held my hand / In hers and coughed out angry tearless sighs.*'

Loss
As we have seen, many of these poems deal with loss of some kind or other: loss of a son in 'Mother of the Groom' and 'Mid-Term Break', loss of innocence in 'Death of a Naturalist'.

Crisis points in life
Heaney's poems are about points of crisis or events of great significance in people's lives. It is a topic to which he returns often. The family wedding is the subject of 'Mother of the Groom', an event that produces both happiness and sorrow, or at least nostalgia, on the part of the mother. It seems as if her reason for living has been taken away: '*Hands in her voided lap / She hears a daughter welcomed.*' That word 'voided' suggests a great emptiness.

'Digging' is really a metaphor for the poet's work, so this poem can be taken as one about career choice—another crisis point in a person's life. The poet chose a different yet poetically similar career to that of his parents and grandparents.

> '*Between my finger and my thumb*
> *The squat pen rests.*
> *I'll dig with it.*'

'Death of a Naturalist' looks at the painful process of growing up, and 'Mid-Term Break' explores a young person's view of death—surely a major crisis in any young life.

Other themes explored by Heaney in these poems are the need for a sense of belonging and family tradition ('Digging'); and the nature of writing poetry ('Digging' and 'St Francis'); but his favourite topics seem to be nature, relationships, people, and moments of crisis in life.

Note
- *You would not be expected to write an answer of this length in 20 or 25 minutes. A very full treatment of one topic or a lesser treatment of two or three topics should be sufficient. Aim to make as many relevant points as you can in the time allowed.*

(b) The poet's special appeal for you.

I like the themes he explores. Many are important issues in the lives of young people—for example, growing up and loss of innocence in 'Death of a Naturalist'. The boy in this poem was young and innocent initially, happy with what he knew of nature.

> '*Here, every spring*
> *I would fill jam pots of the jellied*
> *Specks to range on window-sills at home,*
> *On shelves at school, and wait and watch until*
> *The fattening dots burst into nimble-*
> *Swimming tadpoles.*'

But awakening sexual awareness made life difficult for him, and he could no longer look on life in the same happy-go-lucky way: '*the slap and plop were obscene threats.*' Life becomes more complicated and difficult as one grows up, and the poet deals with this very cleverly through the symbolism of the frogs.

Death is another theme that holds a certain fascination for us all, young or old. I might ask myself how I would cope if someone I loved suddenly died. The boy in this poem is numbed: he notices everything but he doesn't react emotionally at all:

> '*Wearing a poppy bruise on his left temple,*
> *He lay in the four foot box as in his cot.*
> *No gaudy scars, the bumper knocked him clear.*'

Perhaps the boy is really breaking up inside. We get the impression that he does actually feel how awful it is, in the last line: '*A four foot box, a foot for every year.*' This bottling up of emotions makes the poem very tense. It is also very real, which is part of its appeal.

So one of the things I find appealing about Séamus Heaney is that he writes about issues and events that are significant for our lives. He writes about a lot of ordinary yet important events: growing up; death; career choices ('Digging'); humanity's dependence on nature and our relationship with the environment ('Digging', 'The Diviner', 'St Francis and the Birds').

People feature a lot in his poems: mothers, fathers, grandfathers, sons. And he makes it easy to sympathise with the people involved and their human problems: the mother at the wedding or the young boy fleeing from the dam. Heaney is able to create great drama out of ordinary events.

I also like and find appealing the way he writes. He uses images that are simple yet very memorable: *'a four foot box'*. He makes no attempt to shield us from the crude reality of burial: after all, a coffin is just a box. The birds *'Throttled up / Into the blue like a flock of words.'* This is a clever, witty simile linking the sound and meaning of the two words 'birds' and 'words'. It is also easy to visualise, and so it works easily.

'It's as if he kicked when lifted / And slipped her soapy hold' ('Mother of the Groom'). We can picture the anxiety a mother might feel about dropping her baby. He uses this picture as a metaphor for a young person breaking free of family, with hints of danger and worry on the part of the parent.

I also like the way he gets the meaning across through the sounds of the words; for example, the sound of bells as the boy waits to be taken home from boarding school in 'Mid-Term Break'. *'Bells knelling classes to a close.'* Bell, knell: these repeated sounds act like an echo, adding to the sadness and emptiness of the occasion. Sometimes he uses the sounds of the words to carry the meaning, as in the onomatopoeia of *'nicking and slicing'* in 'Digging'. These sharp sounds are exactly what's happening. Or the word 'heaving', which uses the long vowel sound to show the huge effort of lifting up the wet turf. *'The squelch and slap of soggy peat'*—again the sounds evoke accurately the actual work. Or *'gravelly ground'*—the rough *r* sounds bring home to us that tooth-hurting sound of metal on rock.

As well as appealing to the ear, Heaney also appeals to our sense of touch—*'loving their cool hardness in our hands.'* Heaney's poems appeal to our senses and are very effective for this reason.

You could write on any aspect of the poetry you find appealing (simple language; lack of rhyme, yet the flow of the lines has a rhythm; the sense of drama in his poems; etc.). But make clear, analytical points and back up with quotation.

Section 7 — Fiction

Novels and Short Stories

✓ Fiction: Check-list

☐ **1. PLOT**
Details?
Well constructed?
Credible?
Fast-moving story? Action?
Good beginning?
Satisfactory ending?
Quotations or references?

☐ **2. SETTING**
Where?
Interesting, unusual?
Realistically described?
Good sense of place?
Examples?
Study of opening and one other section?

☐ **3. ATMOSPHERE**
Describe: low-key; romantic; adventurous; frightening; horrific?
What and how created?
Suspense or tension? Did it build to a high point or points?
Climax—where and how?

☐ **4. CHARACTERISATION**
Detailed study of main characters
Are they well portrayed? Are they real, complicated, credible characters or just cardboard cut-outs?
Quotations or references?

☐ **5. DIALOGUE**
Does the dialogue fit the characters; i.e. could you really imagine that type of character speaking like that?
Memorable dialogue?

	6. RELATIONSHIPS	Detailed study of main relationships? How well done are they? Credible? Interesting? What and why?
	7. DRAMA, CONFLICT, CONFRONTATION	Explain main cause. Study scene of particular conflict: how it is structured? Quotation or reference?
	8. THEMES, ISSUES, TOPICS	What issues were dealt with? Were issues deeply examined and explored? New insights to the reader? or did issues just get a surface treatment? Quotation or reference?
	9. MESSAGE OR MORAL	Is the story expressing a particular point of view? If so, what? Is there a message or a moral? Explain.
	10. LANGUAGE	Well written? Examine the quality of the language. Good descriptions? Well-chosen words? Colourful imagery: metaphors or similes? symbolism, etc.?
	11. KIND OF NOVEL	What category of novel does it belong to: historical; romance; adventure; thriller; whodunit; drama; study of human relationships; family saga; social satire; poetic description of childhood? etc. How would you classify it?

	12. ENTERTAINMENT VALUE	Is it a good read?
		Would you recommend it?
		Why?

	13. REVIEW	Write a review of it.

Note

The questions on the unseen piece of fiction tend to be of two types: (i) simple comprehension questions like those in the reading question in paper I. For these, you examine the extract carefully and pick out all the evidence you can find in order to answer as fully as possible; (ii) criticism questions, which ask for your evaluation or opinion on how well the piece of fiction has been written. For these, you draw on your experience of fiction studied and read over the course.

Read the 1993 examination extract and study the questions that follow (question 1). Which parts are basically comprehension questions and which ask for literary criticism?

Examination Questions

Read carefully the following passage and answer the questions that follow it. The passage (in edited form) is the opening passage of the novel *The Butcher Boy* by Patrick McCabe. [Junior Certificate examination, 1993]

[60 marks]

1. When I was a young lad twenty or thirty or forty years ago I lived in a small town where they were all after me on account of what I done on Mrs Nugent. I was hiding out by the river in a hole under a tangle of briars. It was a hide me and my friend Joe made. Death to all dogs who enter here, we said. Except us of course.

2. You could see plenty from the inside but no one else could see you. Weeds and driftwood and everything floating downstream under the dark archway of the bridge. Sailing away to Timbuctoo. Good luck now weeds, I said.

3. Then I stuck my nose out to see what was going on. Plink—rain if you don't mind! But I wasn't complaining. I liked rain. The hiss of the water and the earth so soft bright green plants would nearly sprout beside you. This is the life I said. I sat there staring at a waterdrop on the end of a leaf.

It couldn't make up its mind whether it wanted to fall or not. It didn't matter—I was in no hurry. Take your time drop, I said—we've got all the time we want now. We've got all the time in the world.

4. The first day Mrs Nugent's son came to the school my friend Joe says to me Francie did you see the new fellow? Philip Nugent is his name. O, I says, I'll have to see this. He had been to a private school and he wore this blazer with gold braid and a crest on the breast pocket. He had a navy blue cap with a badge and grey socks. What do you make of that says Joe. Woh boy, I said, Philip Nugent. This is Philip Nugent, said the master, he's come to join us Philip used to live in London. Now I want you to make him feel at home won't you? He was like Winker Watson out of the *Dandy* in this get-up of his only Winker was always up to devilment and Philip was the opposite. Every time you saw him he was investigating insects under rocks or explaining to some snottery-nosed young gawk about the boiling point of water. Me and Joe used to ask him all about his school. We said: What about these secret meetings and passwords? Tell us about the tuck shop—come on Philip but I don't think he knew what we were talking about. The best thing about him was his collection of comics. I just can't get over it, said Joe. He had them all neatly filed away in shirt boxes not a crease or a dog-ear in sight. They looked as if they had come straight out of the shop. Mrs Nugent says: Make sure not to damage any of those now they cost money. We said: We won't—but afterwards Joe said to me: Francie we've got to have them. So you could say it was him started it and not me. We talked about it for a long time and we made our decision.

Answer question 1 and question 2.
1. Answer ANY TWO of the following questions (*a*), (*b*), and (*c*). [30 marks]
(*a*) From the things he notices and the language he uses to describe his experiences in the hiding place, what kind of boy do you think Francie, the narrator, is? Explain your answer. Refer to paragraphs 2 and 3 only for your answer.
(*b*) When Philip Nugent came to the local school the master said to the children, 'Now I want you to make him feel at home won't you?' From what you learn from the final paragraph of the passage do you think Philip will feel at home with the other children? Give reasons for your answer.
(*c*) Do you think this is a good opening passage for a novel? Explain your answer.

2. Answer A or B in this question. [30 marks]

A. Select a novel studied by you where at least one of the principal characters is a young person. Discuss what you consider to be the most important influence in the novel in helping that young person to develop. You must give the title of the novel and the author's name.

or

B. From a novel or short story studied by you, select what you consider to be a crisis event for the principal character and show in what way the principal character has been affected by, or has reacted to, the crisis. You must give the title of the novel or short story and the author's name.

Sample answers (to question 1 above)

1.
Remember—how many parts to the question? 'From the THINGS HE NOTICES *and the* LANGUAGE HE USES.*'*

(*a*) He is a very observant boy. We can say this from the details he notices: '*the dark archway of the bridge*' and also the waterdrop at the end of a leaf.
He is very much at home out in the wilds with nature—perhaps he is a loner, happier with nature than people. Certainly he seems part of the landscape: '*bright green plants would nearly sprout beside you.*' This is also reinforced by the language he uses to talk to the raindrop. It is the language of everyday speech, of friendship and intimacy with which he speaks to his friend the raindrop: '*Take your time drop, I said—we've got all the time we want now ...*'
He is a very imaginative boy. He imagines the flotsam on the river, which he has observed in detail, as sailing away to Timbuctoo. He imagines the drop as having a mind. '*It couldn't make up its mind whether it wanted to fall or not.*'
He has an odd, zany sense of humour. '*Good luck now weeds, I said.*' '*Take your time, drop.*'
He can be quite poetic in a simple way. Notice the sounds of the words, how onomatopoeic they are: 'plink', and the 'hiss' of the water.

(*b*) It does not seem likely, as he does not fit in well. Joe and the narrator see him as different, like a figure out of a comic: '*Winker Watson out of the Dandy.*' But he doesn't even have the advantage of being a bit of a rascal.

He does have one thing in his favour: his collection of comics. But even they are different, neatly stored away, no dog-ears. Joe and the narrator are not content with reading them: they plan to steal them. So it certainly does not have all the hallmarks of a beautiful friendship.

(c) Yes. It has a very good opening sentence, which hints at some great misdeed but doesn't reveal it: *'They were after me on account of what I done on Mrs Nugent.'* This opening sentence whets our appetite for the story.

The opening section also gets us on the side of the narrator straight away. We sympathise with the underdog—*'They were all after me.'*

The location of the opening, a boys' hide-out by the river, suggests adventure. Indeed it seems to have echoes of a very famous adventure story, *Huckleberry Finn*.

And of course there is conflict, developing nicely by the fourth paragraph, with the new boy, who is very much an outsider.

So it is a good opening passage, because it draws us into the story, asks questions, and promises some drama.

EXAM PAPERS

Coimisiún na Scrúduithe Stáit
State Examinations Commission

JUNIOR CERTIFICATE EXAMINATION, 2005

ENGLISH—HIGHER LEVEL—PAPER 1

(180 marks)

WEDNESDAY, 8 JUNE — MORNING, 9.30 — 12.00

YOU MUST ATTEMPT ALL 4 SECTIONS ON THIS PAPER

IT IS SUGGESTED THAT YOU SPEND ABOUT HALF AN HOUR ON EACH OF SECTIONS 1, 3, 4, AND ABOUT ONE HOUR ON SECTION 2

SECTION 1: READING [40]

Read carefully the following article (in edited form) by Cyril Kelly and then answer the questions that follow:

Eating An Ice Cream Cone

It was a sweltering day and the sash-windows of our third class were opened as wide as possible to gulp any stray puff of fresh air. Outside, swallows were arcing like black bolts of voltage against the blue sky. Master McMahon had had to call on all his stamina and wizardry to keep forty of us on our collective mettle since early morning. But, as the minute hand of the school clock ticked towards three, there was one delightful twist left in the day.

Pressing the blackboard firmly against the easel, he wrote the title of the story we were getting for homework, namely 'Eating an Ice Cream Cone'. Then turning to face us and, without uttering a word, he pushed up the white cuffs of his shirtsleeves as far as they would go. In the expectant hush, he slowly undid the strap of his rectangular watch and placed it on the table.

From that moment his stern eyes no longer needed to demand our attention. He had become a nine-year-old boy approaching the high windowsill of our classroom to buy a cone. Nobody in the class dared to blink, I hardly allowed myself to breathe. We saw him proffer his money up to some shopkeeper who must have been as gigantic as Fionn MacCumhaill. We were parched as we waited for him to be served. Occasionally, the raucous call of a rook ripped the backdrop of silence which was the only prop for his performance.

As our mime artist turned away from the counter, we were entranced by his widening, expectant eyes. We salivated as, firstly, he licked his lips and then fastened a fond smile on his upheld fist. We, too, agonised on how to best tackle this cone which had materialised before our hungry eyes. Should he lick the quiff of soft ice cream that drooped with a cowlick at the apex, or should he tackle the fronds melting over the crisp edge of the cone?

Forever the *agent provacateur** against predictability, he suddenly raised the ice cream, got his mouth under the golden tip and snipped off the plain bit at the end. The crumbling cone crackled in every inner ear and brought more water to our teeth and we watched as, manfully, he tried to suck the ice cream through the small opening in the end.

The other classes were on their noisy way out of the building but Master McMahon remained motionless, with his knees bent for balance, his head thrown back and his face upturned towards the ceiling. Frozen for a moment in that pose, he was the strong man in the circus, the base of the human pyramid, supporting the combined expectancy of forty spellbound boys. As he resumed sucking for ice cream, his cheeks grew more and more hollow. We could feel the ice cream offering stout resistance and we were craning forward on the edges of the benches, almost asphyxiated with anticipation, our cheeks also concave with phantom pain.

At last with a resounding pop, his cheeks relaxed and we knew that he had, finally, sucked an air hole through the dense ball of ice cream. The relief in that classroom was audible. What an expression of Dennis the Menace satisfaction Master McMahon had on his face! As he put on his watch again and before we could stretch out of our trance, he pointed to the words on the board and said: 'Tomorrow I'll give the price of an ice cream to any boy who makes me taste the flavour of vanilla from his story.'

* One who provokes others into action.

Answer the following **three** questions:

1. Master McMahon wants the boys to make him, 'Taste the flavour of vanilla from his story.' What kind of writing is he trying to encourage from his pupils when he says this? Explain your answer. (10)

2. The writer uses many attractive images in his writing. Pick out one that you particularly enjoyed and say why you liked it. (10)

3. In this passage Cyril Kelly recalls an incident from his childhood. Do you think he is a good storyteller? Support your answer with reference to the text. (20)

Note: A different passage appears on the actual 2005 exam paper which could not be reproduced in this book for copyright reasons. The substituted passage and questions appeared in a previous exam paper.

SECTION 2: PERSONAL WRITING [70]

Write a prose composition on any **one** of the following titles. Except where otherwise stated, you are free to write in any form you wish, e.g. narrative, descriptive, dramatic, short story, etc.

1. The best **OR** worst holiday I have ever had.

2. A case of mistaken identity.

3. You have been granted three wishes: one for yourself, one for Ireland and one for the World.

   What are your wishes and why?

4. Write a modern version of **ONE** of the following:

   • Little Red Riding Hood

   OR

- The Three Little Pigs

  OR

- The Emperor's New Clothes

  OR

- Any other fairytale

5. Write a speech for **OR** against the motion, 'Transition Year should be made compulsory'.

6. 'My mouth was dry and my heart beat so hard I thought it would burst from my chest…'

   Continue with this story.

7. You have spent the summer travelling around Ireland. Write a number of diary entries recording your impressions.

SECTION 3: FUNCTIONAL WRITING [30]

Study **Pages 1 and 4** of **Paper X** and answer **ONE** of the following questions.

You will be rewarded for:

- Well-structured answers
- Clarity of expression
- An appropriate tone
- Good grammar, spelling, punctuation and correct use of capitals

1. Look at the collection of coastal images that appear on Page 1 of Paper X. These images appear on the cover of a brochure about the area. Write a text for the brochure promoting the area as a tourist destination.

   OR

2. Look at the Food Pyramid that appears on Page 4 of Paper X. The recommended servings on the right state the fundamentals of a healthy diet.

   Using the information provided, write a short article for your school magazine promoting healthy eating.

SECTION 4: MEDIA STUDIES [40]

Examine carefully the advertisements that appear on **Page 2 and Page 3** of **Paper X**, which accompanies this examination paper, and answer the following **three** questions.

1. In your opinion is the target audience (target market) the same for both of these advertisements?

    Explain your answer with specific reference to each advertisement. (10)

2. Comment on the visual images used in both of these advertisements. (15)

3. Which of the two advertisements do you find more appealing?
    Give reasons for your answer. (15)

JUNIOR CERTIFICATE EXAMINATION, 2005
PAPER X of ENGLISH — HIGHER LEVEL — PAPER 1

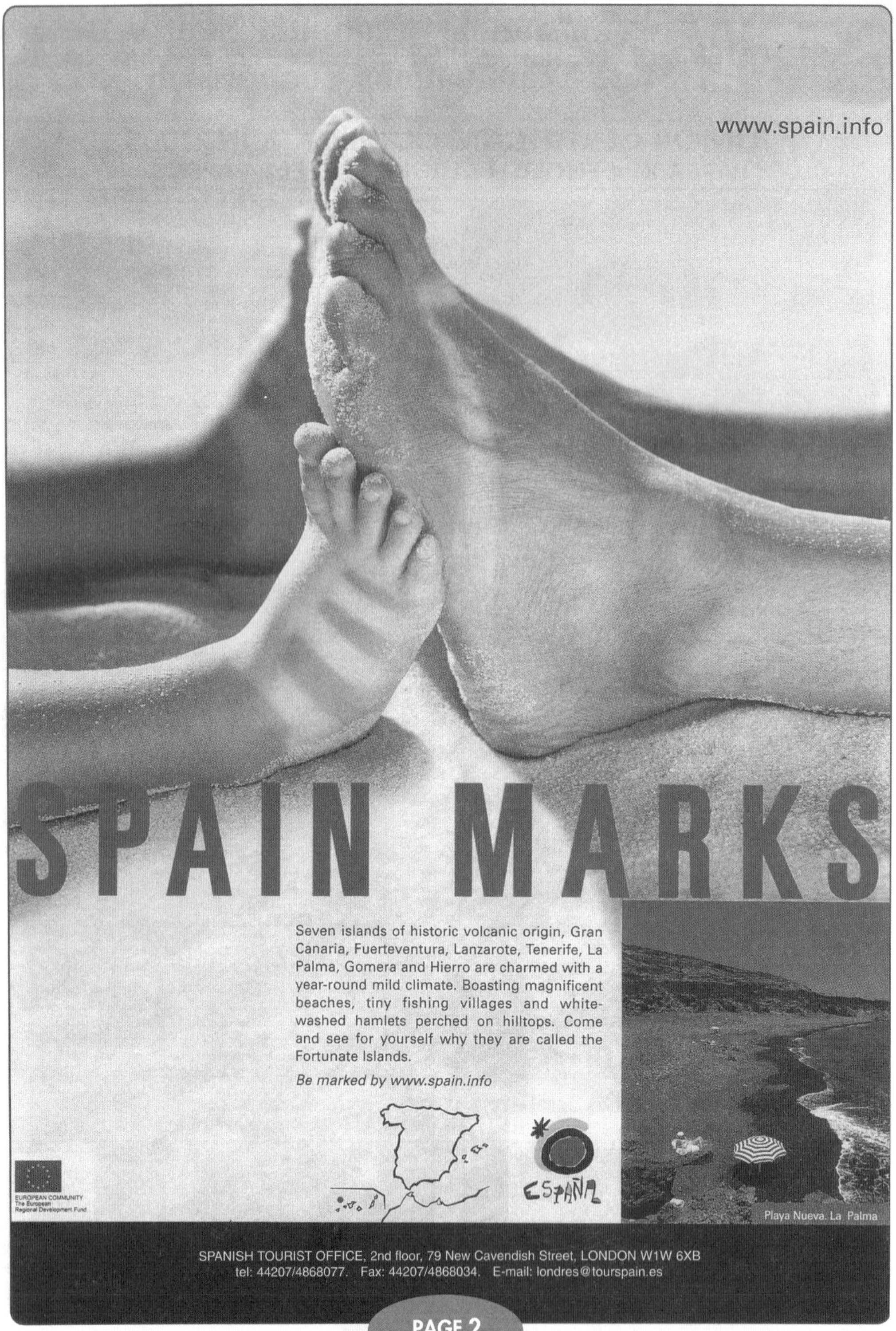
www.spain.info
SPAIN MARKS
Seven islands of historic volcanic origin, Gran Canaria, Fuerteventura, Lanzarote, Tenerife, La Palma, Gomera and Hierro are charmed with a year-round mild climate. Boasting magnificent beaches, tiny fishing villages and white-washed hamlets perched on hilltops. Come and see for yourself why they are called the Fortunate Islands.
Be marked by www.spain.info
EUROPEAN COMMUNITY
The European Regional Development Fund
ESPAÑA
Playa Nueva. La Palma
SPANISH TOURIST OFFICE, 2nd floor, 79 New Cavendish Street, LONDON W1W 6XB
tel: 44207/4868077. Fax: 44207/4868034. E-mail: londres@tourspain.es

PAGE 2

Just as we imagined; the Irish have turned enjoyment into an art form
Any time, any place, turn a corner in Ireland and you'll run into a festival. It might be music; it might be poetry; it might be gastronomic or a heady mixture of all three. Either way, cancel all your plans and join in.
For information telephone 0800 952 2004
or visit theislandofmemories.co.uk
The island of memories Ireland

PAGE 3

The Food Pyramid

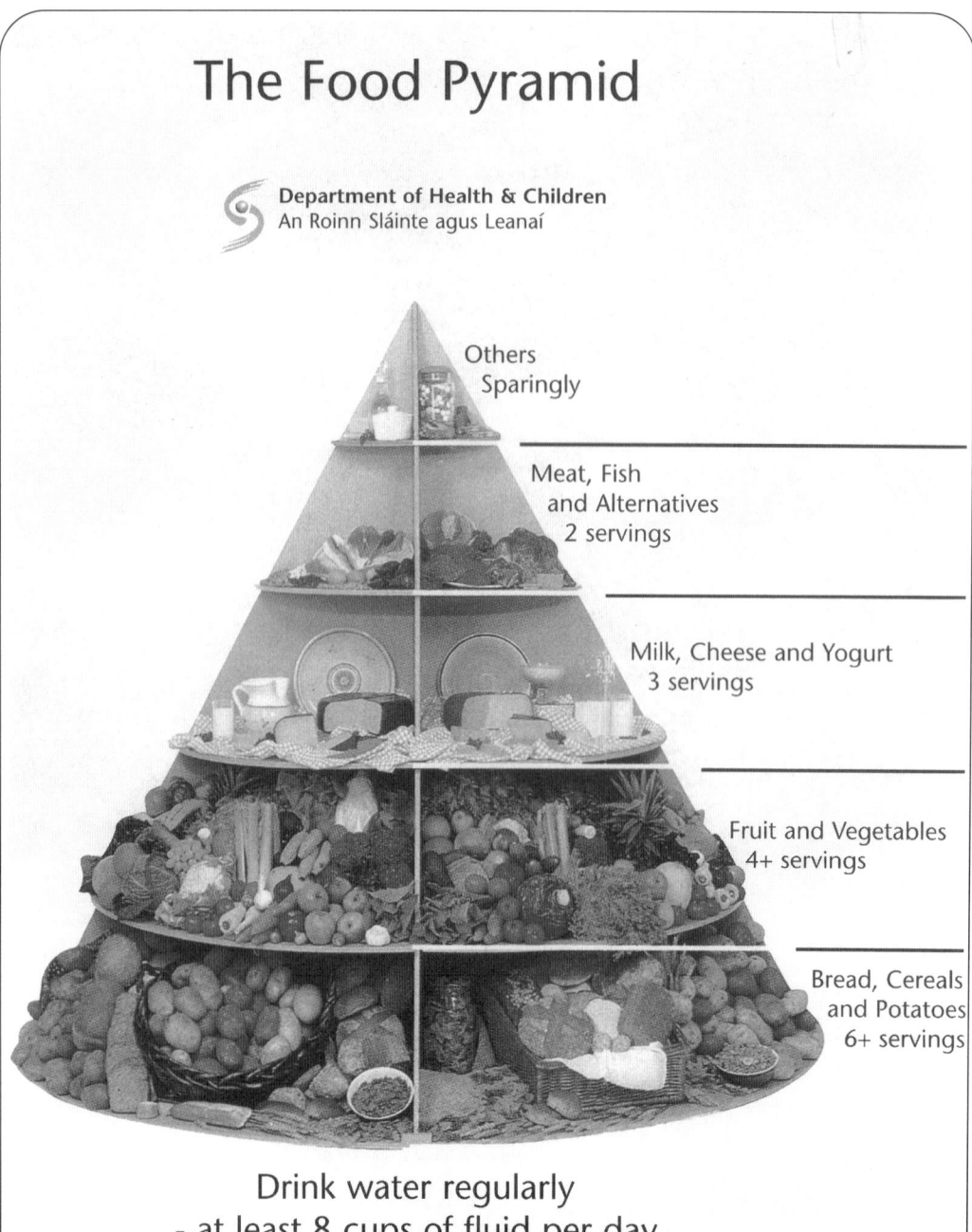

Department of Health & Children
An Roinn Sláinte agus Leanaí

Others
Sparingly

Meat, Fish
and Alternatives
2 servings

Milk, Cheese and Yogurt
3 servings

Fruit and Vegetables
4+ servings

Bread, Cereals
and Potatoes
6+ servings

Drink water regularly
- at least 8 cups of fluid per day

Coimisiún na Scrúduithe Stáit
State Examinations Commission

JUNIOR CERTIFICATE EXAMINATION, 2005

ENGLISH—HIGHER LEVEL—PAPER 2

(180 marks)

WEDNESDAY, 8 JUNE — AFTERNOON, 1.30 — 4.00

YOU MUST ATTEMPT ALL 3 SECTIONS ON THIS PAPER

EACH SECTION CARRIES 60 MARKS

SPEND ABOUT 45 MINUTES ON EACH SECTION

SECTION 1: DRAMA [60]

Answer **QUESTION ONE** and **QUESTION TWO**

QUESTION ONE (30)

Answer either **(A)** or **(B)**.

(A) SHAKESPEAREAN DRAMA

The following extract (in edited form) is taken from *Much Ado About Nothing* by William Shakespeare. Read the extract carefully and then answer the questions which follow.

Background to this extract:
Benedick and Beatrice are discussing Count Claudio and Hero, Claudio's bride to be. Mistakenly, Count Claudio thinks that Hero has been unfaithful to him and cancels their wedding. Beatrice weeps for her cousin Hero who, she strongly believes, has been wronged.

Benedick:	(*With great kindness*) Lady Beatrice have you wept all this while?
Beatrice:	Yea and I will weep a while longer.
Benedick:	I will not desire that.
Beatrice:	You have no reason; I do it freely.
Benedick:	Surely I do believe your fair cousin is wronged.
Beatrice:	Ah, I would be more impressed by some man who would right her situation!
Benedick:	Is there any way to show such friendship?
Beatrice:	It is a man's job but not yours.
Benedick:	I do love nothing in the world so well as you. Is not that strange?
Beatrice:	Strange indeed!
Benedick:	I protest I love thee!
Beatrice:	Why then, God forgive me for what I am thinking!
Benedick:	Come, tell me, come bid me do anything for thee.
Beatrice:	(*Pause*)... Kill Claudio...!
Benedick:	(*Horrified*) Ha, not for the wide world.
Beatrice:	(*Angrily*) You kill me to refuse doing it. Farewell!
Benedick:	(*Calling out*) Wait, sweet Beatrice. (*Benedick tries to stop her leaving*).
Beatrice:	I am gone, though I am here, there is no love in you. Nay, I pray you let me go!
Benedick:	Beatrice...

Beatrice:	Leave me go!
Benedick:	We'll be friends first.
Beatrice:	Friends! You should fight mine enemy first!
Benedick:	Is Claudio thine enemy?
Beatrice:	(*Angrily*) He is a villain that hath slandered, scorned, dishonoured my cousin Hero. O that I were a man! I would eat his heart in the market place!
Benedick:	(*Pleading*) Hear me Beatrice…
Beatrice:	Sweet Hero, she is wronged, she is slandered, she is destroyed.
Benedick:	Listen…
Beatrice:	Princes and Counts! The goodly Count Claudio indeed! O that I had any friend who would be a man for my sake! But manhood is melted into being courteous, giving compliments and having nice speech. There is no honour and truth anymore! I cannot be a man with wishing, therefore I will die a woman with grieving.
Benedick:	Wait, good Beatrice. By this hand I love thee. Think you in your soul that the Count Claudio hath really wronged Hero?
Beatrice:	Yea, as sure as I have a thought or a soul.
Benedick:	Enough, I am convinced. I will challenge him. I will kiss your hand and so I leave you. By this hand Claudio will meet his match. Think of me Beatrice. Go comfort your cousin. And so farewell.

Answer **two** of the following questions. Each question is worth 15 marks.

1. What is your impression of either Benedick **or** Beatrice from this extract? Support your answer by reference to the text.

2. Based on evidence from this extract do you think Beatrice and Benedick are in love with each other? Support your answer by reference to the text.

3. Imagine this scene is to be staged and you are the Director. Outline the directions you would give to either Beatrice **or** Benedick on how to perform their parts.

(B) OTHER DRAMA

The following extract (in edited form) is the opening scene from *Sean, the Fool, the Devil and the Cats* by Ted Hughes. Read the extract carefully and then answer the questions which follow.

Music

Fool: Once upon a time – not very long ago – I was a happy man.
But that's another story.
Now I'm blind, I've no ears, I'm a quilt of scars.
Look at me. Now listen.

There was a boy called Sean.
Not me. Sean was himself.
I'm a fool. Sean was clever. Now listen.
Sean was leaving home.

Mother: You're leaving me alone. O Sean, who'll look after me?

Sean: The neighbours will look after you. Our savings will look after you.
Good-bye, Mother.

Mother: O Sean, where will you go?
Get a job in a bank, get a job on a farm,
Get a job in a canning factory, keep out of harm.
Get a job driving a lorry, if you want to see the world,
But don't go away, don't leave me.

Sean: I'm going for a year.

Mother: You're a dreamer, Sean. You can stay at home. The world will eat you up.

Sean: I'm going to try my luck. So wish me luck.

Mother: Don't go, Sean.

Sean: I'm going.

Mother: Then may an angel go before you, an angel behind you,
An angel to the right of you, an angel to the left,
All lucky angels.

Sean: Good-bye, Mother.
Music

Mother: Write to me, write to me.

Fool: Sean is on the road.
He walks at the roadside in the dust of the cars,
In the exhaust of the diesels,
The racket of the trucks. His head begins to ache.

Sean: Where does the road go?
A road goes to a road.
Roads run into roads, fork into roads, circle and come back into roads.
Roads can never get away from roads.
Roads are a maze with no ending.
People who stick to the roads stick to the maze.
They all end up where they started.
Get off the road, Sean.

Fool:	Sean turns up a lane, over a hill,
	Over a bridge, and he stops at a crossroads.
	It is evening.
Sean:	The sun is setting. Where shall I sleep?
	Four roads meet under my feet.
	Which one shall I take?
First Voice:	(*very distant*):
	This way, Sean. This way for happiness, Sean.
	We like you. We like you.
	This way for smiles and presents and kisses.
Second Voice:	(*distant*):
	This way, Sean, for thrills and adventures.
	This way for hair on end and the skin of
	your teeth and the luck of the devil. This way for the
	seven deadly seas.
Third Voice:	(*distant* – **Mother**'s *voice*):
	Come home, Sean, come home. Wait a year, go next summer, think
	about it, remember your bed. Remember your old dog.
	Remember my puddings.
Fourth Voice:	(*close and urgent*):
	This way, Sean, for a future.
	You are just the chap we need – the very man. Just what we're
	wanting – this way, Sean. There's a fortune in it. For you, Sean. A
	good sound job with a good sound future.
Sean:	Down every road of the four – there's a tempting voice.
	But what about that stile in the hedge? And the path
	that goes over the field beyond into that dark wood?
	That's a fifth way. How about that?
First Voice:	No.
Second Voice:	No.
Third Voice:	Don't go that way, whatever you do.
Fourth Voice:	Good-bye for ever, Sean, if you go that way.
Sean:	Why, what's wrong with it? It's only a path to a wood.
Third Voice:	No.
Fourth Voice:	Don't go that way.
Sean:	Right, then I'll try it.

Answer **two** of the following questions. Each question is worth 15 marks.

1. What is your impression of either Sean **or** Mother from this extract? Support your answer by reference to the text.

2. Do you think that this extract from *Sean, the Fool, the Devil and the Cats* by Ted

Hughes would work well on stage? Give reasons for your answer with close reference to the extract.

3. Imagine you are the costume **or** stage designer for a production of this play. Describe how you would like to see the characters costumed **or** the stage set. Give reasons for your answer with close reference to the extract.

QUESTION TWO (30)

Answer **EITHER 1 OR 2** which follow.

N.B. You must give the name of the play that you choose. You may **NOT** choose either of the scenes quoted on this examination paper as the basis for your answer.

1. Select a play you have studied and choose from it a scene where conflict occurs.

    (a) Outline what happens in this scene. (10)

    (b) What are the underlying causes of the conflict in this scene?

    Support your answer by reference to the play as a whole. (20)

    OR

2. Choose your favourite character from a play you have studied.

    (a) Why do you find this character interesting? Support your answer by reference to the text. (10)

    (b) Discuss the relationship between your chosen character and **ONE** other character in the play. Refer to the text in support of your answer. (20)

SECTION 2: POETRY [60]

Read the following poem (in edited form) and answer the questions which follow.

FIFTEEN

South of the Bridge on Seventeenth
I found, one summer day,
a motorcycle with engine running
as it lay on its side, ticking over
slowly in the high grass. I was fifteen.

I admired all that pulsing gleam, the
shiny flanks, the shy headlights,
grass-fringed where it lay; I led it gently
to the road and stood with that
companion, ready and friendly. I was fifteen.

We could find the end of a road, meet
the sky on out Seventeenth. I thought about
hills, and patting the handle got back a
confident response. On the bridge we indulged
a forward feeling, a tremble. I was fifteen.

Thinking, back farther in the grass I found
the owner, just coming to, where he had flipped
over the rail. He had blood on his hand, was pale –
I helped him walk to his machine. He ran his hand
over it, called me good man, roared away.

I stood there, fifteen.

William Stafford

Answer **QUESTION ONE** and **QUESTION TWO**

QUESTION ONE (30)

Answer the following questions. Each question is worth 10 marks.

1. How does the poet give the impression that the motorcycle is a living creature? Give reasons for your answer with reference to the poem.

2. The fifth stanza consists of one line only: 'I stood there, fifteen.'

   Why do you think the poet has set this stanza apart from the rest of the poem?

   Give reasons for your answer with reference to the poem.

3. Do you think 'Fifteen' is a good poem?

   Give reasons for your answer with close reference to the poem.

QUESTION TWO (30)

Answer **EITHER 1 OR 2** which follow.

N.B. In answering you may **NOT** use the poem given on this paper. You must give the title of the poem you choose and the name of the poet.

1. From the poetry you have studied choose a poem which is set in an interesting time **or** place.

   (a) Describe this setting. (10)

   (b) What does this setting contribute to the effectiveness of the poem?
   Give reasons for your answer based on evidence from the poem. (20)

OR

2. From the poetry you have studied choose a poem which deals with either Youth **or** Old Age.

   (a) What picture does this poem give of either youth **or** old age? (10)
   (b) What is your personal response to the picture of youth **or** old age given in the poem?
   Support your answer with reference to the poem. (20)

SECTION 3: FICTION [60]

Read carefully the following extract (in edited form) from the opening chapter of *The Love Bean* by Siobhán Parkinson.

Chapter 1

Lydia turned the key and gently pushed in the door. No one called out. No one appeared. Good. She pressed the door closed again behind her and leaned her back against it. Made it. A giggle rose up in her. She was behaving like a ridiculous character in a detective movie, sneaking into her own house. It was four o'clock in the afternoon, for goodness' sake. She'd only been to the second-hand CD shop to sell off a bunch of her least favourite CDs and buy a new one with the proceeds. She'd only met Jonathan Walker there and spent five (fabulous) minutes chatting with him. She'd only agreed to go for a coffee with him tomorrow afternoon in the glitzy seafront café, where the stainless steel equipment gleamed like precious metals and the customers shone like superstars – or so it seemed to Lydia, who didn't shine at all.

There was nothing wrong with meeting Jonathan by chance in a music shop. Nothing wrong, either, she told herself, with agreeing to meet him again. He was stunningly good-looking: high cheekbones, lightly tanned skin, a flop of rich wavy hair over his forehead, widely spaced blue eyes – it was all too good to be true. Lydia had said it herself, six months ago. Anyone who looked like that couldn't possibly be good. Beauty like that was bound to corrupt. Still, no one would have had anything against him, or against Lydia's going to meet him, if it hadn't been for Julia. But there *was* Julia. There was no getting around that. It was definitely a problem, no matter what way Lydia looked at it.

Julia was Lydia's identical twin. They had the same pale, freckly skin, the same crinkly, red-gold hair, the same grey-green eyes. But that's where the resemblance stopped. With her unruly mane of hair, Julia managed to look as if she didn't own a hairbrush; Lydia wore her hair pinned back with a hair slide or plaited or swinging in a ponytail. Julia wore spangly bracelets and fluorescent boots and tights with Santa Clauses on them, even in summer, and mad purply embroidered things that swooshed as she walked and got tangled up in machinery; Lydia preferred jeans with runners and T-shirts most of the time, or else just black trousers and what Julia called 'sweet little tops'. Julia spent hours on the phone organising her social life; Lydia had friends, but she didn't much like using the phone.

Officially, Julia was still 'getting over' Jonathan. She had an amazing though short-lived reign last term as Jonathan's girlfriend. But then somebody else, somebody cleverer, prettier, wittier and blonder had stolen him from right under her nose. Julia had been in mourning ever since. Nobody was allowed to mention him. He was like a shadow person attached to Julia, always there, always ignored.

The break-up had been three months ago. But getting over Jonathan seemed to suit Julia. It gave her an excuse to slouch around the house, changing TV channels with her big toe from the sofa – the remote was always missing – and complaining about life's unfairness. It was the excuse she used also for sitting in the twins' shared attic bedroom for hours each day, playing endless music by dead rock musicians too loudly. They had to be dead, Julia explained, because that was in keeping with her feelings. At first, Lydia had thought this a little weird but kind of poetic; now she just thought it was self-indulgent – she was starting to get tired of passionate wailings. It was time to stop feeling sorry for Julia.

Answer **QUESTION ONE** and **QUESTION TWO**

QUESTION ONE (30)

Answer **two** of the following questions. Each question is worth 15 marks.

(a) What did you learn about the character of Lydia from this extract? Support your answer by reference to the text.

(b) Imagine you are Julia. Based on evidence from this extract write a diary entry capturing Julia's thoughts and feelings.

(c) Siobhán Parkinson has been described as a writer of 'infinite skill'. Based on evidence from this extract do you agree?

QUESTION TWO (30)

Answer **EITHER 1 OR 2** which follow.

N.B. In answering you may **NOT** use the extract given above as the basis for your answer. You must give the title of the text that you choose and the name of the author.

1. Choose either the opening **or** the ending of a novel **or** short story you have studied.

    (a) Briefly describe what happens in the opening **or** the ending of your chosen text.
    (10)

    (b) Did this opening **or** ending impress you? Explain your answer by reference to the novel **or** short story you have chosen.
    (20)

OR

2. From a novel **or** short story you have studied choose a character who experiences change.

    (a) Describe this character at the beginning of the novel **or** short story. (10)

    (b) How has this character changed by the end of the novel **or** short story?

    Support your answer by reference to the text. (20)

Acknowledgments (2005 exam paper)

For permission to reproduce copyright material in these examination papers the publishers gratefully acknowledge

extract from the novel *The Love Bean* by Siobhán Parkinson, published by O'Brien Press Ltd, Dublin, © Siobhán Parkinson; Faber and Faber for (adapted) extract from *Sean, the Fool, the Devil and the Cats* by Ted Hughes; and Harper Perennial for 'Fifteen' by William Stafford. These extracts were adapted by the State Examinations Commission exclusively for the purposes of the Leaving Certificate English (Higher Level) examination paper (2005) and do not purport to be the authors' original published texts.

The publishers have made every effort to trace all copyright holders, but if they have inadvertently overlooked any they will be pleased to make the necessary arrangement at the first opportunity.

Coimisiún na Scrúduithe Stáit
State Examinations Commission

JUNIOR CERTIFICATE EXAMINATION, 2004

ENGLISH — HIGHER LEVEL — PAPER 1
180 marks

WEDNESDAY, 9 JUNE – MORNING, 9.30 – 12.00

YOU MUST ATTEMPT ALL 4 SECTIONS ON THIS PAPER

IT IS SUGGESTED THAT YOU SPEND ABOUT HALF AN HOUR ON EACH OF SECTIONS 1, 3, 4, AND ABOUT ONE HOUR ON SECTION 2

SECTION 1: READING [40]

Read carefully the following passage and then answer the questions that follow.

'Call the usher! The pleasure of movie-going is becoming a pain, thanks to noisy, guzzling, mobile-phone-using talkers, kickers and general pests.' So said Irish Times journalist, Hugh Linehan, in an article in his newspaper. The article appears below in edited form.

Shhhhhhhhhh!

Maybe it's because I'm a spoiled snobbish elitist — and that's not something I'm happy about — but I have to confess I'm finding it increasingly painful to go to the movies with the rest of you, the great paying public. It's not because of the cinemas — standards of projection, sound, seating and ventilation have improved out of all recognition over the last ten years — but (and I am sorry to say this) your standards of behaviour seem to be disimproving all the time.

Kickers are a real source of irritation. The kicker problem is exacerbated by the design of modern cinema seats — a kicked seat reverberates right along the row, so that it can be nigh-well impossible to figure out where it's coming from. In the 1970s, they called this Sensurround and people paid to experience it in movies such as *Earthquake* and *Towering Inferno*. Nowadays, you can have your own personal towering inferno as you reach boiling point after two hours of bone-shaking juddering.

Up until recently, the mobile phenomenon seemed to be spinning out of control. Cinemas were buzzing like beehives with the wretched things and some buffoons even had the cheek to strike up conversations on them during the film. There will always be buffoons, but a corner seems to have been turned in recent times. Thankfully, cinemas have now taken to putting reminders on the screen telling people to switch off their phones, and many appear to be doing so. On an electronically related topic, by the way, what, what sort of benighted fool needs a watch that beeps on the hour, every hour?

I have some sympathy for those who feel nauseated by the smell of warm buttery popcorn which is so much a part of the multiplex experience, but it doesn't bother me that much. If people want to eat wildly overpriced, grease-saturated cardboard, then that's their business. At least popcorn has the virtue of being (almost) silent food — far better than the high-pitched crackle of the jumbo crisp packet or the extended kitchen-sink gurgle of the almost-drained Coke.

To my mind the real problem in cinemas these days is talkers. They're everywhere and they come in a variety of species. One kind can't help giving a blow-by-blow commentary on the movie. They're bad enough, but there is worse. Top of the list come those who just utterly ignore the film in favour of their own chat. Western society has devised countless places where people can communicate with each other, but cafes, restaurants or street corners are just not good enough for these people — apparently not when they can have the added pleasure of spoiling other people's enjoyment.

Then, there are those who think that any break in the dialogue has been inserted by the filmmaker expressly for them to start talking. The minute there is a pause of more than a couple of seconds they launch into conversation. This is not to forget the downright stupid, who spend most of the time asking questions: 'Who's she? What happened there?' By the time they've got an answer they've missed the next plot point, and the whole weary rigmarole starts all over again.

What is the reason for this plague? The general decline in politeness in society may have something to do with it, but it doesn't fully explain the seemingly unstoppable desire to talk when the lights go down. We don't want funereal silence; a good comedy, horror or action movie can be immeasurably improved by the communal experience of seeing it with an audience. People can shriek or laugh to their hearts' content, and there is a real sense of a shared magical experience. After all, we're all together in the cinema . . . in the dark. And you never know who is sitting next to you!

Answer the following **three** questions:

1. Hugh Linehan outlines a number of complaints about cinemagoer's behaviour. List two examples of behaviour he finds particularly irritating. Basing your answer on the text, explain why he finds these examples irritating. (10)

2. Hugh Linehan describes himself as a 'spoiled, snobbish elitist' in the opening line of the passage. Based on what you have read, would you agree with this description? Support your answer with reference to the text. (15)

3. Basing your answer on the way the passage is written, how serious do you think the writer is in his criticism of the behaviour of cinema audiences? (15)

SECTION 2: PERSONAL WRITING [70]

Write a prose composition on any **one** of the following titles. Except where otherwise stated, you are free to write in any form you wish, e.g. narrative, descriptive, dramatic, short story, etc.

You will be rewarded for:
- A personal approach to the subject
- An appropriate style
- Liveliness and a good choice of words
- Organisation and accuracy

1. My pet hates.

2. Write a composition beginning, 'Finally the smoke cleared and I could see...'

3. You discover that a close friend of yours has found some money. Write the conversation that takes place between you about what to do with the cash.

4. Movie magic.

5. Your Aunt and Uncle have asked you to mind their house and pets while they are on holiday. Write about your experiences while 'house-sitting'.

6. The future: things I dread and things I look forward to.

7. Look at the picture on **Page 226** and write a composition inspired by it.

8. You are preparing to represent Ireland in a sport of your choice at the 2004 Olympic Games. Write a series of diary entries recording your preparations.

SECTION 3: FUNCTIONAL WRITING [30]

Answer **either** Question 1 **or** Question 2.

You will be rewarded for:
- Well-structured answers
- Clarity of expression
- An appropriate tone
- Good grammar, spelling, punctuation and correct use of capitals

1. Write a review for a young people's magazine of any book, film, computer game or concert you have recently experienced. Your answer should include an introduction, description, evaluation and recommendation.

OR

2. You feel strongly about Hugh Linehan's article in Section 1 of this paper (Page 222 of this book). Write a letter to the Editor of the newspaper in which you outline your views in response to the article.

SECTION 4:   MEDIA STUDIES   [40]

Examine carefully the advertisement that appears on **Page 227** and answer **either** Question 1 **or** Question 2.

1. (a) What elements of this advertisement contribute to its impact? Your answer should refer to at least two elements. (20)

   (b) Who do you think the target audience for this advertisement might be? Explain your answer with reference to the advertisement. (20)

OR

2. (a) What is the function of the editor of a newspaper? (10)

   (b) You are the editor of your school's annual magazine. Write an editorial for the publication on any aspect of student behaviour you wish to encourage or discourage. (30)

Coimisiún na Scrúduithe Stáit
State Examinations Commission
JUNIOR CERTIFICATE EXAMINATION, 2004

PAPER X OF ENGLISH – HIGHER LEVEL – PAPER 1

GREAT WHITE

TOBLERVISION

IT'S BACK! Starring smooth, WHITER than WHITE CHOCOLATE, ALMOND and NOUGAT centre.

Coimisiún na Scrúduithe Stáit
State Examinations Commission

JUNIOR CERTIFICATE EXAMINATION, 2004

ENGLISH — HIGHER LEVEL — PAPER 2

(180 marks)

WEDNESDAY, 9 JUNE — AFTERNOON, 1.30 – 4.00

YOU MUST ATTEMPT ALL THREE
SECTIONS ON THIS PAPER.

EACH SECTION CARRIES 60 MARKS.

SPEND ABOUT 45 MINUTES ON EACH
SECTION.

SECTION 1: DRAMA [60]

Answer **QUESTION ONE** and **QUESTION TWO**

QUESTION ONE (30)

Answer either **(A)** or **(B)**.

(A) SHAKESPEAREAN DRAMA

The following extract (in edited form) is taken from *The Tempest* by William Shakespeare. Read the extract carefully and then answer the questions which follow.

> **Background to this extract:**
> This scene is set on a deserted island where Prospero and his daughter Miranda, a beautiful girl of fifteen, have been living in exile for twelve years. A violent storm strikes the island. Ferdinand, son of the King of Naples, is shipwrecked and washed ashore. He believes that his father and all others on board have been drowned. Miranda and Ferdinand meet and fall in love at first sight. Prospero likes this development, but pretends otherwise in order to test their love.

Prospero:	Say what thou seest yond.
Miranda:	(*Seeing Ferdinand for the first time.*) What is't? A spirit? Lord, how it looks about! Believe me, sir, It carries a brave form. But 'tis a spirit.
Prospero:	No daughter. It eats and sleeps and hath such senses As we have. This youth thou seest Was in the wreck; and, but he's somewhat stained With grief, thou mightst call him A goodly person. He hath lost his fellows, And strays about to find them.
Miranda:	I might call him a thing divine, for nothing natural I ever saw so noble.
Prospero:	(*Aside.*) This love begins as I see it.
Ferdinand:	(*Approaching Miranda.*) Most sure the goddess On whom these airs attend! O you wonder! Be you maid or no?

Miranda:	No wonder, Sir, but certainly a maid.
Ferdinand:	O! Ye gods! Such sadness, and such joy
	Do mingle in my soul this day.
	Ferdinand begins to weep.
Prospero:	(*harshly*) Why weepst thou in such unmanly fashion
	Who are so young and strong?
Miranda:	Why speaks my father so ungently? This
	Is the second man that e'er I saw; the first
	That e'er I sighed for. Pity move my father!
Ferdinand:	(*tearfully*) I weep, who with mine eyes
	Beheld the king, my father, drowned.
Miranda:	Alack for mercy! O noble youth!
Ferdinand:	O you wonder! If a virgin, and your affections
	Not gone forth, I'll make you the Queen of Naples.
Prospero:	(*Aside.*) They are both in either's powers. But this swift love
	I must uneasy make, lest too easy winning
	Make the prize light.
	(*To Ferdinand, with mock severity.*) One word more!
	Thou hast put thyself upon this island as a spy,
	To win it from me, who is Lord of it.
Ferdinand:	No, as I am a man!
Miranda:	There's nothing bad can dwell in such a man. If …
Prospero:	(*Interrupting her abruptly.*) Follow me, traitor!
	(*Turns to Miranda.*)
	Speak not you for him, he's a traitor.
	(*To Ferdinand.*)
	Come!
	I'll bind thy neck and feet together. Sea-water
	Shalt thou drink; thy food shall be the fresh-brook mussels
	Withered roots and husks wherein the acorn cradled.
	Follow!
Miranda:	(*Grabbing Prospero's cloak*) I beg you, father!
Prospero:	Hence! Hang not on my garments.
Miranda:	Sir, have pity. I'll be his guarantor.
Prospero:	Silence! One word more shall make me scold thee, if not hate thee.
	What, pleading for an impostor?
	Hush, foolish wench! Compared to most men, this fellow
	Is a beast, and they to him are angels.

Miranda:	My love is then most humble. I have no ambition to see a goodlier man.
Prospero:	(*To Ferdinand.*) Come! Obey!
Ferdinand:	My spirits, as in a dream, are all bound up. My father's loss, the weakness which I feel, The wrack of all my friends and this man's threats – Yet all are light to me Could I but through my prison once a day, Behold this maid.
Prospero:	(*Aside.*) It works. (*To Ferdinand.*) Come on –
Miranda:	Be of comfort. My father's of a better nature, sir, Than he appears by speech. This is unusual. He speaks not like himself.
Prospero:	Come, follow! (*To Miranda.*) Speak not for him. *Exit all.*

Answer **two** of the following questions. Each question is worth 15 marks.

1. What do we learn of the character of Ferdinand from the above extract?

2. The name Miranda means 'wonder', and Ferdinand certainly thinks that she is a wonder. What is wonderful about the growing relationship between Miranda and Ferdinand? Support your answer by reference to the text.

3. If you were directing this scene, what suggestions would you make to Prospero as to how should play his part in order to convey his true feelings to the audience?

(B) OTHER DRAMA

The following extract (in edited form) is taken from *The Glass Menagerie* by Tennessee Williams. Read the extract carefully and answer the questions which follow.

> **Background to this extract:**
> This play is set in St Louis, USA in the 1930s. This scene is set in the home of Amanda, a deserted wife, who lives with her daughter, Laura, and her son, Tom. Laura is an extremely shy and introverted girl. Amanda is very anxious for Laura to marry and persuades Tom to invite his colleague, Jim, to their home for dinner. Laura and Jim are left alone after dinner.

Jim:	You know – you're – well – very different. Surprisingly different from anyone else I know . . . Do you mind me telling you that?
	Laura is too shy to speak.
Jim:	I mean it in a nice way. Has anyone ever told you that you were pretty?
	Laura looks up slowly with wonder and shakes her head.
Jim:	Well, you are! In a very different way from anyone else. And all the nicer for that difference too.
Laura:	In what respects am I pretty?
Jim:	In all respects – believe me! Your eyes – your hair – are pretty! Your hands are pretty! Laura, you know, if I had a sister like you, I'd do the same thing as Tom. I'd bring fellows home and – introduce them to her. The right type of boys – of a type to appreciate her.
	Only . . . Tom made a mistake about me.
	Maybe I've got no call to be saying this. This may not have been the idea in having me over. But what if it was? There's nothing wrong about that. The only trouble is that in my case – I'm not in a situation to do the right thing . . .
	I can't take down your number and say I'll phone. I can't call up next week and – ask for a date. I thought I'd better explain the situation in case – you misunderstood it and – hurt your feelings . . .
	Pause. Slowly, very slowly, Laura's look changes.
Laura:	(*Faintly.*) You – won't – call?
Jim:	No, Laura, I can't. As I was just explaining, I've got strings on me, Laura. I've been – going steady! I go out all the time with a girl named Betty . . . I met her last summer on a boat trip up the river to Alton. Well, right away from the start it was – love!
	Laura sways slightly forward and grips the arm of the sofa.
	Jim fails to notice.
Jim:	Being in love has made a new man of me! The power of love is really tremendous! Love is something that changes the whole world, Laura.
	He looks at her again.
Jim:	It happened that Betty's aunt took sick. She had to go to Centralia. So Tom – when he asked me to dinner – I naturally

	just accepted the invitation, not knowing that you – that he – that I –
	He stops awkwardly. I wish that you would – say something. Laura bites her lip, which was trembling, and then bravely smiles. At this moment Amanda rushes brightly into the room bearing a jug of fruit punch.
Amanda:	Well, isn't the air delightful after the shower? I've made you children a little liquid refreshment. Why, Laura! You look so serious!
Jim:	We were having a serious conversation.
Amanda:	Good! Now you're better acquainted!
Jim:	(*Uncertainly.*) Ha – ha! Yes.

Answer **two** of the following questions. Each question is worth 15 marks.

1. Jim is described as 'a nice ordinary young man'. Would you agree with this? Refer to the text in support of your answer.

2. Imagine that you are directing a production of *The Glass Menagerie*. What suggestions would you make to the actress who is playing the part of Laura? Consider, for example, body language and tone of voice.

3. Based on what you learn about Amanda from the above text, write the scene you imagine could have taken place between Amanda and Laura after Jim's departure. Use suitable dialogue and stage directions.

QUESTION TWO (30)

Answer **EITHER 1 OR 2**.

N.B. You must give the name of the play that you choose. You may **NOT** choose either of the scenes quoted on this examination paper as the basis for your answer.

1. Name a play you have studied in which one character rebels against another. With which character did you have more sympathy? Give reasons for your answer making reference to the play.

OR

2. Name a play you have studied.
Choose a scene from this play you found either happy **or** sad.
Describe how the playwright conveys this happiness **or** sadness.

SECTION 2: POETRY [60]

Read the following poem by T. S. Eliot and answer the questions that follow.

> The winter evening settles down
> With smell of steaks in passageways.
> Six o'clock.
> The burnt-out ends of smoky days.
> And now a gusty shower wraps
> The grimy scraps
> Of withered leaves about your feet
> And newspapers from vacant lots;
> The showers beat
> On broken blinds and chimney-pots,
> And at the corner of the street
> A lonely cab-horse steams and stamps.
>
> And then the lighting of the lamps.
>
> *T. S. Eliot* (1888–1965)

Answer **QUESTION ONE** and **QUESTION TWO**

QUESTION ONE (30)

Answer **both 1 and 2**.

1. What title would you give to this poem?
   Explain your choice with detailed reference to the poem. (15)

2. Do you think that this is a well-written poem?
   Defend your point of view with reference to the text of the poem. (15)

QUESTION TWO (30)

Answer **EITHER 1 OR 2**.

N.B. In answering you may **NOT** use the name of the poem given on this paper. You must give the title of the poem you choose and the name of the poet.

1. Being in love has always inspired men and women to express their feelings in verse.

    Select a love poem you have studied.

    (a) Describe what happens in this poem.
    (b) How does the lover express her/his feelings?
    (c) Would you like to have this poem written for you for St Valentine's Day? Give reasons for your answer. (30)

    OR

2. It is said that every reader brings to the same poem a new life.

    Choose a poem you have studied which has a special and very personal meaning for you.

    (a) Explain why this poem has a special meaning for you.
        Describe how the poet has made it possible for you, the reader, to identify with the message in this poem.
    (b) What is there in the language and imagery of the poem that attracts you? (30)

SECTION 3: FICTION [60]

Read the following short story carefully and then answer the questions that follow. The story (in edited form), is called *Fear*, by Rhys Davies.

As soon as the boy got into the compartment he felt there was something queer in it. The only other occupant was a slight Indian man who sat in a corner. There was also a faint sickly scent. For years afterwards, whenever he smelled that musk odour again, the terror of this afternoon came back to the boy.

He went to the other end of the compartment and sat in the opposite corner. There were no corridors in these local trains. The man smiled at him in a friendly fashion. The boy became aware of a deep vague unease, but it would look silly to jump out of the compartment now. The train began to move.

Immediately, the man began to utter a low humming chant. The hum penetrated above the noise of the train's wheels. Startled, the boy turned from staring out of the window and forced himself to glance at the man. The man was looking at him. Something coiled up in the boy. It was as if his soul took primitive fear. The humming chant continued. The musk scent was stronger. Yet, this was not all. The boy felt that some fearful thing lurked in the compartment, a secret power of something evil.

Abruptly, the compartment was plunged into darkness as the train entered a tunnel. The boy crouched. He knew that the man's eyes were gazing at him. What was this strange presence of evil in the air, stronger now in the dark?

Suddenly, daylight came crashing into the compartment. The boy stared dully at the man. He saw the man's lips part in a full enticing smile. 'You not like dark tunnels?' The smile continued seductively as flecks of light danced wickedly in his eyes.

'Come!' he beckoned with a long finger. The boy did not move. 'You like pomegranates?'* He took from the luggage rack a brown basket, crossed over and sat down beside the boy. 'Nice pomegranates,' he smiled with good humour.

The boy was aware of the sickly perfume beside him and of a presence that was utterly alien. The man, still humming, lifted the basket's lid. There was no glow of gleaming fruits. But from the basket's depth rose the head of a snake, swaying towards the man's lips. It was a cobra.

Something happened to the boy, some primitive warning. He leaped and flung himself across the compartment. He gave a sharp shriek. But his eyes could not tear themselves from that reared head. Somehow, the boy knew that he had evoked rage. The cobra was writhing in anger. More fearful was the dilation of the throat, its skin swelling evilly into a hood. The boy sensed the destructive fury of the hood. He became very still. The man did not stop humming. The snake was pacified. Its head ceased to lunge and its body sank into the basket. The man closed the basket and fastened it securely. Then, he turned angrily to the boy, making a contemptuous sound. 'I show you cobra and you jump and shout, heh! Make him angry. I give you free performance with cobra and you hump and scream. I sing to keep cobra quiet in train'. 'Cobra not like train! Not liking you jump and shout!'

The boy was not stirred.

The train was drawing into a station, not the boy's station, but he made a sudden blind leap, opened the door, saw it was not on the platform side, but he jumped. He ran up the track and dived under some wire railings, like a hare that knows its life is precarious among the colossal dangers of the world.

* Tropical fruit

Answer **QUESTION ONE** and **QUESTION TWO**

QUESTION ONE (30)

Answer **two** of the following questions. Each one is worth **15 marks**.

1. Do you find the boy's reaction to the Indian snake charmer normal or exaggerated? Give reasons for your answer.

2. 'We enjoy reading stories like this one because they enable us to explore the outer edges of the unknown, strangeness, things that cannot be explained — without feeling any danger to ourselves.'

   Do you agree with this statement? Why? Why not? Support your answer with reference to this story.

3. The title of this story is *Fear*. In your opinion, is the writer successful in conveying a sense of the boy's fear to the reader? Give reasons for your opinion and support your answer by reference to the text.

QUESTION TWO (30)

Answer **EITHER 1 OR 2**.

N.B. In answering you may **NOT** use the extract given above as the basis for your answer. You must give the title of the text you choose and the name of the author.

1. Many novels or short stories show the conflict between good and evil.

   Name a novel **or** short story you have studied where there is conflict between good and evil. Trace how the author presents this conflict. (30)

   OR

2. Choose a novel **or** a short story you have studied which contains a strong element of surprise.

   (a) Describe the setting of the novel or short story. (10)
   (b) Describe the events leading up to the surprise in this novel or short story. (10)
   (c) How did the surprise in the novel or short story affect one or more of the characters? (10)

Acknowledgments (2004 exam paper)

For permission to reproduce copyright material grateful acknowledgment is made to the following:

The Irish Times for an edited form of 'Shhhhhhhhhh!' by Hugh Linehan, first published by The Irish Times;

Methuen Publishing Limited for an extract from *The Glass Menagerie* by T.S. Eliot published by Methuen Publishing Limited Copyright © 1945 renewed 1973 The University of the South and for 'Preludes' by T.S. Eliot from *Collected Poems 1909–62* published by Methuen Publishing Ltd. Copyright © 1945, renewed 1973 The University of the South;

The author and publishers have made every effort to trace copyright holders, but if any has been overlooked they will be pleased to make the necessary arrangement at the first opportunity.